DUMBARTON OAKS
MEDIEVAL LIBRARY

Jan M. Ziolkowski, General Editor

THE *BEOWULF* MANUSCRIPT

DOML 3

The *Beowulf* Manuscript

Complete Texts and *The Fight at Finnsburg*

Edited and Translated by

R. D. FULK

DUMBARTON OAKS
MEDIEVAL LIBRARY

HARVARD UNIVERSITY PRESS
CAMBRIDGE, MASSACHUSETTS
LONDON, ENGLAND
2010

Printed in the United States of America

Library of Congress Cataloging-in-Publication Data
Beowulf. English & English (Old English)
The Beowulf manuscript : complete texts ; and The fight at Finnsburg / edited and translated by R. D. Fulk.
p. cm.—(Dumbarton Oaks medieval library ; DOML 3)
In Old English with a facing modern English translation.
Includes bibliographical references and index.
ISBN 978-0-674-05295-6 (alk. paper)
1. Epic poetry, English (Old) 2. Scandinavia—Poetry. 3. Monsters—Poetry. I. Fulk, R. D. (Robert Dennis) II. Fight at Finnesburg (Anglo-Saxon poem). English & English (Old English) III. Title.
PR1583.F85 2010
829′.3—dc22 2010017540

Contents

Introduction

The *Beowulf* Manuscript

Visitors to the British Library in London can see so many famous and finely made manuscripts on display in the public galleries that they may not be inclined to linger over an unassuming and rather exhausted-looking book from the Cottonian collection of medieval codices that bears the shelf mark Vitellius A. xv. It is nonetheless a most important book, as it contains, along with some other unique texts, the sole copy of the poem *Beowulf,* the finest and most intensively studied work of vernacular literature from Anglo-Saxon England. The manuscript has been so ill treated over the centuries that it seems an unlikely accident that the poem has managed to survive mostly intact into modern times.

Two separate manuscripts were bound together to form the present book in the early seventeenth century. The first, of the twelfth century, is now commonly referred to as the Southwick Codex, as it is known to have been in the library of the priory of Southwick, Hampshire, in the late thirteenth century. It contains several vernacular texts of a pious nature. The second manuscript is commonly called the Nowell Codex, since its first known owner was the antiquary Laurence Nowell, who wrote his name and the date 1563 on the first leaf. It is also sometimes referred to as the

Beowulf Manuscript, and it is the contents of this second component of Vitellius A. xv that are edited and translated in the present volume. The manuscript is in two rather different hands. The prose texts and *Beowulf* to line 1939 are in a variety of Insular minuscule written by Scribe A, while the remainder of *Beowulf* and *Judith* are in a more old-fashioned minuscule, that of Scribe B. The occurrence of the two scripts in one codex suggests that the book cannot have been made much before or after the first decade of the millennium. However, we know nothing of the whereabouts of the manuscript before Nowell acquired it. Presumably it was preserved in the library of a religious house until the dissolution of the monasteries under Henry VIII, at which time it must have joined the mass of monastic books that, if they were fortunate enough to be preserved at all, found their way into private hands.

The manuscript must already have been in a mutilated state when it was in Nowell's possession, as the first leaf on which he wrote his name begins in the middle of the text of *The Passion of Saint Christopher,* of which the beginning is missing. Very likely the beginning of the poem *Judith* was wanting by then as well, since there are reasons to believe that *Judith* originally preceded the prose texts in the manuscript. That it did not precede them when Nowell wrote his name in the book suggests that the poem was already a fragment at that time.

Sometime after Nowell's death the manuscript came into the possession of Sir Robert Bruce Cotton (1571–1631), and presumably it was he who had the Southwick and Nowell Codices bound together. Cotton's collection of medieval books later served as the foundation on which the manuscript collections of the British Museum were built. This collection was temporarily housed in Ashburnham House in Westminster when a catastrophic fire broke out there in 1731. Many of the books were damaged, some destroyed. Vitellius A. xv was saved when, it seems, it was tossed from a window, but the top and outer edges of each leaf were burned, with the result that today many letters are missing from the texts. Fortunately, *Judith* had been transcribed before the fire, so that nothing is lost of the poem. *Beowulf* was transcribed some years after the fire, as explained in the introduction to that text below, apparently when many charred fragments around the edges of the leaves still remained. No early transcripts of the prose texts that precede *Beowulf* in the manuscript were made, however, so that the book in its present state remains our sole witness to all these texts but *The Wonders of the East,* of which another medieval copy survives.

In 1845, further deterioration around the edges of the leaves was halted by the rebinding of the manuscript. The folios were slit at the folds and each leaf was mounted in a heavy paper frame in which a hole had been cut to match the contours of the damaged folio. This is the present state of the manuscript, as may be seen in the published facsimiles. On one side of each leaf the frame inevitably covers some letters in the damaged areas; on the other side the letters are visible through the transparent tape that holds the leaf in place.

The texts of the Nowell Codex must have been copied from a written exemplar, since they show examples of the sorts of copying errors that result when a scribe misreads a written text. Their linguistic features, however, differ in ways that suggest that the texts were not all copied from a single source. Why these particular texts were collected in one book is not plain, but one influential explanation that has been offered is that the manuscript is devoted to narratives about monsters.

The Passion of Saint Christopher

Because the *Beowulf* Manuscript is defective at the beginning, about two-thirds of the legend of St. Christopher has been lost (see the first note in the Notes to the Translations for a summary of the corresponding Latin source, the *Passio S. Christophori*). The specific version of the source employed, of no later than the eighth century, was itself probably an abridgment of the legend, beginning not with Christopher's conversion to Christianity but with his later mission to the realm of King Dagnus. Certainly Christopher's legend was known from early times in Anglo-Saxon England, since it is abstracted in two of the four surviving manuscripts of the ninth-century *Old English Martyrology,* translated from a Latin text that, it has been argued, may have been composed by Acca of Hexham in the third decade of the eighth century; there is also an Anglo-Saxon manuscript of the Latin *Passio* from about 900. Outside these texts, however, evidence for Christopher's popularity is obtainable only from late in the Anglo-Saxon period, since his feast is not noted in Anglo-Saxon liturgical calendars before about 975. When the Old English translation was first made cannot be determined, but, like all the texts in the *Beowulf* Manuscript, some of its linguistic features suggest composition north of the Thames, though the language of the extant fragment is chiefly that of the southwest. What was probably another copy of the present text was once preserved in another manuscript in the Cottonian collection (see the first note in the Notes to the Translations).

The Wonders of the East

The Wonders of the East, also sometimes called *The Marvels of the East,* was translated into Old English from a Latin text now generally referred to as *De rebus in oriente mirabilibus,* a title given it in modern times. This Latin text was in turn rendered from a Greek one sometime before the death of Isidore of Seville in 636, since Isidore used the Latin text as a source for his *Etymologiae.* The Old English is rather faithful to the Latin, with only minor omissions and errors. Occasionally a brief explanation is added, as in regard to Latin *Homodubii* ("þæt beoð twi-men," 33) and *Gorgoneus* ("þæt is Wælkyrging," 34). Sometimes two alternate translations are offered for a single Latin word or phrase, as in the case of *pisces crudos manducant* ("be hreawum fixum hy lifiað ond þa etaþ," 33).

The Wonders of the East is the only text in the *Beowulf* Manuscript of which a copy survives in another Anglo-Saxon codex, London, British Library, Cotton Tiberius B. v. The latter copy is slightly longer and fuller. Indeed, the first scribe of the *Beowulf* Manuscript seems to have had little regard for the text, which he frequently shortened to make fit the space available among the illustrations, most notably in sentences 15–16, 51, and 102–8. The differences between the texts, however, are not infrequently due to the Vitellius scribe's lack of care, exceptional by comparison to his work on the other texts he copied, and perhaps an indication of faltering interest in such a sensational, implausible, and fairly discontinuous account. And yet while the Tiberius version is somewhat fuller, the Vitellius is of greater linguistic import, preserving a wider variety of features that appear to be archaic and dialectal. It is particularly interesting that a number of Old English words in the Vitellius manuscript have been supplied with interlinear glosses in Middle English, attesting to study of the text after the Norman Conquest.

Unlike the other texts in the *Beowulf* Manuscript, *The Wonders of the East* is accompanied by numerous illustrations, which attest to the allure of its contents, the most exotic of any of the texts in the manuscript, though all are devoted to wonders of various kinds. The drawings are not exceptionally skilled by Anglo-Saxon standards, but neither are they artless, especially given the difficulty of helping readers to visualize unimaginably foreign peoples, fauna, and flora. The illustration of the process of stealing riches from the gold-gathering ants of India (sentences 34–41) is particularly ambitious. But the even more numerous illustrations in the Tiberius manuscript show considerably greater skill, reinforcing the impression that the Vitellius manuscript is provincial in origin.

The Letter of Alexander the Great to Aristotle

Within a very few years of the death of Alexander III of Macedon (356–323 BCE) there circulated already in the ancient world outlandish tales of his life and exploits. These were transmitted to later times chiefly in the form of the "Alexander Romance," a compilation that was falsely ascribed to the historian Callisthenes of Olynthus (ca. 360–328 BCE), although it was actually compiled in Alexandria in the first or second century CE. One source used by the compiler of the romance was a Greek text of a purported letter of Alexander to his teacher Aristotle. The Greek letter no longer survives, but the Latin *Epistola Alexandri ad Aristotelem* is a translation of it made no later than the seventh century. The Old English *Letter of Alexander the Great to Aristotle* uniquely preserved in the *Beowulf* Manuscript is a translation of this Latin text.

The Old English translator is rather faithful to the Latin, though he omits the account of Alexander's adventures after leaving the grove of the sacred trees. This passage is admittedly somewhat repetitive, and at all events it is anticlimactic after the prophecy of Alexander's approaching death, so that the swift conclusion of the Old English text is more satisfying and effective. The reference to sexual relations between men and boys has been omitted from sentence 246, but the reference is also discarded in at least one Latin manuscript. Names of unfamiliar peoples, places, and things are also sometimes omitted, as so commonly happens in Old English texts—for example, *Seres* in sentence 43 and *Caspii* in sentence 46, and the comparison in sentence 64 of the bitterness of the water to that of hellebore. Aside from altered numbers, substantive differences otherwise are mostly the result of misapprehension of the Latin; some of the more interesting instances are indicated in the Notes to the Translations on sentences 4, 46, 118, 144, and 243.

Beowulf

Beowulf is valued among Old English texts for a variety of reasons, especially for its exceptional poetic qualities, for its information about Anglo-Saxon heroic culture and early Scandinavian history, and for the insights into earlier stages of the Old English language that its linguistic conservatism affords. Yet much remains undecided in scholarship on the poem because there is little agreement among literary scholars about the cultural context in which the poem was produced, simply because it is impossible to prove conclusively when and where the poem was composed, except within very broad limits.

Although the manuscript was probably made in the first decade of the millennium, many of the errors committed by the scribes can be plausibly explained only on the assumption that the text is a copy of another written text. A certain number of linguistic and paleographical considerations suggest that the first written copy of the poem could have been recorded as early as the late seventh century, though very few would now date the poem's composition so early. Early Welsh and Irish texts nonetheless furnish ample evidence for the derivation of extant texts from exemplars at several centuries' remove. In recent years a number of scholars have argued for composition in the ninth, tenth, or even the eleventh century, and almost none of these proposals can be dismissed out of hand. Undeniably, Old English poetry is a linguistically conservative genre, employing many forms that must have seemed distinctly archaic by contemporary standards, so that antiquated linguistic forms cannot prove beyond doubt that a poem such as this is genuinely much older than the extant copy of it. Some of the poem's linguistic and formal archaisms, however, are poorly explained by the assumption of late-preserved poetic traditions, and certainly the balance of probability favors the supposition that the poem dates from a time much earlier than the manuscript itself, though it must have undergone significant change in the course of its manuscript transmission, at the very least in regard to its more superficial linguistic features. The most compelling linguistic evidence suggests composition in the early eighth century, a dating supported by the resemblance of some of the poem's formal characteristics, especially of meter, to those of the text preserved in the Exeter Book known as *Guthlac A,* a poem that, by the narrator's account, was composed when Guthlac, who died in 714, was still remembered by many living persons. As for the place of composition, the language of the text is chiefly that of the southwest of England after the middle of the tenth century, but very many linguistic forms argue for composition both earlier and in a more northerly area, most plausibly between the Thames and the Humber.

Because early historiographers are exceedingly spare in their references to Scandinavian affairs, almost nothing in the poem can be confirmed in recorded history. The one striking historical fact is Hygelac's raid on Frisia, which can be dated probably to the period 516–531 on the basis of certain Frankish annals. No historical reference in the poem can definitely be dated later than this, though the poem must have been composed much later.

The poem's account of events in Scandinavia chiefly of the sixth century is corroborated only in part by later, legendary records from Scandinavia itself, and less directly by recent excavations at Lejre in Denmark, identified in legend as the royal seat of the Scylding dynasty. The great Danish king Hrothgar is a relatively minor figure in northern legends, certainly subordinate to his nephew Hrothulf, who figures prominently in Icelandic or Norwegian sagas as Hrólfr kraki. It is hard to believe, though, that the Old English poet alone elevated Hrothgar to his prominent position. If he did not, the poem must preserve traditions that antedate by centuries those preserved in the much later sagas. Similarly, the dragon fight attributed to Sigemund is attached in Scandinavian and late Continental tradition to his son, the greatest of the Scandinavian legendary heroes, though certain early Scandinavian poetry suggests that Sigemund was originally the greater champion, as might be inferred from *Beowulf*. The poet's information about early events in the north presents a remarkable appearance of historicity in its degree of detail, especially in regard to the wars between Geats and Swedes, in comparison to the plainly semi-fictionalized accounts of later Scandinavian records. It is hardly plausible that the *Beowulf* poet's account of these wars could be based on the much vaguer and apparently evolving memories recorded in the surviving Scandinavian records. His narrative certainly must not be regarded as factual, but by comparison to the Scandinavian records, it inspires considerably greater confidence and thus suggests the genuine antiquity of the Old English material, regardless of when that material was actually put into roughly its present form. The hero Beowulf himself, however, has no convincing analogue in Scandinavian records, and he must be regarded as a literary interloper in the legends that form the historical background of his life's story.

The history of these wars between Swedes and Geats, neighboring peoples in what is now central Sweden, plays a prominent role in the final third of the poem. The poet plainly expected some degree of familiarity on the part of his audience with the figures mentioned in his scattered references to the prolonged conflict—another reason to suspect relatively early composition of the poem, since the scribes themselves were plainly unfamiliar with many of the persons mentioned, miscopying many names. Modern readers will most likely require some guidance to follow the course of the action. The poet attributes the origin of the conflict to attacks by Ohthere and Onela, the sons of the Swedish king Ongentheo (2472ff.). These were avenged by Hæthcyn and Hygelac, the surviving sons of the Geatish king Hrethel, though Hæthcyn perished in the campaign. The conflict initially went badly for the Geats, with Ongentheo assuming the upper hand and threatening doom for the Geats (2922ff.), but Hygelac arrived to save the day, and Ongentheo succumbed to the Geatish brothers Wulf and Eofor. Subsequently there developed a struggle for the throne between the Swede Ongentheo's son Onela and his grandsons Eanmund and Eadgils, the sons of Ohthere (2379ff.). The grandsons sought refuge at the Geatish court, and for harboring them Hygelac's son Heardred was attacked and killed by Onela, as was Eanmund. The surviving Swedish heir to the throne, Eadgils, with the support of the Geats, attacked his uncle Onela, defeated him, and assumed the throne. Although Eadgils thus has reasons to owe allegiance to the Geatish realm, it is not plain who occupies the Swedish throne at the time of Beowulf's death, and presumably there lingered resentment in some quarters of the Swedish kingdom about former encounters with the Geats.

Some doubts have been raised at times about the compositional integrity of the poem. The sharp change of tone at line 2200, when the narrative suddenly advances fifty years, has prompted some to conclude that the work is a composite of two earlier works, perhaps with a transitional section (lines 1888–2199?) composed to link the two. However, more recent studies, especially of the poem's peculiar linguistic features and their fairly homogeneous distribution across the supposed separate compositional parts, argues strongly in favor of regarding the poem as the work of a single poet with a coherent design.

The modal contrast between Beowulf's youthful exploits in Denmark and his confrontation with the dragon as an old man in his own country has in fact been analyzed influentially as integral to the poet's purpose. In 1936, J. R. R. Tolkien argued, to great effect, that the poem is constructed as a study in contrast between the hero's youthful exploits abroad, exemplifying the pinnacle of vigor and achievement under the heroic code, and the tragic close of his life, in which noble resistance to malign forces, to the very end, is conquered, in heroic grandeur, by the human inevitability of decline. The poem is thus elegiac in nature, as the opening account of the funeral of Scyld Scefing suggests it will be, celebrating heroic accomplishments but finally lamenting how even the noblest spirit must succumb ultimately to the mutability of earthly things. Alternatively, the poem may be viewed as tripartite in structure, with the particularly difficult fight with Grendel's mother at the center of the three battles with monsters, suggesting the possibility that gender and a questioning attitude toward the impulse to vengeance urged by the heroic code are themselves the poet's chief concerns. Tolkien's view of the poem's structure as binary, however, is lent support by the pointed juxtaposition of contrasting elements at multiple levels of analysis, from the individual verse (e.g., "young and old," 72; "one against all," 145) to the long alliterative line (e.g., "then after feasting, wailing was lifted up," 128; "they dissuaded him little, though he was dear to them," 203) to the passing allusion (e.g., the construction and destruction of Heorot, 81–85, and Hygd's nobility of spirit versus Fremu's treachery, 1926–32) to the episode (Sigemund's success versus Heremod's failure, 875–97, and the awarding and loss of the Brosings' neck-ornament, 1195–1214). This principle of contrastive juxtaposition is in fact to a considerable extent responsible for the poet's perceived digressiveness: the poem's frequent interposed episodes and divagations can to a remarkable extent be explained as intended to reflect contrastively on the main line of the narrative. This is nowhere plainer than in the portion of the poem set in Beowulf's home country, in which the frequent allusions to the Geats' prior wars with Swedes and Franks serve to intensify the tragedy of Beowulf's self-sacrifice in fighting the dragon, since the implication is that without Beowulf's protection, after a long period of calm the Geats face a difficult future of armed hostility with old enemies.

A few other rhetorical features merit notice. One is the employment of kennings, which are poetic circumlocutions of a relatively fixed form. An example is "whale-road" in line 10, referring to the sea. Neither element of the kenning refers literally to the intended referent, and the effect of the combination is distinctly metaphorical. Kennings may be compound words, as in this example, or they may comprise close syntactic groups, especially noun-plus-dependent-possessive, for example "herder of crimes" (750), in reference to Grendel. A reduced form of the kenning is encountered when a single word takes on metaphorical meaning, as when "sweat" (no doubt an abbreviation of "battle-sweat") assumes the meaning "blood." Another favored pattern is direct contrast at the local level, in which a decided opposite is indicated by a negative construction contrasted with a positive. An example is "Neither, certainly, did they criticize their benevolent lord, gracious Hrothgar, but that was a good king" (862–63), which emphasizes Hrothgar's cherished status by rejecting the opposite proposition. Sometimes the positive element is suppressed, and the result is a kind of litotes, or poetic understatement, for example in "that was not a good exchange" (1304), describing the vengeance exacted by Grendel's mother. There is also the device of aural punctuation, comprising a lone, grammatically independent verse in the second half of the poetic line that serves to mark the rhetorical end of a poetic passage. Examples are "Things always go as they must" (455) and "There hell received him" (852).

Despite the poem's position of importance in Anglo-Saxon studies, it elicited no sustained scholarly interest until 1787, when the Icelandic historian and archivist to the Danish crown Grímur Jónsson Thorkelín had the poem transcribed and undertook a transcription of his own shortly thereafter. This was many years after the fire of 1731 that had damaged the manuscript so disastrously, but apparently there remained many charred fragments attached to the manuscript leaves when the amanuensis did his work, since his transcript appears to preserve very many manuscript readings that are now otherwise lost to us. Thorkelín's own transcript (referred to as Thorkelín B) is less reliable, being in many places clearly indebted to the transcript of his amanuensis (referred to as Thorkelín A). Occasionally some help in the reconstruction of the text is afforded by other early records. These include the 1705 manuscript catalogue of Humphrey Wanley (the second volume of the *Thesaurus* of George Hickes) and the collations recorded in Thorkelín's 1815 edition by John Josias Conybeare and Frederic Madden (which are reproduced in Kiernan's *Electronic Beowulf* of 2003). The final folio of *Beowulf* seems at one time to have served as an outside cover for the manuscript, since the writing is worn and the parchment torn. Although there is scholarly disagreement, it appears that someone, perhaps Laurence Nowell, retouched much of the writing on the verso of this leaf, and not always correctly, so that restoring the text of lines 3150–82 entails some difficulty. Even greater difficulties attend the reconstruction of the text in lines 2207–52, since the folio on which these verses are preserved has been particularly ill treated, and it appears likewise to have been retraced, with even less accuracy than on the final leaf. This passage also contains a mostly erased dittograph that has been omitted from the present text. The text is, as a consequence, one line shorter than is usually assumed, and to preserve congruence with the lineation of other editions, the expedient has been adopted of omitting line 2229 without renumbering the remainder.

The translation in nearly all respects accords with the interpretations offered in *Klaeber's Beowulf* (corrected reprint

2009), though the vocabulary employed ranges more widely than what is to be found in the glossary of that edition. Since some of the original writing is also discernible under the retouching on the leaves of the manuscript containing lines 2207–52 and 3150–82, the later hand is remarked in the apparatus of variants in regard to these verses. That is, although the later hand is often wrong, earlier readings sometimes show through.

Judith

The fragmentary *Judith* is a very free rendering of portions of the deuterocanonical book of Judith, which was regarded as canonical in Anglo-Saxon times. Precisely which Latin version the poet used cannot be determined with certainty, but undeniably he made use of a version resembling the Vulgate, though his source may also have incorporated certain aspects of an earlier Latin version called *Vetus Latina.*

The poem, like *Beowulf,* is divided into fitts, the numbers X, XI, and XII appearing after lines 14, 121, and 235, respectively. The fitts preserved entire thus average a bit more than 111 lines in length, and if the missing initial fitts were of the same approximate length, it would appear that about a thousand lines have been lost at the beginning. Since the extant fragment corresponds to chapters 12:10 to 16:1 in the Vulgate, the loss of some thousand lines would at first appear to be a plausible estimate. However, the poet is selective in his treatment of the source material, and elements that he omitted from the preserved portion entail extensive related omissions from the lost portions of the poem, so that it is difficult to believe that chapters 1:1 to 12:9 of the book of Judith could alone have provided material for a thousand lines of verse. Since fitt numbering is continuous in the first three poems of Oxford, Bodleian Library, Junius 11, it may be, as most scholars seem to believe, that the fitts of *Judith* were similarly numbered consecutively with those of a lost, preceding poem on a related theme. Alternatively, it may be that the translator incorporated material from a source or sources other than the book of Judith into the lost material, on a structural plan that is no longer recoverable.

The end of the poem also raises questions about the state of preservation of the text, because the portion recorded in the hand of the Anglo-Saxon scribe, the same who copied lines 1939–3182 of *Beowulf,* ends at the foot of the final page of the manuscript with the word "sigor-lean" (344), the remainder having been copied into the bottom margin by an unidentified early modern hand (probably ca. 1600) imitating an Insular script. The final six lines thus appear to have been copied from a subsequent leaf, now lost, which was most likely the first leaf of a new quire. It is possible that yet more of the poem followed these added lines in that lost quire, since there remains one entire chapter of the book of Judith in the Vulgate that the poet has not translated; but the poem gives the impression of being complete at this point. This analysis also is most congruent with the argument that *Judith* preceded the St. Christopher fragment in the original construction of the manuscript, as mentioned above.

It is fortunate that a transcript of the poem was made by the Dutch scholar Franciscus Junius, probably between 1646 and 1651. As a result, the Cottonian fire of 1731 had no serious consequences for the recovery of the text.

The poet's treatment of his source is by no means slavish. Like so many Old English poets, he omits the names of people and places that would not have been familiar to a monoglot audience, and he reduces the cast of named characters to Judith and Holofernes alone. He also "polarizes" the characters, making Holofernes more fiendish, and perhaps higher in rank, than the Assyrian general of his source, and similarly having all the Assyrian officers lie in a drunken stupor as an explanation for their inability to resist the Hebrews' onslaught. Conversely, he makes of Judith a more unambiguously virtuous figure. In the Vulgate she is more devious, willing to lie and to use her charms to encourage Holofernes in his folly, plotting all the while his assassination. In the Old English she is all virtue, guided as she is by the will of God, and there is no hint of her intent to use her attractiveness against her adversary. The reduction of detail in characterization is matched by the general omission of most features of the Latin text that are not essential to the plot, and particularly elements that do not contribute to the tradition-bound portrayal of a heroic world of arms and armed conflict presided over by divine will.

A formal peculiarity of *Judith* is the proliferation of so-called hypermetric verses, sometimes described as comprising three measures each, whereas normal verses comprise two. In *Beowulf* there are perhaps just eleven hypermetric lines (i.e., verse pairs) out of 3,181, while in *Judith,* 68 of the 349 lines (indicated by leftward movement of the left margin in the text) are hypermetric. In poetry, the hypermetric form tends to be employed for passages of elevated dignity (as when, for example, God speaks in *Genesis A*), though the motivation for such a distinction is not always obvious in *Judith.*

Like most Old English verse, *Judith* evinces linguistic features that indicate composition in the Midlands or the north, though the language is in the main that of the southwest. More remarkable are certain neologisms that are wanting in the conservative language of most verse, suggesting relatively late composition. The poem does not, however, show the alliterative peculiarities found in datably late poems such as *The Battle of Maldon* (composed no earlier than 991) in regard to the matching of palatal and velar varieties of *g*.

The most substantial text in the codex, and the most difficult, is thus *Beowulf*. If it seems an improbable stroke of good fortune that the manuscript should have survived into modern times, it is equally the baldest improbability that a text such as *Beowulf* should have been recorded at all. For manuscripts were precious objects in the early Middle Ages, requiring considerable expense and labor to produce, and thus they tend to contain only such texts as the ecclesiastics who compiled them were likely to find useful in the service of the Church. That *Beowulf* had grown obscure by the time it was copied into the extant manuscript is demonstrated by the sorts of errors committed by the scribes, especially in the copying of proper names, which, it is apparent, were often entirely unfamiliar to the copyists. That such a lengthy poem, full of puzzling allusions to a vanished world and of no obvious ecclesiastical use, should have been copied at about the millennium is thus perhaps the greatest wonder presented by this book of many wonders.

THE PASSION OF SAINT CHRISTOPHER

. . . mines Dryhtnes hælendes Cristes, ac þu eart dysig ond unsnotor, þu ðe ne ondrætst Dryhten, se ys ealra þinga scyppend.

Se cyningc þa yrre geworden wæs ond het gebindan his handa ond hys fet tosomne, ond he hyne het swingan mid isernum gyrdum, ond he het settan on his heafde þry weras. Þa cempan, þa ðe hyne swungan, gecwædon to ðam cyninge, "Eadig wære ðu, Dagnus, gyf þu næfre geboren nære, þu ðe þus wæl-hreowlice hetst tintregian þillicne godes cempan." Se cyningc þa yrre geworden wæs, ond he het þære ylcan tide þa weras acwellan.

5 Se halga Cristoforus cigde to þæm cynige ond cwæð, "Gyf þu hwylce maran witu be me geþoht hæbbe, hrædlice do ðu þa, forðon þine tintrego me synt swettran þonne huniges beo-bread." Se cyningc þa het bringan isenne scamol, se wæs emn-heah þæs mannes up-wæstme, þæt wæs twelf fæðma lang, ond he hyne het asettan on middan þa ceastre, ond þone halgan Cristoforus he het þær to gebindan, ond he het beneoðan him þæt unmætoste fyr onælan, ond myt ty þe þæs fyres lig on þære mæstan hæto wæs, he þær ofer þæt het geotan tyn orcas fulle eles, þæt he wolde þæt þæs fyres hæto þe reðre wære ond þe ablæstre on þone halgan man.

. . . of my Lord the savior Christ, but you are deluded and unwise, you who do not fear the Lord, who is the creator of all things.”

The king by then had become angry and ordered that his hands and his feet be bound together, and he directed that he be beaten with iron rods, and he commanded that three men be set on his head. The soldiers who beat him said to the king, “You would be fortunate, Dagnus, if you had never been born, you who thus bloodthirstily order that such a soldier of God be tortured.” The king by then had grown angry, and he ordered that those men be executed that very hour.

Saint Christopher cried out to the king and said, “If you 5
have any greater torments planned for me, apply them quickly, since your tortures are sweeter to me than honeycomb with honey.” The king then directed that an iron bench be brought that was equal in height to the man’s stature—it was twelve fathoms tall—and he commanded that it be set in the midst of the town, and he ordained that Saint Christopher be bound to it, and he directed that beneath it the most immense fire be kindled; and as soon as the flame of that fire was at its hottest, he ordered that ten pitchers full of oil be poured over it, inasmuch as he wanted the heat of the fire to be the fiercer and the more furious against the saintly man.

Se halga Cristoforus þa, on middum þam reðestan ond þam unmætostan liges bæle he cigde to Drihtne beorhtre stefne, ond he cwæð to ðam cyninge, "Þas tintrego þe ðu on me bringan hehst to þinre gescyndnesse ond to þinre forwyrde becumað. Ond ic me næfre þine tintrego ne ondræde ne þin yrre."

Ond mit ty þe he þis cwæð, se halga on middes þæs fyres mænigo, se scamull him wæs geworden eallswa geþywed weax. Þa geseah Dagnus se cyningc þone halgan Cristoforus on middum þam fyre standende, ond he geseah þæt his ansyn wæs swylce rosan blostma. Myt ty þe he þæt geseah, he wæs on micelre modes wafunga, ond for þæs eges fyrhto he wæs swa abreged þæt he gefeol on eorðan ond þær læg fram þære ærestan tide þæs dæges oð ða nigoþan tide. Þa þæt geseah se halga Cristoforus, he hyne het up arisan, ond myt ty þe he up aras, he him to cwæð, "Þu wyrresta wild-deor, hu lange dyrstlæcest þu þæt ðu þis folc fram me tyhtest, swa þæt him nis alyfed þæt hi minum godum onsecgen?

Se halga Cristoforus him andswarode ond cwæð, "Nu git micel folces mænio þurh me gelyfað on minne Drihten hælend Crist, ond æfter þon þu selfa."

Se cyningc þa him andswarode bysmerigende ond him to cwæð, "Is þæs wen þæt ðu me swa beswican mæge þæt ic þinne god gebidde ond minum wiðsace? Wite þu, þonne, þæt ðys mergenlican dæge æt þisse sylfan tide ic wrece minne teonan on þe, ond ic gedo þæt ðu byst forloren ond þin nama of þys gemynde ond of þyssum life adilgod, ond þu scealt wesan ealra bysen þara þe ðurh þe on ðinne god gelyfað."

Oðre dæge þa se cyningc het þone halgan Cristoforus to

Then Saint Christopher, in the midst of the fiercest and most immense burning of the flame, called out to the Lord with a clear voice, and he said to the king, "These torments that you commanded be inflicted on me will result in your disgrace and your perdition. And I shall never be intimidated by your tortures or your anger."

And as soon as the saint had said this in the midst of the multitude of flames, the bench became for him just like pressed wax. King Dagnus then saw Saint Christopher standing in the midst of the fire, and he perceived that his countenance was like the bloom of a rose. When he saw that, he was greatly astonished, and in the fright of that panic he was so alarmed that he fell to the earth and lay there from the first hour of the day until the ninth hour. When Saint Christopher saw that, he told him to get up, and as soon as he had risen, the king said to him, "You vilest brute, how long will you presume to entice this populace away from me, so that they are not allowed to offer sacrifice to my gods?"

Saint Christopher answered him and said, "Already by means of me a great host of people believe in my Lord and savior Christ, and after this, you yourself."

The king then answered him, mocking him, and said to him, "Is it to be expected that you can so delude me that I should pray to your god and forsake mine? Take heed, then, that tomorrow at this very hour I shall exact satisfaction on you for my injury, and I shall arrange it that you will be destroyed and your name blotted out of memory and out of existence, and you will be made an example of all those who by means of you believe in your god."

The next day, then, the king ordered that Saint Christo-

him gelædan ond him to cwæð, “Ongit min word ond onsaga minum godum, þæt ðu on swa manegum tintregum ne forweorðe swa ðe gegearwode synt.”

Se halga him andswarode ond cwæð, “Symle þine goda ic laðette ond him teonan do, forþon þe minne geleafan ic unwemne geheold, þone þe ic on fulwihte onfeng.”

Se cyningc þyder þa het bringan unmætre micelnesse treow þæt wæs efn-heah þæs halgan mannes lengo, ond he hit het asettan beforan þære healle, ond he hyne het þær on gefæstnian ond bebead þæt ðry cempan hyne scotedon mid hyra strælum oð þæt he wære acweald. Þa cempan hyne þa scotedon fram þære ærestan tide þæs dæges oð æfen. Se cyningc þa wende þæt ealle þa strælas on his lic-haman gefæstnode wæron, ac ne furþon an his lic-haman ne gehran, ac Godes mægen wæs on ðam winde hangigende æt þæs halgan mannes swyðran healfe. Ond se cyningc þa, æfter sunnan setl-gange, he sende to ðam cempum, ond he bead þæt hi hyne swa gebundenne geornlice heoldon, forðon he wende þæt þæt cristene folc hyne wolde onlysan þy mergenlican dæge.

Þa se cyningc wæs ut gangende to þam halgan Cristoforus ond him to cwæþ, “Hwær ys þin god? For hwon ne com he ond þe gefreolsode of minum handum ond of þyssum egeslican strælum?”

Hraðe þa myt ty þe he þas word gecwæð, twa flana of þam strælum scuton on þas cyninges eagan, ond he þurh þæt wæs ablend. Þæt þa geseah se halga Cristoforus; he him to cwæð, “Þu wæl-grimma ond þu dysega, wite þu þæt ðis mergenlican dæge æt þære eahtoðan tide þæs dæges ic onfo minne sigor, ond ðurh dryhten sylfne me wæs ætywed þæt Cristene men cumað ond onfoð mines lic-haman ond hyne gesettaþ

pher be brought to him and said to him, "Understand what I said and offer sacrifice to my gods, lest you perish from as many tortures as are prepared for you."

The saint answered him and said, "I shall always despise your gods and do them injury, because I have held unblemished my faith, which I received at baptism."

The king then commanded that there be brought a piece of timber of immense size that was as tall as the man's stature, and he ordered that it be set before the hall, and he had him affixed to it and directed that three soldiers should shoot at him with their arrows until he was killed. The soldiers then assailed him from the first hour of the day until evening. The king then supposed that all the arrows were fixed in his body, but not even one touched his body; rather, the might of God was hanging on the wind to the right-hand side of the saintly man. And the king then, after the setting of the sun, sent for the soldiers and requested that they carefully guard him, bound thus, since he supposed that the Christian community wished to release him the next day.

Then the king was out on a walk to Saint Christopher, and he said to him, "Where is your god? Why did he not come and liberate you from my hands, and from these horrid arrows?"

At once, then, upon his speaking those words, two barbs from those arrows darted into the king's eyes, and by that he was blinded. Saint Christopher saw that then; he said to him, "You bloodthirsty fool, take heed that tomorrow at the eighth hour of the day I shall receive my victory, and by the Lord himself it was revealed to me that Christian people will come and take my body and deposit it in the place that

on þa stowe þe him fram Drihtne ætywed wæs. Cum þonne to minum lic-haman ond nym þære eorðan lam þe ic on gemartyrod wæs ond meng wið min blod ond sete on þine eagan. Þonne gif þu gelyfst on God of ealre heortan, þære sylfan tide þu bist gehæled fram þinra eagena blindnesse. Wite þu þæt seo tid nealæceð þæt Cristforus, Godes se gecorena, onfehð his gewinna mede and gelif-fæsted ferð to Drihtne."

Þy mergenlican dæge, ær þam þe he fram þam cempum acweald wære, þyssum wordum he ongan gebiddan ond cweþan: "Drihten ælmihtig, þu ðe me of gedwolan gehwyrfdest ond godne wisdom gelærdest, þæt ic þin þeow nu on þysse tide þe bidde gearwa, hyt unne þætte on swa hwylcre stowe swa mines lic-haman ænig dæl sy, ne sy þær ne wædl ne fyres broga. Ond gif þær neah syn untrume men and hig cumon to þinum þam halgan temple, ond hig ðær gebiddon to þe of ealre heortan, ond for þinum naman hi ciggen minne naman, gehæl þu þone, Drihten, fram swa hwylcere untrumnesse swa hie forhæfde."

Ond on ðære ylcan tide stefn wæs gehyredu to him cweþendu, "Cristoforus min þeow, þin gebed ys gehyred. Þeah þin lic-hama ne sy on þære stowe, swa hwyllce geleaffulle men swa þines naman myndgien on heora gebedum, beoð gehælede fram hyra synnum, ond swa hwæs swa hie rihtlice biddaþ for þinum naman ond for þinum geearningum, hig hyt onfoð."

Mit ty þe þeos wuldorlice spræc of heofenum wæs gehyredu ond gefylledu, hraðe fram þam cempum he wæs slegen, ond he on þære mæstan blisse ond unasecgendlican wuldre he ferde to Criste. Ond þæt wæs wundor þæs folces þe se halga Cristoforus þurh his lare Gode gestrynde: þæt wæs eaht ond feowertig þusenda manna and hundteontig and fiftyne.

was manifested to them by the Lord. Come then to my body and take the soil of the earth on which I was martyred, and mix it with my blood and set it on your eyes. Then if you believe in God with all your heart, that very hour you will be healed of the blindness of your eyes. Take heed that the time approaches when Christopher, God's chosen, will receive the reward of his labors and, ever-living, will go to meet the Lord."

The next day, before he was to be killed by the soldiers, with these words he began to pray and speak: "Lord almighty, you who converted me from error and taught me good wisdom, I your servant now at this time earnestly request it, grant it that in whatever place any part of my body may be, let there not be want there or the danger of fire.
And if there are any infirm people there by, and they come 30
to your holy temple, and they pray to you there with all their heart, and in your name they invoke my name, heal them, Lord, from whatever infirmity has afflicted them."

And at that same hour a voice was heard saying to him, "Christopher my servant, your prayer is heard. Even if your body is not at that place, whichever people of faith make mention of your name in their prayers, they will be healed of their sins, and whatever they reasonably request in your name and on your merits, they will receive it."

As soon as this miraculous speech from heaven was heard and completed, immediately he was killed by the soldiers, and in the greatest happiness and inexpressible glory he journeyed to Christ. And that was a wonder, the people Saint Christopher acquired for God through his teaching: that was forty-eight thousand one hundred fifteen.

35 Oþre dæge þa se cyningc cwæð to his þegnum, "Uton
gangan ond geseon hwær þa cempan hyne gesett habbon."
Ond mit ty þe hie becomon to þære stowe þær se halga lic-
hama wæs, se cyningc cigde micelre stemne ond cwæð,
"Cristoforus, ætyw me nu þines godes soð-fæstnesse, ond ic
gelyfe on hyne." Ond he genam dæl þære eorðan þær þæs
Cristes martyr wæs on þrowigende ond medmicel þæs blo-
des ond mengde tosomne ond sette on his eagan, ond he
cwæð, "On naman Cristoforus godes ic þis dom." Ond hraðe
on ðære ylcan tide his eagan wæron ontynde, ond gesihþe he
onfeng, ond he cigde micelre stemne, ond he cwæð beforan
eallum þam folce, "Wuldorfæst ys ond micel Cristenra manna
God, þæs wuldor-geworces nane mennisce searwa ofercu-
man ne magon. Ic þonne nu fram þyssum dægenlican dæge
ic sende mine bebodu geond eall min rice þætte nan mon þe
to mines rices anwealde belimpe ne gedyrstlæce nan-wuht
do ongean þæs heofonlican Godes willan þe Cristoforus
40 beeode. Gif þonne ænig man þurh deofles searwa to þon
beswicen sy þæt hyt gedyrstlæce, on þære ylcan tide sy he
mid swyrde witnod, forþon ic nu soðlice wat þæt nan eorðlic
anweald ne nan gebrosnodlic nys noht, butan his anes."

Ond swa þa wæs geworden þurh Godes miht ond þurh geearnunga þæs eadigan Cristoforus þætte se cyningc gelyfde se wæs ær deofles willan full. Þæs eadigan Cristoforus wuldor-geworc synd nu lang to asecgane þe Dryhten þurh hyne geworhte to herennesse his naman ond nu oð þyssne dæg wyrcð, forþon þe þær nu blowað ond growað his þa halgan gebedu, ond þær ys Drihtnes hyrnes mid ealre sybbe ond gefean, ond þær ys gebletsod Crist, Godes sunu lyfigendes,

The next day, then, the king said to his retinue, "Let's go 35
and see where the soldiers have set him." And upon their coming to the place where the holy body was, the king called out in a loud voice and said, "Christopher, show me now the righteousness of your god, and I shall believe in him." And he took some of the earth where Christ's martyr had suffered and a bit of the blood and mixed them together and put it on his eyes, and he said, "In the name of Christopher's god I do this." And immediately at that very hour his eyes were opened, and he recovered his sight, and he called out in a loud voice, and before all the people he said, "Glorious and great is the God of Christian peoples, whose wondrous work no human stratagem can overcome. Now then from this very day I shall send my orders throughout all my realm that no one who is subject to the jurisdiction of my rule do anything in opposition to the will of the heavenly God
which Christopher served. Then if anyone is so deluded 40
through the devil's wiles that he attempt that, in that same hour let him be punished with the sword, since I now know it for a truth that there is no earthly and no perishable authority at all, but his alone."

And so it came to pass through the power of God and through the merit of the blessed Christopher that the king who had been full of the devil's will became a believer. The wondrous works of the saintly Christopher which the Lord performed and still to this day performs through him to the praise of his name are now too long to relate, for now his holy prayers blossom and grow there, and there is obedience to the Lord with all love and contentment, and there Christ

se rixað mid Fæder ond mid Suna ond mid þam Halgan Gaste a butan ende.

Þyses eac bæd se halga Cristoforus of þære nihstan tide ær he his gast onsende ond cwæð, "Drihten min God, syle gode mede þam þe mine þrowunga awrite, ond þa ecean edlean þam þe hie mid tearum ræde."

is blessed, son of the living God, who reigns with the Father and the Son and the Holy Ghost for ever and ever.

Saint Christopher also prayed for this from the last hour before he gave up his spirit, and said, "My Lord God, give good reward to whoever writes about my passion, and eternal recompense to whoever reads it with tears."

THE WONDERS OF THE EAST

Seo land-bunis is on fruman from Antimolime þæm lande. Þæs landes is on gerime þæs læssan mil-getæles þe *stadio* hatte fif hund, ond þæs miclan þe *leones* hatte þreo hund ond eahta ond .lx. On þæm ea-lande bið micel mænegeo sceapa, ond þanon is to Babilonian þæs læssan mil-getæles *stadio* hundteontig ond eahta ond .lx., ond þæs miclan mil-getæles þe *leones* hatte fiftyne ond hundteontig.

5 Seo lond-bunis is swyðust cepe-monnum geseted. Þær beoð weðras acenned on oxna micelnesse, þa buað oð Meda burh. Þære burge nama is Archemedon; sio is mæst to Babilonia burh, þonon syndon þæs læssan mil-getæles *stadi* .ccc. ond þæs maran þe *leon* hatte .cc. from Archemedon. Þær syndon þa miclan mærða, þæt syndon þa weorc þe se micla macedonisca Alexsander het gewyrcan. Ðæt land is on lenge ond on brædc .cc. þæs læssan mil-getæles *stadi* ond þæs miclan þe *leones* hatte .cxxx. ond healf mil.

Sum stow is þonne mon fereð to þære Readan Sæ seo is
haten Lentibelsinea, þæm beoð henna acenned onlice ðam
10 þe mid us beoð reades heowes. Gif hi hwylc man niman wile
oþþe him o æthrineð, þonne forbærnað hy sona eal his lic.
Þæt syndon ungefrægelicu liblac.

Eac þonne þær beoð wildeor acenned; þa deor þonne hy

The settled area starts from the country Antimolima. The length of that country by count of the smaller measure of distance called stades is five hundred; of the large variety called leagues, three hundred sixty-eight. On that island there is a vast multitude of sheep, and from there to Babylon it is one hundred sixty-eight of the lesser measure of distance stades, and of the large measure of distance called leagues one hundred fifteen.

The settled area is inhabited chiefly by merchants. Rams propagate there the size of oxen, which populate the area as far as the city of the Medes. The name of the city is Archemedon; it is the largest city excluding Babylon, to which it is three hundred of the smaller measure of distance, stades, and two hundred of the larger called leagues from Archemedon. Those great monuments are there, that is, the works that the Macedonian Alexander the Great directed to be made. That country is in length and breadth two hundred of the lesser measure of distance, stades, and of the large that is called leagues one hundred thirty, plus one half mile.

There is a certain place when one is going to the Red Sea that is called Lentibelsinea, where hens are hatched like those that are among us of a red color. If anyone wants to capture them or touch them at all, they immediately burn up his entire body. That is unparalleled black magic.

In addition, wild animals are native there; when those

mannes stefne gehyrað, þonne fleoð hy feor. Þa deor habbað eahta fet ond wælcyrian eagan ond twa heafdu; gif him hwylc mon onfon wille, þonne hiera lic-homan þæt hy onælað. Þæt syndon þa ungefrægelicu deor.

Hascellentia hatte þæt land, þonne mon to Babilonia færð, þæt is þonne ðæs læssan mil-getæles þe *stadia* hatte .ix. mila lang ond brad; þæt bugeð to Meda rice. Þæt land is eallum godum gefylled. Þeos stow hafað nædran; þa nædran habbað twa heafdu, þara eagan scinað nihtes swa leohte swa blæc-ern.

On sumon lande eoselas beoð acende þa habbað swa micle hornas swa oxan. Þa syndon on ðam mæstan westene þæt is on þa suð-healfe from Babiloniam. Þa bugað to þæm Readan Sæ, for þara nædrena mænego þe in þæm stowum beoð þa hatton *corsias*. Þa habbað swa micle hornas swa weðeras. Gif hy hwilcne man sleað oþþe a æthrineð, þonne swylteð he sona. On þam landum bið pipores genihtsumnis; þone pipor healdaþ þa næddran on heora geornfulnysse. Þone pipor mon swa nimeð þæt mon þa stowe mid fyre onæleð, ond þa nædran þonne of dune on þa eorþan þæt hi fleoð; forþon se pipor bið sweart.

From Babiloniam oð Persiam þa burh þar se pipor weaxeð is þæs læssan mil-geteles þe *stadia* hatte eahta hund mila; of þæm is geteald þæs miclan mil-geteles þe *leones* hatte .vi. hund ond .xxiii. ond an healf mil. Seo stow is unwæstmberenlicu for þara nædrena mænego.

Eac swylce þær beoð cende healf-hundingas þa syndon hatene *conopenas*. Hy habbað horses mana ond eoferes tuxas ond hunda heafdu, ond heora oroð bið swylce fyres leg. Þas

animals hear a human voice, they flee far away. The animals have eight feet and Valkyries' eyes and two heads; if anyone wants to capture them, they send their body up in flames. Those are unique creatures.

Hascellentia is the name of that country, when one is going to Babylon, which in length and breadth is nine of the smaller measure of distance called stades; it is subject to the kingdom of the Medes. That region is filled with all good things. This place has snakes; the snakes have two heads, of which the eyes shine at night as bright as a lamp.

In a certain region asses propagate that have horns as large as oxen have. They are in the greatest desert that is to the south of Babylon. They retreat to the Red Sea, on account of the multitude of snakes that are called *corsiae* which are in those places. They have horns as large as rams have. If anyone strikes them or touches them at all, he will die immediately. In that region there is an abundance of pepper; the snakes keep the pepper under their watch. The pepper is obtained in such a way that the area is set ablaze, and the snakes then flee down into the earth; therefore the pepper is black.

From Babylon to the city called Persia where the pepper grows is eight hundred of the smaller measure that is called stades; from the same the count is six hundred twenty-three of the large measure of distance called leagues, plus one half mile. The area is unfruitful on account of the multitude of snakes.

Likewise, cynocephali are born there which are called *conopenae.* They have the mane of a horse and the tusks of a boar and dogs' heads, and their breath is like the blaze of a fire. These regions are near the cities that are filled with all

land beoð neah þæm burgum þe beoð eallum world-welum gefylled; þæt is on þa suð-healfe Egyptana landes.

30 On sumon lande beoð men acende þa beoð on lenge syx fot-mæla. Hi habbað beardas oþ cneow side ond feax oð helan. *Homodubii* hy syndon hatene, þæt beoð twi-men, ond be hreawum fixum hy lifiað ond þa etaþ.

Capi hatte seo ea in þære ilcan stowe þe is haten Gorgo-
neus, þæt is Wælkyrging. Þær beoð cende æmetan swa micle
35 swa hundas. Hy habbaþ fet swelce swa græs-hoppan; hy
syndon reades heowes ond blaces heowes. Þa æmettan del-
fað gold up of eorþan from foran-nihte oð ða fiftan tid
dæges. Þa men þe to þon dyrstige beoð þæt hi þæt gold ni-
men, þonne lædað hy mid him olfendan meran mid hyra fo-
lan ond stedan. Þa folan hy gesælað ær hy ofer þa ea faren.
Þæt gold hio gefætað on þa meran ond hy sylfe onsittað, ond
40 þa stedan þær forlætað. Þonne þa æmettan hy onfindað, ond
þa hwile þe þa æmettan embe þone stedan abysgode beoð,
þonne þa men mid þam merun ond mid þam golde ofer þa
ea fareð. Hy beoð swa hrædlice ofer þære ea þæt men wenað
þæt hy fleogan.

Betwih þysson twam ean is lond-bunis Locotheo hatte; þæt is betwih Nile ond Bryxontes geseted. Seo Nil is ealdor eallicra ea, ond heo floweð of Egypta lande, ond hi nemnað þa ea Archoboleta, þæt is haten þæt micle wæter. On þyssum stowum beoð acende þa miclan mænego ylpenda.

45 Ðær beoð cende men, hy beoð fiftyne fota lange, ond hy habbað hwit lic ond twa neb on anum heafde, fet ond cneowu swyðe reade ond lange nosa ond sweart feax. Þonne hy cennan willað, þonne farað hi on scipum to Indeum, ond þær hyra gecynda in world bringaþ.

Ciconia in Gallia hatte þæt land, þær beoð men acende

worldly treasures; that is to the south of the land of the Egyptians.

In a certain region there are native people who are six feet in height. They have beards down to the knee and hair to the heel. They are called *Homodubii,* that is, "maybe-people," and they live on raw fish and eat them.

Capi is the name of the river in the same place that is called Gorgoneus, that is, "Valkyriean." Ants as large as dogs propagate there. They have feet such as grasshoppers have; they are of red color and of black color. The ants dig gold up out of the earth from dusk until the fifth hour of the day. People who are daring enough to go after the gold take with them female camels with their calves and males. They tie up the calves before they cross the river. They load the gold on the females and seat themselves on them, and they leave behind the males. When the ants find them, and while the ants are busy with the male, the people cross the river with the females and the gold. They are across the river so quickly that people suppose they fly.

Between these two rivers is a settled area called Locotheo; it is situated between the Nile and the Brixontes. The Nile is the parent of all rivers, and it flows out of the land of the Egyptians, and they call the river Archoboleta, which is to say "the big water." In these places great herds of elephants propagate.

People are native to the place who are fifteen feet tall, and they have a white body and two faces on a single head, very red feet and knees and a long nose and dark hair. When they intend to reproduce, they go on ships to India, and there they bring their offspring into the world.

The region in Gallia is called Ciconia wherein people of

on ðrys heowes, þara heafdu beoð gemonu swa leona heafdu, ond hi beoð .xx. fota lange, ond hy habbað micelne muð swæ fon. Gyf hi hwylcne monnan on þæm landum ongitað oððe geseoþ, oððe him hwilc folgiende bið, þonne feor þæt hi fleoð, ond blode hy swætað. Þas beoð men gewende.

Begeondan Brixonte ðære ea, east þonon beoð men acende lange ond micle, þa habbað fet ond sconcan .xii. fota lange, sidan mid breostum seofan fota lange. Hi beoð sweartes hiwes, ond *Hostes* hy synd nemned. Cuþlice swa hwylcne man swa hy gelæccað, þonne fretað hi hyne.

Ðonne seondon on Brixonte wildeor þa hatton *lertices.* Hy habbað eoseles earan ond sceapes wulle ond fugeles fet.

Þonne syndon oþere ealond suð from Brixonte, on þon beoð men acende buton heafdum, þa habbað on hyra breostum heora eagan ond muð. Hy seondon eahta fota lange ond eahta fota brade. Ðar beoð dracan cende þa beoð on lenge hundteontige fot-mæla lange ond fiftiges; hy beoð greate swa stænene sweras micle. For þara dracena micelnesse ne mæg nan man na yþelice on þæt land gefaran.

From þisse stowe is oðer rice on þa suð-healfe garsegcges þæt is geteald þæs læssan mil-geteles þe *stadia* hatte .ccc. ond .xxxiii., ond þæs miclan þe *leones* hatte .cc.liii. ond an mil. Þær beoð cende *Homodubii,* þæt byð twi-men. Hi beoþ oð ðone nafolan on menniscum gesceape ond syþþan on eoseles gelicnesse; ond hy habbað longe sconcan swa fugelas ond liþelice stefne. Gif hy hwilcne man on þæm landum ongytað oððe geseoð, þonne fleoð hy feor.

Ðonne is oþer stow el-reordge men beoð on, ond þa habbað cynigas under him þara is geteald .c. Þæt syndon ða

three colors are born whose heads are maned like lions' heads, and they are twenty feet tall, and they have a mouth as big as a fan. If they notice or see any person in that region, or someone is following them, they flee a long distance, and they sweat blood. They are thought to be humans.

Beyond the river Brixontes, east of there, big and tall 50
people are native who have feet and legs twelve feet long, flanks with chests seven feet long. They are of a dark color, and they are called Enemies. Evidently, whatever person they get hold of, they eat him.

Then in the Brixontes there are wild animals called *lertices.* They have the ears of an ass and the wool of a sheep and the feet of a bird.

Then there are other islands south from the Brixontes on 55
which there are born people without heads, who have their eyes and mouth on their chest. They are eight feet tall and eight feet wide. There dragons propagate that are one hundred fifty feet long; they are as thick as large columns. On account of the abundance of the dragons, no one can travel easily to that region.

From this place there is another realm on the southern side of the ocean that is measured at three hundred thirty-three by the smaller measure of distance called stades, and by the large one that is called leagues two hundred fifty-
three plus one mile. *Homodubii* are native to the place, that 60
is, "maybe-people." They are in human shape as far as the navel and then similar to an ass; and they have long legs like birds and a pleasant voice. If they notice or see any person in the region, they flee far away.

Then there is another place in which there are speakers of barbaric tongues, and they have kings under them who

wyrstan men ond þa el-reordegestan. Ond þar syndon twegen seaþas; oþer is sunnan oþer monan. Se sunnan seað, se bið dæges hat ond nihtes ceald, ond se monan seað, se bið nihtes hat ond dæges ceald. Heora widnes is .cc. þæs læssan mil-geteles *stadia,* ond þæs maran þe *leones* hatte .cxxxiii. ond an healf mil.

On þisse stowe beoð treow-cyn þa beoð lawern-beame ond ele-treowum onlice. Of þæm treowum balzamum se deor-weorðesta ele bið acenned. Seo stow is þæs læssan mil-geteles þe *stadia* hatte .c.li. ond þæs miclan þe *leones* hatte . lii.

Đonne is sum ea-lond in þære Readan Sæ, þær is man-cyn þæt is mid us Donestre nemned, þa syndon geweaxene swa frihteras fram þam heafde oð ðone nafolan, ond se oðer dæl bið mennisce onlic, ond hy cunnon eall mennisce gereord. Þonne hy fremdes cynnes mannan geseoð, þonne nemnað hy hyne ond his magas cuþra manna naman, ond mid leaslicum wordum hy hine beswicað ond hine gefoð, ond æfter þan hy hine fretað ealne buton þon heafde ond þonne sittað ond wepað ofer þam heafde.

Đonne is east þær beoð men acende þa beoð on wæstme fiftyne fota lange ond .x. on brade. Hy habbað micel heafod ond earan swæ fon. Oþer eare hy him on niht underbredað, ond mid oþran hy wreoð him. Beoð þa earan swiðe leohte ond hy beoð swa on lic-homan swa hwite swa meolc. Gyf hy hwilcne mannan on þæm lande geseoð oððe ongytað, þonne nymað hy hyra earan him on hand ond fleoð swiðe, swa hrædlece swa is wen þæt hy fleogen.

Đonne is sum ea-lond on þæm beoð men acende þara ea-

number one hundred. Those are the worst people and the most barbaric. And there are two lakes there: one is of the sun, the other of the moon. The lake of the sun is hot by day and cold by night, and the lake of the moon is hot by night and cold by day. Their breadth is two hundred of the smaller measures of distance, stades, of the larger that are called leagues, one hundred thirty-three plus one half mile.

In this place there are species of trees that are like laurels and olive trees. From those trees balsam, the most precious oil, is produced. The area is one hundred fifty-one of the smaller measure of distance that is called stades, and fifty-two of the large one that is called leagues.

Then there is a certain island in the Red Sea where there are humans who are called Donestre among us, who are formed like soothsayers from the head to the navel, and the other part is similar to a human, and they know all human languages. When they see a person of a foreign race, they name him and his kinsmen with the names of acquaintances, and with devious words they delude him, and they get hold of him, and after that they eat him, all but the head, and then sit and weep over the head.

Then it is to the east where people are native who are fifteen feet tall in stature and ten wide. They have a large head and ears like a fan. One ear they spread under them at night, and with the other they cover themselves. The ears are very light, and in their body they are as white as milk. If they spot or notice any person in that region, they take their ears in their hands and flee like mad, so quickly that it is supposed they fly.

Then there is a certain island on which people are born

gan scinaþ swa leohte swa man micel blac-ern onele on þeostre nihte.

Đonne is sum ea-lond þæt is þæs læssan mil-geteles þe *stadia* hatte on lenge ond on bræde .ccc. ond .lx., ond þæs miclan þe *leones* hatte .cx. Þær wæs getymbro on Beles dagum þæs cyninges ond Iobes templ of isernum geworcum ond of glæs-gegotum. Ond on þære ilcan stowe is æt sunnan up-gange ðanon eac oþer templ sunnan halig, to þam is sum geþungen ond gedefe sacerd to gesett, ond he ða hofa gehealdeð ond begymeþ ond setl *Quietus* þæs stillestan bisceopes, se nænine oþerne mete ne þige buton sæ-ostrum, ond be þam he lifede.

Đonne is gylden win-geard æt sunnan up-gonge se hafað bergean hundteontiges fot-mæla ond fiftiges. Of þæm bergean beoð cende sara-gimmas.

Đonne is oþer rice on Babilonia landum þær is seo mæste dun betwih Meda dune ond Armoenia. Seo is ealra duna mæst ond hyhst. Þær syndon gedefelice menn þa habbað him to cynedome þone Readan Sæ ond to anwalde. Þær beoð cende saro-gimmas.

Ymb þas stowe beoð wif acenned þa habbað beardas swa side oð hyra breost, ond horses hyda hy habbað him to hrægle gedon. Þa syndan hunticgean swiðast nemde, ond fore hundum tigras ond leon ond loxas þæt hy fedað, þæt syndon þa cenestan deor, ond ealra þara wildeora cyn þe on þære dune acende beoð, mid heora scinlace þæt hy gehuntiaþ.

Đonne syndan oþere wif þa habbað eoferes tuxas ond feax oð helan side, ond oxan tægl on lendunum. Þa wif syn-

whose eyes shine as bright as if a large lamp were lighted on a dark night.

Then there is a certain island that is in length and breadth three hundred sixty of the smaller measure of distance that is called stades, and one hundred ten of the large that are called leagues. A building was there in the days of King Belus, and a temple of Jove made out of ironwork and of molten glass. And in the same place there is in the direction of the rising sun also another temple sacred to the sun, to which a certain virtuous and proper priest is dedicated, and he tends and maintains the tabernacle and the seat "Quiet" of the most serene bishop, who takes no other food than sea-oysters and lived on them.

Then there is a golden vineyard in the direction of the rising sun that has grapes a hundred fifty feet across. From those grapes are produced jewels.

Then there is another realm in the region of Babylonia where there is the greatest mountain between the mountain of the Medes and of Armenia. It is the largest and tallest of all mountains. There are estimable men there who hold the Red Sea in their rule and in their control. Jewels are produced there.

About that area women are born who have beards as far down as their breast, and they have put to use horsehide for their clothing. They are known foremost as huntresses, and to serve as hunting dogs they raise tigers and lions and lynxes, that is, the fiercest animals, and with their illusion they hunt the species of all the wild animals that propagate on that mountain.

There are other women who have the tusks of a boar and hair down to the heel, and an oxtail on their hindquarters.

don þryttyne fota lange, ond hyra lic bið on marmor-stanes hiwnesse, ond hy habbað olfendan fet ond eoseles teð. Of hyra unclennesse hie gefylde wæron from þæm miclan macedoniscan Alexandre. Þa cwealde he hy þa he hy lifiende oferfon ne mehte, forþon hy syndon æwisce on lic-homan ond unweorþe.

Be þæm garsecge is wildeora cyn þa hatton *catinos,* þa syndon frea-wliti deor, ond þær syndon men þe be hreawum flæsce ond be hunie hy lifiað. On þæm wynstran dæle þæt rice is þe þa deor on beoþ *catinos,* ond þær beoð gæst-liþende men, cyningas þa habbaþ under him monigfealde leodhatan. Heora land-gemæra buaþ neah þæm garsecge; þanon fræm þæm wynstran dæle syndon fela cyninga. Ðis man-cyn lyfið fela geara, ond hy syndon fremfulle men. Gif hwilc mon him to cymð, þonne gifað hy him wif ær hy hine onweg læten. Se Macedonisca Alexander, þa he him to com, þa wæs he wundriende hyra menniscnesse, ne wolde he hi cwellan ne him nan lað don. Ðonne syndon treow-cyn on þæm þa deor-wyrþystan stanas synd of acende, þonon hy growað. Ðær moncyn is; seondan sweartes hyiwes on onsyne, þa mon hateð Sigel-wara.

Ðonne is sum land win-geardas weaxat on swiðast; þær bið rest of elpenda bane geworht, seo is on lenge þreo hund fot-mæla lang ond syxa.

Ðonne is sum dun Aðamans hatte. On ðære dune bið þæt fugel-cynn þe *grifus* hatte. Þa fugelas habbað feower fet ond hryðeres tægl ond earnes heafod.

On þære ylcan stowe byð oðer fugel-cynn *fenix* hatte, þa habbað cambas on heafde swa pawan, ond hyra nest þætte hi wyrcaþ of ðam deor-weorðestan wyrt-gemangum þe man

Those women are thirteen feet tall, and their body has the appearance of marble, and they have the feet of a camel and the teeth of an ass. For their filthiness they were slaughtered by the Macedonian Alexander the Great. He killed them when he could not capture them alive, because they are obscene and disgraceful of body.

By the ocean is a species of wild animal called *catini,* which are noble-looking beasts, and there are people there who live on raw meat and on honey. On the left-hand edge is that realm wherein are the animals *catini,* and there are hospitable people there, kings who have under them various despots. Their regional borders lie near the ocean, and along it from the left-hand edge there are many kings. This race lives many years, and they are well-disposed people. If any man comes to them, they give him a woman before they will let him go away. The Macedonian Alexander, when he visited them, was amazed at their humanity, and he would not kill them or do them any harm. Then there are species of trees from which the most precious stones are produced, [trees] on which they grow. There are humans there; they are of a dark color in their appearance, who are called Ethiopians.

Then there is a certain region in which grapevines grow profusely; there is there a couch made of elephants' bone which is three hundred six feet long.

Then there is a certain mountain called Adamant. On the mountain is the species of bird which is called a griffin. These birds have four feet and the tail of an ox and the head of an eagle.

In the same place there is another species of bird called the phoenix, which have crests on their head like peacocks, and they build their nest of the most precious mixtures of

cinnamomum hateð. Ond of his æðme æfter þusend gearum he fyr onæleð ond þonne geong upp of þam yselum eft ariseþ.

Ðonne is oðer dun þær syndon swearte menn, ond nænig oðer man to ðam mannum geferan mag forðam þe seo dun byð eall byrnende.

the spice that is called cinnamon. And with its breath after a thousand years it kindles a fire and then rises up again young from the ashes.

Then there is another mountain where there are dark people, and no other person can travel to those people because the mountain is all aflame.

THE LETTER OF ALEXANDER THE GREAT TO ARISTOTLE

Her is seo gesetenis Alexandres epistoles þæs miclan kyninges ond þæs mæran Macedoniscan, þone he wrat ond sende to Aristotile his magistre be gesetenisse Indie þære miclan þeode, ond be þære wid-galnisse his siðfato ond his fora þe he geond middan-geard ferde. Cwæþ he þus sona ærest in fruman þæs epistoles:

“Simle ic beo gemindig þin, ge efne betweoh tweondan frecennisse ura gefeohta, þu min se leofesta lareow, ond efne to minre meder ond geswystrum þu me eart se leofesta freond; ond forþon þe ic þe wiste wel getydne in wisdome, þa geþohte ic forþon to þe to writanne be þæm þeod-londe Indie ond be heofenes gesetenissum ond be þæm unarimdum cynnum nædrena ond monna ond wildeora, to þon þæt hwæthwygo to þære ongietenisse þissa niura þinga þin gelis ond gleawnis to geþeode. Þeoh to þe seo gefylde gleawnis ond snyttro, ond naniges fultumes abædeð sio lar þæs rihtes, hwæþere ic wolde þæt þu mine dæde ongeate, þa þu lufast, ond þa þing þe ungesewene mid þe siond, þa ic in Indie geseah þurh monigfeald gewin ond þurh micle frecennisse mid Greca herige.

5 “Þa ic þe write ond cyþe, ond æghwylc þara is wyrðe synderlice in gemyndum to habbanne æfter þære wisan þe ic hit oferseah. Ne gelyfde ic æniges monnes gesegenum swa fela

Here is the text of the letter of Alexander, the great and renowned Macedonian king, which he composed and sent to his teacher Aristotle concerning the composition of the great nation of India, and about the extensiveness of his experiences and his expeditions that he undertook throughout the world. Thus he said immediately at the very outset of the letter:

"I am always thinking of you, even amidst the uncertain risks of our combats, my dearest instructor, and next to my mother and sisters you are my dearest friend; and since I knew you to be well endowed with wisdom, I thought on that account to write to you about the land of India and about the constellations of the firmament and about the countless varieties of snakes and humans and wild animals, so that your learning and acuity might add somewhat to the understanding of these novel things. Although you have consummate intellect and prudence, and the teaching of what is right requires no aid, still I wanted that you should know of my accomplishments, which you love, and of those things that are unseen where you are, which I saw in India in the course of numerous engagements and amidst great danger with my army of Greeks.

"I shall write to you and describe them, and each of them 5
is worth keeping specially in mind according to the manner that I observed it. I would not have believed anyone's asser-

wundorlicra þinga þæt hit swa beon mihte ær ic hit self minum eagum ne gesawe. Seo eorðe is to wundrienne, hwæt heo ærest oþþe godra þinga cęnne, oððe eft þara yfelra, þe heo þæm sceawigendum is æteowed. Hio is cennende þa ful-cuþan wildru ond wæstmas ond wecga oran ond wunderlice wyhta, þa þing eall, þæm monnum þe hit geseoð ond sceawigað, wæron uneþe to gewitanne for þære missenlicnisse þara hiowa.

"Ac þa ðing þe me nu in gemynd cumað ærest, þa ic þe write, þy læs on me mæge idel spellung oþþe scondlic leasung beon gestæled. Hwæt, þu eac sylfa const þa gecynd mines modes, mec a gewunelice healdon þæt gemerce soðes ond rihtes, ond ic sperlicor mid wordum sægde þonne hie mid dædum gedon wærun. Nu ic hwæþre gehyhte ond gelyfe þæt þu þas þing ongete swa þu me ne talige owiht gelpan ond secgan be þære micelnisse ures gewinnes ond compes, forðon ic oft wiscte ond wolde þæt hyra læs wære swa gewinfulra.

"Ic ðæs þoncunge do Greca herige ond swyðost þæm mægene þære iuguþe ond þæm unforswyþdum urum weorode, forþon on ieþum þingum hie me mid wæron ond on þæm earfeðum no from bugon, ac hie on þære geþylde mid me a wunedon þæt ic wæs nemned ealra kyninga kyning. Þara weorð-mynta blissa þu min se leofa lareow. Ond ic nu þas þing write to þe gemænelice ond to Olimphiade minre meder ond minum geswustrum, forþon incer lufu sceal beon somod gemæne; ond gif hit oþor bið, þonne æteawest þu læsson þonne ic nu ær to þe gelyfde.

"On þæm ærrum gewritum þe ic þe sende, ic þe cyþde

tion about so many miraculous things that it could be so before I saw it with my own eyes. The world is to be wondered at, what it first produces either of good things or in turn of bad, by which it is revealed to observers. It continually produces those well-known wild animals and plants and ores of metals and amazing creatures, all which things would be, for people who witness and observe it, difficult to understand on account of the variety of their forms.

"But the things that come to my mind first, those I shall write you about, so that idle hearsay or shameless fabrication cannot be imputed to me. Now, you yourself know, too, that characteristic of my mind, as a constant practice to confine myself to the bounds of truth and uprightness, and I have described things more sparingly with words than they were done in deeds. Now, however, I hope and trust that you will understand these matters in such a way that you will not assume me to be boasting at all and dwelling on the magnitude of our struggles and combat, for I would often have wished and preferred that fewer of them were so hard-won.

"I give thanks to the Greek army, and most of all to the force of young recruits and our indomitable troop of veterans, since they were with me in easy circumstances, and in straits they did not desert, but with patience they remained with me all along until I was named king of all kings. For these marks of distinction, be glad, my dear instructor. And now I am writing about these matters jointly to you and to my mother Olimphias and my sisters, since your affection ought to be shared on both sides; and if it is otherwise, then you show yourself to be less than I have all along expected of you.

"In the earlier messages that I sent you, I related and ex-

ond getacnode be þære asprungnisse sunnan ond monan ond be tungla rynum ond gesetenissum ond be lyfte tacnungum. Þa ðing eall ne magon elcor beon buton micelre gemynde swa geendebyrded ond forestihtod. Ond nu þas niwan spel ic þe ealle in cartan awrite. Ðonne þu hie ræde, þonne wite þu þæt hie ealle swylce wæron swa þam gemyndum gedafenode þines Alexandres þe to sendanne.

"On Maius þæm monþe Persea se kyning Dariun æt Gande þære ea we hine oforcwomon ond oferswyðdon ond us þær in onweald geslogon eal his lond-rice. Ond we þær settan ond geendebyrdedon ure gerefan þæm east-þeodum, ond monegum cynelicum weorð-myndum we wæron gewelgode. On þæm ærron epistole ic þe þæt sægde, ond þy læs þæt eow seo sægen monifealdlicor bi þon þuhte to writanne, ic þa wille swa lætan, ond þa secgon þe nu ðær gewurdon. On Iulius monðe on þæm ytemestum dagum þæs monðes we cwomon in Indie lond in Fasiacen þa stowe. Ond we þa mid wunderlicre hreðnisse Porrum þone cyning ofercwomon ond oferswyðdon, ond we ealle his þeode on onwald onfengon, ond on þæm londe we wæron monegum cynelicum weolum geweorðode.

"Ac ic wolde þæt þu þa ðing ongeate þa ðe weorðe sindon in gemyndum to habbanne. Ærest ic þe write be þære unarimedlican mengeo his weoredes, þæs wæs buton unarimedlican feþum sixtene þusend monna ond eahta hund eoredmanna, ealle mid here-geatwum gegerede. Ond we þa þær genoman feower hund elpenda, ond on þam ufan stodon gewæpnode scyttan, ond þa torras ond þa scylfas on him bæron þa elpendas þe ða byrn-wigon on stodan. Æfter þon we ða cynelican burh Porres mid urum wæpnum in eodon ond his healle ond þa cynelican geseto his sceawedon. Þar

plained the eclipses of the sun and moon and the courses and constellations of the stars and signs in the atmosphere. All these things cannot otherwise be so arranged and foreordained without a great purpose. And now I shall write you all these new observations in a scroll. When you read them, understand that they are all just as seemed right to the purposes of your Alexander to send you.

"In the month of May we fell upon and defeated Darius, the king of the Persians, at the river Gande and there brought under our control his entire empire. And there we established and ordained our viceroys over the Asian peoples, and we were enriched with many regal dignities. In the earlier letter I told you about that, and lest the matter thereby seem to you too repetitious to write about, I shall thus leave off, and narrate those things that have since taken place there. In the month of July, during the last days of the month, we arrived in the country of India, in the place Fasiacen. And then with amazing swiftness we fell upon and defeated Porus, the king, and we gained control of his entire nation, and in that country we were dignified with many regal riches.

"But I wanted you to know about those things that are worth keeping in mind. First I shall write to you about the numberless multitude of his forces, of which there were, aside from countless infantry, sixteen thousand men and eight hundred cavalry, all equipped with full battle gear. And there we captured four hundred elephants, and on top of them stood armed archers, and the elephants carried on them the turrets and platforms that the fighters in chain mail stood on. After that we entered Porus's capital with our weapons and explored his hall and the royal palace. There

wæron gyldene columnan swiðe micle ond trumlice ond fæste, ða wæron unmetlice greate heanisse upp, ðara wæs þe we gerimdon be þæm gemete .cccc. Þa wagas wæron eac gyldne mid gyldnum þelum anæglede fingres þicce. Mid þy ic ða wolde geornlicor þa þing geseon ond furðor eode, þa geseah ic gyldenne win-geard trumlicne ond fæstlicne, ond þa twigo his hongodon geond þa columnan. Ða wundrode ic þæs swiðe. Wæron in þæm win-gearde gyldenu leaf, ond his hon ond his wæstmas wæron cristallum ond smaragdus, eac þæt gim-cyn mid þæm cristallum ingemong hongode. His bryd-buras ond his heah-cleofan ealle wæron eorcnan-stanum *unionibus* ond *carbunculis* þæm gim-cynnum swiðast gefrætwode. Uton hie wæron elpend-banum geworhte þa wæron wunderlice hwite ond fægere, ond cypressus styde ond laurisce hie utan wreþedon, ond gyldne styþeo ond aþrawene ðær ingemong stodon, ond unarimedlicu gold-hord þær wæron inne ond ute, ond monifealdlicu hie wæron ond missenlicra cynna, ond monig fatu gimmiscu ond cristallisce drync-fatu ond gyldne sestras ðær wæron forð borenne. Seldon we þær ænig seolfor fundon.

"Siðþan ic þa me hæfde þas þing eall be gewealdum, þa wilnode ic Indeum innanwearde to geseonne. Ða becwom ic on Caspiam þæt lond mid ealle mine herige. Þa wæs ðær seo wæstm-berendeste eorþe ðæs þeod-londes, ond ic swiðe wundrade þa gesælignesse þære eorðan, ond ic efne gefeonde in minum mode geornlicor ða lond sceawigean wolde. Þa sægdon us ða bigengean þæs londes þæt we us warnigan scoldon wið þa missenlican cynd nædrena ond hrifra wildeora þy læs we on ða becwomon. Þæra mænego in ðissum dunum ond denum ond on wudum ond on feldum eardigeað, ond in stan-holum hie selfe digliað. Ac hwæþre

were very large and firm and immovable golden columns
that were immensely tall, of which we counted a quantity of
four hundred. The interior walls were also golden, paneled
with golden planks the thickness of a finger. When I wished 30
to examine these things in more detail and moved further, I
saw a golden vine, firm and immovable, and its branches
hung among the columns. I was quite amazed at that. There
were on the vine golden leaves, and its clusters and its fruits
were of crystal and emerald, in addition to which gems hung
among the crystals. His women's chambers and upper gal-
leries were all profusely decorated with the precious stones
known as pearls and with the gemstones known as carbun-
cles. On the exterior they were fashioned with ivories that
were amazingly white and beautiful, and posts of cypress
and laurel supported them on the outside, and golden Solo-
monic columns stood among them, and there were count-
less caches of gold inside and out, and they were abundant
and of various kinds, and many jeweled vessels and crystal
goblets and golden pitchers were brought forth there. Sel- 35
dom did we find any silver there.

"After I had all these things under my control, I desired
to see the interior of India. I then entered the region Caspia
with my entire army. There was the most fertile soil of the
country, and I was quite amazed at the productivity of the
earth, and, exulting inwardly, I wanted to explore those re-
gions in even greater detail. The inhabitants of the region
told us that we should take precautions against the various
species of snakes and predatory wild animals in case we en-
countered them. An abundance of them live in these hills 40
and dales and in jungles and in plains, and they conceal
themselves in gaps in the rocks. Nonetheless, I wanted to

ma ic wolde þæm frecnan wege ond siðfatum foeran ðonne þæm gehyldrum wegum, to ðon þæt ðone fleondon Porrum of þæm gefeohte þæt ic hine gemette ær he on þa westenu middan-geardes gefluge. Ic me ða mid genom .cc. lad-þeowa ond eac .l. þe ða genran wegas cuðan þara siðfato.

"Ða ferde we in Agustes monþe þurh þa weallendan sond ond þurh þa wædlan stowe wætres ond ælcere wætan; ond ic mede gehet þæm us cuþlice gelæddon þurh þa uncuðan land Indie ond mec woldon mid mine herige onsund gelædon in Patriacen þæt lond. Ond swiðast ic wilnade þæt hie me gelæddon to þæm dioglum god-web-wyrhtum ða þone þræd wunderlice of sumum treow-cynne ond of his leafum ond of his flyse þæs treowes spunnon, ond swa eac to gode-webbe wæfon ond worhtan. Ac hie þa lond-liode tiolodon ma ussa feonda willan to gefremmanne þonne urne, forþon þe hie us gelæddon þurh þa lond þe þa unarefnedlican cyn nædrena ond hrifra wildeora in wæron. Ða ongeat ic selfa ond geseah of dæle þæt me þa earfeðu becwoman, forþon ic ær forlet ond ne gymde þara nytlicra geþeahta minra freonda ond heded þara monna þe me þæt logon þæt ic þæm wegum ferde. Ða bebead ic minum þegnum ond hie het þæt hie hie mid heora wæpnum gereden ond mid þy herige forðferdon. Ond hie eac swylce þæt min weorod ond þa mine þegnas ond eal min here, goldes ond eorcnan-stana þæt hie gehergad ond genumen hæfdon micel gemet, mid him wægon ond læddon, forþon hie wendon ond ondredon gif hie hit behindon forleton þæt hiora fynd hit þonne deagollice genomon ond onweg aleddon.

"Ond efne swiðe þa mine þegnas ond eal min weorod wæs

travel that perilous way and on those ventures even more than on the more secure ways, for the purpose of meeting up with Porus, who was avoiding confrontation, before he should escape into the wilds of the world. I took with me two hundred fifty guides who were familiar with the more direct routes for those travels.

"Then in the month of August we passed through the boiling sands and through those places poor in water and any kind of moisture; and I promised payment for those who would lead us expertly through the *terrae incognitae* of India and were willing to lead me with my army safely into the region Patriacen. And most of all I wanted them to bring me to those obscure makers of fine cloth who amazingly spun thread from a certain species of tree and from its leaves and from the fleecy growth of the tree, and likewise wove and worked it into fine cloth. But they, the natives, aimed 45
more to cultivate our enemies' good will than ours, since they led us through those regions in which the intolerable species of snakes and ferocious wild animals were. Then I perceived and understood for my own part that these difficulties were befalling me because I had abandoned and ignored the profitable advice of my friends and listened to those people who misadvised me that I should go that way. Then I enjoined my officers and commanded that they arm themselves with their weapons and set out with the army. And likewise my veterans and my officers and my entire army, since they had seized a large quantity of gold and precious stones, transported and brought it with them, because they suspected and feared that if they left it behind, their enemies would get hold of it by stealth and carry it away.

"And my officers and likewise all my veterans were so very

gewelgod þæt hie uneðe ealle þa byrðene þæs goldes mid him aberan ond alædan meahton. Swelce eac heora wæpena noht lytel byrðen wæs, forþon eal heora wæpenu þæra minra þegna ond ealles mines weoredes ond heriges ic het mid gyldenum þelum bewyrcean. Ond eall min weorod wæs on þa gelicnesse tungles oððe ligite for þære micelnisse þæs goldes. Hit scan ond berhte foran swa ymb me uton mid þrymme, ond here-beacen ond segnas beforan me læddon, ond swa micel wundor ond wæfer-sien wæs þæs mines weoredes on fægernisse ofer ealle oþre þeod-kyningas þe in middan-gearde wæron. Ða sceawede ic seolfa ond geseah mine gesælinesse ond min wuldor ond þa fromnisse minre iuguðe ond gesælignisse mines lifes, þa wæs ic hwæthwugo in gefean in minum mode ahafen.

“Ac swa hit oft gesæleð on þæm selran þingum ond on þæm gesundrum þæt seo wyrd ond sio hiow hie oft oncyrreð ond on oþer hworfeð, þa gelomp us þæt we wurdon earfoðlice mid þurste geswencte ond gewæcte. Ðone þurst we þonne earfoðlice abæron ond aræfndon. Þa wæs haten Seferus min þegn funde þa wæter in anum holan stane ond þa mid ane helme hlod hit ond me to brohte, ond he sylfa þursti wæs se min þegn, ond hwæþre he swiðor mines feores ond gesynto wilnade þonne his selfes. Þa he þa þæt wæter me to brohte swa ic ær sægde, þa het ic min weorod ond ealle mine duguþe tosomne, ond hit þa beforan heora ealra onsyne niðer ageat, þy læs ic drunce ond þone minne þegn þyrste ond minne here ond ealne þe mid me wæs. Ond ic þa beforan him eallum herede Seferes dæde þæs mines þegnes, ond hine beforan hiora ealra onsione mid deor-weorðum gyfum gegeafede for ðære dæde. Ond þa mid þy þe þæt min werod gehyrted ond gestilled wæs, þa ferdon we forð þy wege þe

enriched that only with difficulty could they carry off and bring along the entire burden of gold. Likewise there was no small encumbrance of weapons, since I had ordered that all the weapons of my officers and of all my veterans and army be embellished with gold plate. And my entire force resembled a constellation or lightning on account of the volume of that gold. It shone and gleamed in front of me and around me with majesty, and they carried standards and ensigns before me, and such a great wonder and spectacle there was of my army in its splendor over all other emperors who have been on earth. When I myself observed and perceived my own felicity and my glory and the vigor of my youth and the excellent condition of my life, I was somewhat pleasurably exalted in my spirits.

"But as it often turns out in better and more secure circumstances that events and one's condition often change and go awry, it then happened to us that we were painfully afflicted and weakened by thirst. We bore and suffered that thirst oppressively all the while. Then an officer of mine named Severus found water in a hollow stone and drew it with a helmet and brought it to me, and my officer was himself thirsty, and yet he cared more for my life and well-being than his own. When he brought that water to me, as I said before, I called my veterans and all my recruits together, and then in the sight of them all I poured it on the ground, lest I drink and my officer and my army and all who were with me should go thirsty. And then before them all I praised my officer Severus's action, and in the sight of them all I rewarded him with valuable gifts for that deed. And now that my troop was heartened and calmed, we proceeded the way

60 we ær ongunnon. Ða næs long to þon in þæm westenne þæt
we to sumre ea cwoman. On þære ea ofre stod hreod ond
pin-treow, ond *abies* þæt treow-cyn ungemetlicre gryto ond
micelnysse þy clyfe weox ond wridode.

"Þa we to þære ea cwoman, ða het ic for ðæm unarefnedli-
can þurste þe me selfum getenge wæs ond eac eallum minum
herige ond þæm nytenum þe us mid wæron mine fyrd restan
ond wician. Mid þy we ða gewicod hæfdon, ða wolde ic
minne þurst lehtan ond celan. Þa ic þæt wæter bergde, ða
wæs hit biterre ond grimre to drincanne þonne ic æfre ænig
oðer bergde, ond nowþer ne hit se mon drincan meahte ne
65 his ænig neat onbitan ne meahte. Þa wæs ic swiðe on minum
mode generwed for ðæm dumbum nytenum, forþon ic wiste
þæt men yþelicor meahton þone þurst arefnan þonne þa
nietenu. Wæs þæra feðer-fota nietena micel mænigeo mid
me ond micel mænigeo elpenda þa þe gold wægon ond læd-
don, ungemetlicre micelnisse ðusend, ond twa þusenda
horsa ond .cccc. buton þæm eoreda, ond .xx. þusenda
feþena. Þonne wæs þridde healf þusend mula ðe þa seamas
wægon, ond .xxx. þusenda ealfarena ond oxna þa ðe hwæte
bæron, twa þusenda olfenda, fif hund hryðra þara þe mon
dæg-hwamlice to mete dyde. Wæs unrim getæl eac þon on
horsum ond on mulum ond on olfendum ond on elpen-
dum ungemetlicu mængeo us æfter ferde. Ealle þa wæron
70 mid unarefnedlice þurste geswencte ond gewæcte. Ða men
þonne hwilum hie þa iren-geloman liccodan; hwilum hie ele
byrgdon ond on þon þone grimman þurst celdon. Sume men
ðonne of hiora scome þa wætan for þæm nyde þigdon.

"Seo wise wæs þa in me on twa healfa uneþe, seo ærest be minre seolfre ned-þearfe, ond mines weorodes. Het ic þa

we had begun. It was not long then in the desert till we came to a certain river. On the bank of the river stood rushes and pine trees, and trees of the species silver fir of immense height and girth grew and flourished on the incline.

"When we came to the river, on account of the unendurable thirst that was oppressing me, for my own part, as well as my entire army and the animals that were with us, I called for my troops to rest and pitch camp. When we had made camp, I wished to slake and cool my thirst. When I tasted the water, it was more bitter and acrid to drink than any other I had ever tasted, and neither could any human drink it nor could any animal consume it. Then I was sorely concerned at heart for the dumb animals, because I knew that men could more easily endure that thirst than the animals. There was a great multitude of four-footed animals with me and a great multitude of elephants that carried and transported the gold, a thousand of immense size, and two thousand four hundred horses, excluding the cavalry, and twenty thousand infantry. Then there were two and a half thousand mules that transported the packs, and thirty thousand packhorses and oxen that carried wheat, two thousand camels, five hundred cattle that were made into food daily. There was an untold number in addition to that of horses and of mules, and of camels and of elephants an immense multitude traveled behind us. All these were oppressed and weakened by unendurable thirst. The men then sometimes licked the iron implements; sometimes they tasted oil and thereby cooled the harsh thirst. Some men then in their need consumed the liquid from their private parts.

"The matter was disturbing to me on two counts, the first in regard to my own need, and that of my troops. Then I di-

ælcne mon hine mid his wæpnum gegerwan ond faran forð, ond þæt eac fæstlice bebead ðæt se mon se ne wære mid his wæpnum æfter fyrd-wison gegered, þæt hine mon scolde mid wæpnum acwellan. Ða wundredon hie swiðe for hwon hie þa hefignesse ond micelnisse ðara wæpna in swa miclum þurste beran scoldon þær nænig feond ne æteowde. Ac ic wiste hwæþre þæt ure for ond siðfæt wæs þurh þa lond ond stowe þe missenlicra cynna eardung in wæs, nædrena ond rifra wildeora, ond we ðe þæs londes ungleawe ond unwise wæron, þæt usic ðonne semninga hwelc earfeðọ on becwome.

"Ferdon we þa forð be þære ea ofre. Ða wæs seo eatoðe tid dæges, þa cwoman we to sumre byrig; sėo burh wæs on midre þære ea in anum eglonde getimbred. Wæs seo burh mid þy hreode ond treow-cynne þe on þære ea ofre weox ond we ær bi writon ond sægdon asett ond geworht. Ða gesawon we in þære byrig ond ongeaton Indisce men fea healf nacode eardigende. Ða hie þa us gesawon, hie selfe sona in heora husum deagollice hie miþan. Ða wilnade ic þara monna onsyne to geseonne, þæt hie us fersc wæter ond swete getæhton. Mid þy we ða longe bidon ond us nænig mon to wolde, þa het ic fea stræla sendan in þa burh innan, to þon gif hie hiera willum us to noldon, þæt hie for þæm ege þæs gefeohtes nede scoldon. Ða wæron hie þy swyðor afyrhte ond hie fæstor hyddan. Þa het ic .cc. minra þegna of greca herige leohtum wæpnum hie gegyrwan, ond hie on sunde to þære byrig foron ond swumman ofer æfter þære ea to þæm eg-lande. Þa hie ða hæfdon feorðan dæl þære ea geswummen, ða becwom sum ongrislic wise on hie. Þæt wæs

rected everyone to equip himself with his weapons and set out, and also I strictly demanded that the man who was not equipped with his weapons in military fashion should be killed with weapons. They wondered very much why they had to bear the weight and bulk of the weapons in so great thirst where no enemy was to be seen. However, I knew that our direction and route were through those regions and places in which was the habitat of various species of snakes and ferocious wild animals, and we were so ignorant of and unfamiliar with that region that some trouble might therefore overtake us suddenly.

"Then we proceeded along the river bank. When it was the eighth hour of the day, we came to a certain town; the town was built on an island in the middle of the river. The town was made up and constructed of the reeds and species of trees that grew on the river bank and which we have already written about and described. Then we looked and noticed a few half-naked Indian people living in the town. When they saw us, they immediately concealed themselves furtively in their houses. I desired to get a close look at those people then, so that they could direct us to fresh and sweet water. Since we waited a long time and no one was willing to come to us, I had a few arrows launched into the town, so that if they would not come to us willingly, they should out of necessity, for fear of a fight. Then they were all the more afraid and hid themselves more securely. Then I had two hundred of my officers from the Greek army equip themselves with light weapons, and they set out for the town by swimming, and swam over across the river to the island. When they had swum a quarter of the river, a certain grisly circumstance overtook them. It was a multitude of water-

þonne nicra mengeo on onsione maran ond unhyrlicran þonne ða elpendas, in ðone grund þære ea ond betweoh ða yða þæs wæteres þa men besencte, ond mid heora muðe hie sliton ond blodgodon ond hie ealle swa fornamon, þæt ure nænig wiste hwær hiora æni cwom. Ða wæs ic swiðe yrre þæm minum lad-þeowum, þa us on swylce frecennissa gelæddon. Het hiera ða bescufan in þa ea .l. ond .c., ond sona þæs ðe hie inne wæron, swa wæron þa nicoras gearwe, to-brudon hie swa hie þa oðre ær dydon, ond swa þicce hie in þære ea aweollon swa æmettan ða nicras, ond swilc unrim heora wæs.

"Þa het ic blawan mine byman ond þa fyrd faran, þa hit ða wæs sio endlefte tid dæges, ond we forð ferdon. Ða gesawon we men æfter þære ea feran, hæfdon of þæm hreode ond of þæm treow-cynne þe in ðære ea ofre stodon on scip-wisan geworht þæt hie onufan sæton. Þa men þa mid þy we æfter ferscum wætre hie frunon, þa onswaredon hie us ond sædon hwær we hit findan mehton in hiora gereorde ond cwædon þæt we fundon sumne swiðe micelne mere in þæm wære fersc wæter ond swete genog, ond þæt we genog raðe to þæm becwoman gif we geornfulle wæron. Ond þa for þæm þingum swa monigra geswencnissa wæs þæt we ealle þa niht ferdon mid þurste gewæcte ond mid ura wæpna byrþenum swiðe geswencte. Ond ofer ealle þa niht ðe we ferdon þus, symle leon ond beran ond tigris ond pardus ond wulfas ure ehtan, ond we þæm wiðstodon. Þa ðy æftran dæge ða hit wæs seo eahtoðe tid dæges, þa cwomon we to þæm mere ðe us mon ær foresæde. Þa wæs he eall mid wudu beweaxen mile brædo, wæs hwæþre weg to ðæm wætre. Ða wæs ic ge-feonde þæs swetan wætres ond þæs ferscan, ond þa sona

monsters, larger and fiercer in appearance than the elephants, sank the men to the river bed and between the waves of the water, and with their mouths they lacerated and bloodied them and thus carried all of them off, so that none of us knew where any of them had gone. Then I was extremely angry with my guides, who had led us into such jeopardy. I ordered that one hundred fifty of them be tossed into the river, and as soon as they were in it, the water-monsters were ready and tore them apart the way they had done the others, and the water-monsters swarmed in the river as thick as ants, there was such a countless number of them.

"Then I directed that my trumpets be blown and the troops depart, when it was the eleventh hour of the day, and we set out. We then saw people traveling along the river who had made of the reeds and species of trees that stood on the river bank a kind of vessel that they sat on top of. When we asked them about fresh water, they answered us and said in their language where we could find it, and said that we should come upon a certain very large lake in which there was plenty of fresh and sweet water, and that we should reach it quickly enough if we were diligent. And then it was on account of so many threats that we traveled all that night weakened with thirst and sorely troubled by the weight of our weapons. And through the whole night that we traveled thus, lions and bears and tigers and panthers and wolves continually attacked us, and we fended them off. Then the next day, when it was the eighth hour of the day, we arrived at the lake that we had been told about. It was hemmed about with jungle the breadth of a mile, but there was a path to the water. I reveled in that sweet and fresh water, and

minne þurst ærest gelehte ond þa eal min weored, ða het ic wætrian sona ure hors ond ure nieteno; eall wæron hie swiðe mid þurste fornumene. Ða het ic sioððan sona þa fyrd wician. Wæs seo wic-stow ða on lengo .xx.es furlonga long, ond swa eac in brædo. Sioðþan hie þa gewicod hæfdon, þa het ic ceorfan ða bearwas ond þone wudu fyllan þæt monnum wære þy eþre to þæm wæterscipe to ganganne, ond to þæm mere þe we bi gewicod hæfdon. Þa het ic ða gesamnian eall þa ure hors ond nietenu ond elpendas ond hie het gebringan on middum þæm urum wicum, ond betwih þæm geteldum, þy læs hiora ænig to lore wurde, forþon us wæs uncuð hwæt us on nihtlicum fyrste gesælde. Ond þa het ic eac of þæm wudo þe ðær gefylled wæs þæt mon fyr onælde. Sio fyrd þe mid me wæs, þa didon hie swa, ond þa ðær onældon þusend fyra ond eac fif hund. Forþon ic þæt dyde, gif us on niht uncuðes hwæt on becwome, þæt we hæfdon æt þæm fyre leoht ond fullaste.

"Þa we þara fyra hæfdon onæled swa fela swa us þa ðuhte, þa bleow man mine byman ond ic mete þigde ond eall min fyrd swa dyde. Wæs hit þa an tid to æfenes, ond þa het ic onbærnan ðara gyldenra leoht-fato þe ic mid me hæfde twa þusendo. Ða toforan monan upgonge, þa cwomon þær *scorpiones* þæt wyrm-cyn swa hie ær gewunelice wæron toweard þæs wætersciepes. Wæs þæra wyrma micel mænegeo ond heora wæs unrim, ond hie swiðe on þa ure wic onetton ond in þa feollon. Ða æfter þon cwoman þær hornede nædran *carastis* þæt næder-cyn. Þa wæron ealle missenlices hiwes, forþon hie wæron sume reode, sume blace, sume hwite. Sumum þonne scinan þa scilla ond lixtan swylce hie wæron gyldne þonne mon onlocode. Eall þæt lond hleoðrade for þara wyrma hwistlunge, ond us eac noht lytel ege from him

then as soon as I had slaked my thirst and then my whole troop theirs, I had our horses and livestock watered; they were all devastated by thirst. Then right away I told the troops to pitch camp. The encampment was twenty furlongs in length and likewise in breadth. After they had made camp, I ordered that the groves be cut and the jungle felled, so that it would be easier for the men to get to the water source, and to the lake that we had camped by. Then I had all our horses and livestock and elephants assembled and placed in the midst of our camp, and among the tents, lest any of them go missing, since it was not plain to us what might happen to us over the course of the night. And then I ordered also that fires be kindled from the wood that had been felled. The troops that were with me did so, and there they kindled one thousand five hundred fires. I did this so that if anything unanticipated happened to us during the night, we should have light and the benefit of the fire.

"When we had kindled as many fires as we intended, there was a blast of my trumpets and I took a meal, and all my troops did likewise. It was then one hour till evening, and I directed that two thousand of the golden lamps that I had with me be lighted. Then before moonrise those vermin called scorpions came, as they were accustomed, toward the water source. There was a great multitude of the vermin and their number was countless, and they rushed in force upon our camp and fell upon it. Then after that there came horned snakes, the kind of snake called *cerastes*. They were all of various colors, for some of them were red, some black, some white. When observed, the scales of some shone and gleamed as if they were made of gold. All that region buzzed with the hissing of those pests, and we also had no little

wæs, ac we þa mid scyldum us scyldan, ond eac mid longsceaftum sperum hie slogan ond cwealdon, monige eac in fyre forburnon. Þas ðing we þus drugon þæt we swa wið þam wyrmum fuhtan ond wunnan huru twa tida þære nihte.

"Sioðþan hie þa wyrmas hæfdon ondruncen þæs wætres, þa gewiton hie þonon ond ure no ne ehton. Ða wæs seo þridde tid þære nihte; þa wolde we us gerestan. Þa cwoman þær nædran eft wunderlicran þonne ða oþre wæron ond egeslicran, þa hæfdon tu heafdo ond eac sume hæfdon þreo. Wæron hie wunderlicre micelnisse: wæron hie swa greate swa columnan ge eac sume uphyrran ond gryttran. Cwoman þa wyrmas of þæm neah-dunum ond scrafum þider to þon þæt hie þæt wæter drincan woldon. Eodon þa wyrmas ond scluncon wundorlice: wæron him þa breost upgewende ond on ðæm hricge eodon, ond a swa hie hit geforan gelice mid þæm scillum gelice mid ðe muþe ða eorþan sliton ond tæron. Hæfdon hie þa wyrmas þrie slite tungan, ond þonne hie eðedon, þonne eode him of þy muðe mid þy oroþe swylce byrnende þecelle. Wæs þæra wyrma oroð ond eþung swiðe deað-berende ond æterne, ond for hiora þæm wol-beorendan oroðe monige men swulton. Wið þissum wyrmum we fuhton leng þonne ane tide þære nihte, ond hie þa wyrmas acwealdon .xxx.tig monna þære fyrde, ond minra agenra þegna .xx.

"Ða bæd ic þa fyrde hwæþre þæt hie hæfdon god ellen þara þinga þe us on becwomon, swa monigra geswencnissa ond earfeðo. Þa hit wæs seo fifte tid þære nihte, þa mynton we us gerestan, ac þa cwoman þær hwite leon in fearra gelicnisse swa micle, ond hie ealle swiðe grymetende ferdon. Mid þy ða leon þyder cwoman, þa ræsdon hie sona on us, ond we us wið him sceldan þæs ðe we mihton, ond us wæs swælc

dread on their account, but we shielded ourselves from them with our shields, and also with long-shafted spears we struck and killed them, as well as burned many in the fire. We thus endured these conditions so that we fought with those vermin and struggled as much as two hours of the night.

"After the pests had drunk the water, they departed and did not attack us. Then it was the third hour of the night; we wanted to rest then. Then there came again snakes more amazing than the others had been, and more dreadful, which had two heads, and some even had three. They were of amazing size: they were as large as columns, and some were even taller and thicker. The vermin came there from the neighboring hills and caves because they wanted to drink the water. The pests moved and slithered in amazing fashion: their breasts were turned up, and they went on their backs, and ever as they moved they slit and tore the earth as much with their scales as with their mouths. Those vermin had three slits of the tongue, and when they exhaled, out of their mouths with their breath came something like a burning torch. The breath and exhalations of the pests were very deadly and venomous, and on account of their pestilential breath, many men died. With these pests we fought longer than one hour in the night, and the vermin killed thirty men of the troops, and twenty of my own officers.

"I told the troops, though, to have good courage in the face of those conditions that had affected us, so many trials and difficulties. When it was the fifth hour of the night, we intended to get some rest, but then there came white lions the likes of bulls for size, and they all came roaring fiercely. When the lions came there, they immediately rushed at us, and we shielded ourselves against them as we could, and

geswencnis ond swilc earfeþo mid deorum becymen in þære sweartan niht ond in þære þystran. Swelce eac eoforas þær cwoman unmætlicre micelnisse, ond monig oþer wildeor, ond eac tigris us on þære nihte þar abisgodon. Swelce þær eac cwoman hreaþe-mys þa wæron in culefrena gelicnesse swa micle, ond þa on ure ondwlitan sperdon ond us pulledon. Hæfdon hie eac þa hreaþe-mys teð in monna gelicnisse, ond hie mid þæm þa men wundodon ond tæron.

"Eac ðæm oþrum bisgum ond geswencnissum þe us on becwomm, þa cwom semninga swiðe micel deor sum mare þonne þara oðra ænig. Hæfde þæt deor þrie hornas on foranheafde, ond mid þæm hornum wæs egeslice gewæpnod. Þæt deor Indeos hatað *dentes tyrannum.* Hæfde þæt deor horse gelic heafod, ond wæs blæces heowes. Ðis deor mid þy ðe hit þæs wætres ondronc, þa beheold hit þa ure wic-stowe, ond þa semninga on us ond on ure wic-stowe ræsde. Ne hit for þæm bryne wandode þæs hatan leges ond fyres þe him wæs ongean, ac hit ofer eall wod ond eode. Mid þy ic þa getrymede þæt mægen Greca heriges, ond we us wið him scyldan woldon, þa hit ofsloh sona minra þegna .xxvi. ane ræse, ond .lii. hit oftræd ond hie to loman gerenode, þæt hie mec nænigre note nytte beon meahton. Ond we hit þa unsofte mid strælum ond eac mid long-sceaftum sperum of scotadon ond hit ofslogon ond acwealdon.

"Þa hit wæs foran to uhtes, þa æteowde þær wol-berende lyft hwites hiowes, ond eac missenlices wæs heo on hringwisan fag, ond monige men for heora þæm wol-berendan stence swulton mid þære wol-beorendan lyfte þe þær swelc æteowde. Þa ðær cwoman eac Indisce mys in þa fyrd in foxa gelicnisse ond in heora micle, ða þonne ure feþer-fot-nietenu

such trials and difficulties were visited on us with animals in the black night and in the dark. So, too, there came boars of immense size, and many other wild animals, and also tigers kept us busy there during the night. Likewise there came bats that were the likes of doves for size, and they struck us in the face and plucked out our hair. The bats also had teeth like humans', and with them they wounded and lacerated the men.

"In addition to the other trials and afflictions that happened to us, there came suddenly a certain very large animal, greater than any of the others. That animal had three horns on its forehead, and it was dauntingly armed with those horns. Indians call that animal 'teeth-despot'. The animal had a head like a horse, and it was of black color. When this animal had drunk the water, it noticed our encampment, and then suddenly it rushed upon us and our camp. It did not hesitate on account of the burning of the hot flame and fire that it faced, but it moved along and walked over everything. While I was positioning the force of the Greek army, and we intended to shield ourselves against it, it at once killed twenty-six of my officers in a single onslaught, and it trampled fifty-two and made cripples of them, so that they could be of no use to me. And then we fiercely shot it with arrows and also with long-shafted spears and felled and killed it.

"When it was before daybreak, a poisonous vapor appeared, of white color and also marked here and there by whorls, and many men died on account of the poisonous odor with the noxious vapor wherever such appeared. Then there came also Indian mice into the army similar to foxes and of their size, which bit and wounded our livestock, and

bitan ond wundedon, ond monige for hiora wundum swultan. Þara monna hit þonne ælc gedigde, þeah hie heora hwelcne gewundodan. Ða hit wæs toforan dæges, þa cwoman þær þa fugelas, *nocticoraces* hatton; wæron in wealhhafoces gelicnesse. Wæron hie þa fugelas brunes hiowes, ond him wæron þa nebb ond þa clea ealle blace. Þa fuglas ybsæton eallne þone ofer þæs meres, ond þa fuglas us nænige laðe ne yfle ne wæron, ac hie þa gewunelican fixas þe in þæm mere wæron mid hiora cleum uptugon ond þa tæron. Ða fuglas þa we hie ne onweg flegdon ne him lað dydon, ac hi him selfe eft gewiton þonon.

"Þa hit ða on morgen dæg wæs, ða het ic ealle mine ladþeowas þe mec on swelc earfeðo gelæddon, het hie þa gebindan ond him þa ban ond sconcan forbrecan, ðæt hie on niht wæron from þæm wyrmum asogone þe þæt wæter sohton. Ond ic him het eac þa honda of aheawan, þæt hie be gewyrhtum þes wites wite drugon, þe hie ær hiora þonces us on gelæddon ond gebrohton.

"Het ða blawan mine byman ond þa fyrd faran forð þy wege þe we ær ongunnen hæfdon. Foran we ða þurh ða fæstlond ond þurh þa ungeferenlican eorþan. Þa wæs þær eft gesomnad micel fyrd Indiscra monna ond þæra el-reordigra þe ða lond budon, ond we þa wið þæm gefuhton. Mid þy we þa us eft ongeaton maran gefeoht toweard ond mare gewin, ða forleton we þa frecnan wegas ond siðfato, ond þa þæm selran we ferdon. Ond swa mid mine werode onsunde in Patriacen þæt lond we becwoman mid golde ond oþrum weolum swiðe gewelgode, ond hie us þær fremsumlice ond luflice onfengon. Mid þy we þa eft of þæm londe foron of Patriacen, ða becwoman we on þa lond-gemæro Medo ond

many died on account of their wounds. Each of the men sur-
vived it, though they wounded all of them. When it was be-
fore sunrise, there came those birds called 'night-ravens';
they resembled falcons. The birds were of a glossy appear- 140
ance, and their beaks and claws were all black. The birds en-
circled the entire shore of the lake, and none of the birds
were hostile or harmful to us, but with their claws they
snatched up and lacerated the native fish that were in the
lake. We did not drive the birds away or do them harm, but
they themselves at length departed.

"In the morning when it was day, I commanded that all
the guides who had led me into such straits be bound, and
that their thighbones and shanks be broken, so that during
the night they would be consumed by the vermin that came
looking for water. And I also commanded that their hands
be cut off, so that by virtue of that torment they would suf-
fer the torment that they had willingly invited and brought
upon us.

"Then I had my trumpets sounded and the troops set out 145
the way we had started. We traveled then through rough ter-
rain and trackless expanses. A large force of Indian men and
of the gibberish-speaking people who inhabited those re-
gions was assembled there anew, and we fought against
them. Thereupon, when we perceived fiercer combat and a
greater struggle impending for us, we abandoned those per-
ilous routes and avenues, and we traveled on better ones.
And so with my forces intact, handsomely endowed with
gold and other riches, we entered the province Patriacen,
and there they received us graciously and gladly. Thereafter 150
when we departed from the province of Patriacen, we came

Persa. Þa we ðær eft edniowunga hæfdon micle gefeoht, ond .xx. daga ic þær mid minre fyrde wið him wicode.

“Sioðþan we þa þonon ferdon, þa wæs hit on seofon-nihta fæce þæt we to þæm londe ond to þære stowe becwoman þær Porrus se cyning mid his fyrde wicode. Ond he swiðor þæs londes fæstenum truwode þonne his gefeohte ond gewinne. Þa wilnade he þæt he me cuðe ond mine þegnas, þa he þæs frægen ond axsode from þæm ferendum minra wic-stowa. Þa wæs þæt me gesæd þæt he wilnade mec to cunnenne ond min werod. Ða alede ic minne kyne-gyrylan ond me mid uncuþe hrægle ond mid lyþerlice gerelan me gegerede, swelce ic wære hwelc folclic mon ond me wære metes ond wines þearf. Þa ic wæs in þæm wicum Porres, swa ic ær sæde, ða sona swa he me þær geahsode ond him mon sægde þæt þær mon cymen wæs of Alexandres here-wicum, þa het he me sona to him lædan. Mid þy ic þa wæs to him gelæded, þa frægn he me ond ahsode hwæt Alexander se cyning dyde ond hulic mon he wære ond in hwylcere yldo. Ða bysmrode ic hine mid minum ondswarum ond him sæde þæt he forealdod wære ond to þæs eald wære þæt he ne mihte elcor gewearmigan buton æt fyre ond æt gledum. Þa wæs he sona swiðe glæd ond gefeonde þara minra ondswaro ond worda, forþon ic him sæde þæt he swa forealdod wære. Ond ða cwæð he eac, ‘Hu mæg he la ænige gewinne wið me spowan swa forealdod mon, forþon ic eom me self geong ond hwæt?’ Þa he ða geornlicor me frægn be his þingum, ða sæde ic þæt ic his þinga feola ne cuþe ond hine seldon gesawe ðone cyning, forþon þe ic wære his þegnes mon ond his ceapes heorde ond wære his feoh-bigenga. Þa he ðas word gehyrde, ða sealde he me an gewrit ond ænne epistolan ond me

to the frontiers of the Medes and Persians. There again we had pitched battles, and twenty days I was encamped with my troops opposite them.

"After we had departed from there, it was the space of seven nights till we came to the region and to the place where King Porus was encamped with his forces. And he trusted more in the defenses of the region than in his fighting ability and prowess. Then he desired to be acquainted with me and my officers, when he heard of and received intelligence from travelers about my camp. I was told then that he desired to be acquainted with me and my corps. I then put aside my royal robes and dressed myself in rough clothing and humble garb, as if I were a plebeian man and I had need of food and wine. When I was in Porus's camp, as I said before, as soon as he learned of me there and he was told that someone had arrived from Alexander's camp, he demanded that I be brought to him at once. When I was brought to him, he questioned me and asked what King Alexander was doing and what sort of man he was and of what age. Then I mocked him with my answers and told him that he (Alexander) was decrepit with age and was so old that he could not stay warm otherwise than at a fire and at coals. Straightway he was very pleased and delighted at my responses and my remarks, because I had said that he was so decrepit with age. And then he said also, 'How in the world can a man so decrepit with age prevail against me in any combat, since I am myself young and vigorous?' When he asked me more particularly about his affairs, I said that I did not know much about his affairs and seldom saw the king, because I was his officer's man and his herdsman and tender of his cattle. When he heard these remarks, he gave me a

bæd þæt ic hine Alexandre þæm kyninge ageafe, ond me eac mede gehet gif ic hit him agyfan wolde, ond ic him gehet þæt ic swa don wolde swa he me bæd. Swa sona ic ða þonon gewiten wæs ond eft cwom to minum here-wicum, þa ægþer ge ær ðon þe ic þæt gewrit rædde ge eac æfter þon þæt ic wæs swiðe mid hleahtre onstyred. Ðas þing ic forþon þe secge, *magister,* ond Olimphiade minre meder ond minum geswustrum, þæt ge gehyrdon ond ongeaton þa oferhygdlican gedyrstignesse þæs el-reordgan kyninges.

"Hæfde ic þa þæs kyninges wic ond his fæstenu gesceawod þe he mid his fyrde in gefaren hæfde. Ða sona on morgne þæs ða eode Porrus se kyning me on hond mid ealle his ferde ond dugoþe þa he hæfde ongieten þæt he wið me gewinnan ne meahte. Ond of þæm feondscipe þe us ær betweonum wæs, þæt gesælde þæt he seoðþan wæs me freond ond eallum greca herige ond min gefera ond gefylcea. Ond ic him ða eft his rice ageaf, ond þa wæs he swa gefeonde for ðære unwendan are þæs rices, þe he him seolfa næniges rices ne wende, þæt he ða me eall his gold-hord æteowde, ond he þa ægþer ge mec ge eac eall min werod mid golde gewelgode. Ond Herculis gelicnisse ond Libri ðara twegea goda, he buta of golde gegeat ond geworhte ond hie butu asette in þæm east-dæle middan-geardes. Ða wolde ic witan hwæþer ða gelicnissa wæron gegotene ealle swa he sæde; het hie þa þurhborian. Þa wæron hie buta of golde gegotene. Ða het ic eft þa ðyrelo þe hiora mon þurh cunnode mid golde forwyrcean ond afyllon ond het þa ðæm godum bæm onsægdnisse onsecgan.

"Þa ferdon we forð ond woldan ma wunderlicra þinga geseon ond sceawian ond mærlicra. Ac þa ne gesawon we swa swa we þa geferdon noht elles buton þa westan feldas ond

letter and a missive and asked that I give it to King Alexander, and he promised me a reward if I should give it to him, and I promised that I would do as he asked me. As soon as I had departed from there and I came back to my encampment, both before I read the letter and after, I was overcome
with laughter. I am telling these things to you, teacher, and 165
to my mother Olimphias and my sisters, so that you may hear and comprehend the arrogant presumption of that gibberish-speaking king.

"I had then studied the king's camp and the fortifications into which he had gone with his troops. Then at once the next day King Porus submitted to me with all his force and troops when he had perceived that he could not fight against me. And out of the enmity that had been between us, it happened that he afterward was a friend to me and to the entire Greek army, and my comrade and ally. And then I gave his kingdom back to him, and he was so happy about the unexpected favor of his kingdom, since he himself had not expected any kingdom, that he showed me his entire treasury,
and he endowed both me and all my troops with gold. And 170
he cast and formed images of the two gods Hercules and Liber, both of gold, and he erected both on the eastern edge of the world. Then I wanted to know whether the statues were cast just the way he had said; I ordered that they be drilled into. They were both cast of solid gold. I then directed that the holes by which they had been tested be done away with and filled with gold again and commanded that sacrifices be offered to both gods.

"Then we went on our way and wanted to see and explore
more wonderful and more splendid things. But as we trav- 175
eled we saw nothing else but the uncultivated plains and

wudu ond duna be þæm garsecge, ða wæron monnum ungeferde for wildeorum ond wyrmum. Þa ferde ic hwæþre be þæm sæ to þon þæt ic wolde cunnian meahte ic ealne middan-geard ybferan swa garsecg beligeð. Ac þa sægdon me þa lond-bigengan þæt se sæ wære to þon þiostre ond se garsecg eall, þæt hine nænig mon mid scipe geferan ne meahte. Ond ic þa ða wynstran dælas Indie wolde geondferan þy læs me owiht in þæm londe beholen oððe bedegled wære.

"Ða wæs þæt lond eall swa we geferdon adrugad ond fen, ond cannon ond hreod weoxan. Ða cwom þær semninga sum deor of þæm fenne ond of ðæm fæstene. Wæs þæm deore eall se hrycg acæglod. Swelce snoda hæfde þæt deor, seono-wealt heafod swelce mona, ond þæt deor hatte *quasi caput luna,* ond him wæron þa breost gelice niccres breastum ond heardum toðum ond miclum hit wæs gegyred ond geteþed. Ond hit þa þæt deor ofsloh mine þegnas twegen. Ond we þa þæt deor nowþer ne mid spere gewundigan ne meahte ne mid nænige wæpne, ac we hit uneaþe mid isernum hamerum ond slecgum gefyldon ond hit ofbeoton.

"Ða becwoman we syðþan to þæm wudum Indie ond to þæm ytemestum gemærum þæs londes, ond ic þa het þa fyrd þær wician be þære ea þe Biswicmon hatte. Wæron þa wic on lengo .l. furlanga long ond swa eac in brædo. Woldon we þa to urum swæsendum sittan; wæs hit þa seo endlefte tid dæges. Þa wæs semninga geboden þæt we wæpenu noman ond hie tioloden, ond us wære micel þearf þæt we us scyldan. Þa dydon we swa, fengon to ussum wæpnum swa us beboden wæs. Ða cwom þær micel mængeo elpenda of þæm wudo, ungemetlic weorod þara diora. Cwoman hie to þon þyder þæt hie on ða ure wic feohtan. Þa het ic sona þa hors

jungles and hills by the sea, which were inaccessible on account of wild animals and vermin. I traveled nonetheless beside the sea because I wanted to test whether I could circle the entire earth that the ocean surrounds. But then the inhabitants told me that the sea was so dark, and all the ocean, that no one could navigate it by ship. And then I wanted to explore the left-hand parts of India, lest anything in that country be concealed or withheld from me.

"That entire region which we visited was parched and marshy, and cane and reeds grew. Then there suddenly appeared a certain animal from the fen and from the wilderness. The animal's entire back was serrated. The animal had something like head-dresses, a head round like the moon, and the animal was called 'head-like-moon', and its chest was like the chest of a sea-serpent, and it was equipped and toothed with hard, large teeth. And the animal killed two of my officers. And we could wound that animal neither with a spear nor with any weapon, but with effort we felled it with hammers and mallets and beat it to death.

"Then afterward we came to the jungles of India and to the remotest borders of the country, and I directed the troops then to make camp there by the river called Biswicmon. The encampment was fifty furlongs in length and likewise in breadth. We wanted then to sit down to our dinner; it was the eleventh hour of the day. Then suddenly word came that we were to go for our weapons and grab them, and it was a dire necessity that we protect ourselves. We did so, seized our weapons as we were told. There came then a vast herd of elephants out of the jungle, an immense army of the beasts. They had come there for the purpose of attacking our camp. I then immediately ordered that the horses be

gerwan ond eored-men hleapan up, ond het geniman swina micelne wræd ond drifan on horsum ongean þæm elpendum, forþon ic wiste þæt swin wæron ðæm deorum laðe, ond hiora rying hie meahte afyrhton. Ond þa sona þæs þa elpendas ða swin gesawon, þa wæron hie afyrhte ond sona on þone wudu gewiton. Ond we þa niht on þære wic-stowe gesundlice wicodon, ond ic hæfde hie mid fæstene gefæstnad, þæt us nowþer ne deor ne oðer earfeðo sceððan meahten.

"Ða hit þa on morgen dæg wæs, þa ferdon we on oþer þeod-lond India; ða cwoman we on sumne micelne feld. Ða gesawe we þær ruge wif-men ond wæpned-men; wæron hie swa ruwe ond swa gehære swa wildeor. Wæron hie nigon fota uplonge, ond hie wæron þa men nacod, ond hie næniges hrægles ne gimdon. Ðas men Indeos hatað *ictifafonas,* ond hie of ðæm neaheum ond merum þa hron-fiscas up tugon ond þa æton ond be þæm lifdon ond þæt wæter æfter druncon. Mid þy ic þa wolde near þa men geseon ond sceawigon, ða flugon hie sona in þa wæter ond hie þær in þæm stan-holum hyddon. Þa æfter þon gesawon we betweoh þa wudu-bearwas ond þa treo healf-hundinga micle mængeo, ða cwoman to þon þæt hie woldon us wundigan. Ond we þa mid strælum hie scotodon ond hie sona onweg aflymdon, ða hie eft on þone wudu gewiton. Þa syððan geferdon we in þa westenn India, ond we þa þær noht wunderlices ne mærlices gesawon.

"Ond we þa eft in Fasiacen þæt lond becwoman þanan we ær ferdon, ond we þær gewicodon be þæm neah-wætrum, ond we þær ure geteld bræddon ealle on æfen, ond þær wæron eac fyr wel monigo onæled. Ða cwom þær semninga swiðe micel wind ond gebræc, ond to þæs unheorlic se wind geweox þæt he þara ura getelda monige afylde, ond he ða eac

prepared and the cavalry mount them, and I ordered that a large herd of swine be taken and driven by cavalry toward the elephants, because I knew that swine were noxious to those animals, and their grunting could frighten them. And then as soon as the elephants saw the swine, they were abashed and immediately departed into the jungle. And that night we camped safely in that encampment, and I had it reinforced with fortifications, so that neither animals nor other annoyances could visit us.

"When it was daylight on the next day, we traveled to another province of India; then we came into a certain large plain. There we saw shaggy women and men; they were as shaggy and hairy as wild animals. They were nine feet tall, and the people were naked, and they did not bother with clothing. Indians call those people 'fish-fauns', and they swept up the whales from the nearby rivers and lakes and ate them and lived on them and afterward drank the water. When I wished to see and examine them more closely, they fled abruptly into the water and hid themselves in gaps in the rocks. After that we saw among the groves and the trees a large group of cynocephali, which came with the intention of wounding us. And when we shot at them with arrows and immediately drove them off, they went back into the jungle. Afterward we traveled into the wastes of India, and we saw nothing there of a marvelous or memorable nature.

"And then we went back to the region Fasiacen from which we had set out, and we made camp there by the neighboring waters, and there we erected all our tents in the evening, and there were also quite a few fires lighted. Then suddenly there came a very strong wind and a blast, and the wind grew so fierce that it leveled many of our tents, and

usse feþer-fot-nietenu swiðe swencte. Ða het ic gesomnigan eft þa geteld ond seamas ealle tosomne, ond hie mon þa seamas ond þa þing ðara ura wic-stowa earfoðlice tosomne for þæm winde gesomnode. Ond ða on gehliuran dene ond on wearmran we gewicodan. Mid þy we gewicod hæfdon ond ure þing eall gearo, þa het ic eallne þone here þæt he to swæsendum sæte ond mete þigde, ond hie þa swa dydon. Mid þy hit æfenne nealehte, ða ongunnon þa windas eft weaxan ond þæt weder hreogan, ond ungemetlic cele geweox on þone æfen. Ða cwom þær micel snaw, ond swa miclum sniwde swelce micel flys feolle. Ða ic þa unmætnisse ond micelnisse ðæs snawes geseah, ða þuhte me þæt ic wiste þæt he wolde ealle þa wic-stowe forfeallan. Ða het ic þone here þæt hie mid fotum þone snaw trædon, ond þa fyr eall wæron forneah for þære micelnesse þæs snawes adwæscte ond acwencte. Hwæþere us þær wæs anes þinges eþnes, þæt se snaw ðær leng ne wunede þonne ane tide. Ða sona wæs æfter þon swiðe sweart wolcen ond genip, ond þa eac cwoman of þæm sweartan wolcne byrnende fyr. Þa fyr ðonne feollon on þa eorþan swelce byrnende þecelle, ond for þæs fyres bryne eall se feld born. Ða cwædon men þætte hie wendon þæt þæt wære goda eorre þæt usic þær on becwome. Ða het ic eald hrægl toslitan ond habban wið þæm fyre ond sceldan mid. Þa seoððan æfter þon we hæfdon smolte niht ond gode siðþan usic þa earfeðo forleton, ond we ða sioðþan butan orenum þingum mete þigdon ond usic restan.

"Ond ic þær þa bebyrgde minra þegna .v. hund þe ðær betweoh ða snawas ond earfeþo ond þa fyr þe us þær in þæm wicum on becwoman þæt hie forwurdon ond deade wæron. Ond þa het ic of þære wic-stowe sioððan þa ferd faran forð,

likewise it took a heavy toll of our livestock. I then ordered that the tents be assembled again and the bags all brought together, and the bags and gear of our encampment were gathered with difficulty on account of the wind. And then we camped in a milder and warmer valley. When we had encamped and put all our things in order, I told the whole army to sit down to dinner and have a meal, and they did so. When it came near to evening, the winds began to rise again and the weather to grow rough, and an intense chill developed in the evening. Then there came a heavy snow, and it snowed as much as if a thick fleece had descended. When I saw the magnitude and thickness of the snow, it appeared such that I realized it would overwhelm the encampment. I then directed the troops to tread the snow with their feet, and the fires were all nearly smothered and extinguished on account of the depth of the snow. However, we were fortunate in one respect, that the snow did not remain there longer than one hour. Then immediately after that there was a very dark cloud and gloom, and also there came from the dark cloud consuming fires. The fires fell on the earth like burning torches, and due to the burning of the fire, the entire plain was ablaze. People said then that they expected that it was thc gods' anger that had visited us there. Then I ordered that old clothing be torn up and used against the fire as protection. After that we had a calm and a fine night when those hardships had passed us by, and then afterward we took a meal without harmful incidents and rested ourselves.

"And there I buried five hundred of my officers who had perished there and lay dead between the snows and mishaps and the fires that had visited us in that camp. And I

ond we þa foron forð be þæm sæ, ond þær ða hean hos ond
220 dene ond garsecg ðone Æthiopia we gesawon. Swelce eac þa
miclan ond þa mæron dune we gesawon þa mon hateð *Ene-*
sios ond þæt scræf Libri þæs godes. Ða het ic þær in bescu-
fan forworhte men, þæt ic wolde gewitan hweþer sio segen
soð wære þe me mon ær be þon sægde, þæt þær nænig mon
in gan mehte ond eft gesund æfter þon beon nymþe he mid
asegendnisseum in eode in þæt scræf. Ond þæt wæs eac æf-
ter þon gecyðed in þara monna deaðe, forþon ðy þriddan
dæge hie swulton ðæs þe hie in þæt scræf eodon. Ond ic
eaþ-modlice ond geornlice bæd þa god-mægen þæt hie mec
ealles middan-geardes kyning ond hlaford mid hean sigum
geweorþeden, ond in Macedoniam ic eft gelæded wære to
Olimphiade minre meder ond to minum geswustrum ond
gesibbum. Ða wolde ic eft in Fasiacen þæt lond feran.

225 "Mid þy ic þa ferde mid mine weorede, ða cwoman us þær
on ðæm wege twegen ealde men togeanes. Ða frægn ic hie
ond ahsode hwæþer hie owiht mærlic in þæm londum wis-
ten. Ða ondsworadon hie mec ond sægdon þæt nære mara
weg þonne ic meahte on tyn dagum geferan. Hwæþre mid
ealle mine weorede somod ic hit geferan ne mehte for ðara
wega nerwette, ac mid feower þusendum monna ic hit gefe-
ran meahte, þæt ic mærlices hwæthwugo gesawe. Ða wæs ic
230 swiðe bliðe ond gefeonde for þæm hiora wordum. Ða cwæð
ic eft to him ond him spræc liðum wordum to: 'Secgað, la,
mec, git ealdon, hwæt þæt sie mærlices ond micellices þæt
git mec gehatað þæt ic þær geseon mæge.' Ða ondswarode
me hiora oðer ond cwæð: 'Þu gesiehst, kyning, gif þu hit ge-
ferest, þa tu trio sunnan ond monan on Indisc ond on Gre-
cisc sprecende. Oþer þara is wæpned-cynnes, sunnan trio,
oþer wif-kynnes, þæt monan trio, ond hie gesecgað þæm

then ordered the army to set out from that encampment, and we made our way along the sea, and there we saw the steep promontories and valley and the ocean of Ethiopia. Likewise we saw the great and famous mountains that are called *Enesii,* and the cave of the god Liber. I ordered then that condemned men be thrown in there, since I wanted to know whether the report was true that I had been given, that no one could go in there and be fit again after that, unless he went into the cave with offerings. And that was also shown thereafter by the death of those men, because on the third day after they had gone into that cave they died. And I humbly and earnestly prayed of the divine powers that they would exalt me with high victories as king and ruler of the entire world, and that I would be guided back to Macedonia to my mother Olimphias and to my sisters and kin. Then I wanted to return to the region Fasiacen.

"As I was en route with my troops, two old men came toward us on the road. I questioned them and asked whether they knew of anything extraordinary in that region. They answered me that it was no greater distance than could be covered in ten days. However, I could not cover it with all my assembled army on account of the narrowness of the paths, but I could cover it with four thousand men, in which case I might see something extraordinary. I was very happy and elated at their report. I then said in turn to them, speaking with mild words, 'So, tell me, you old men, what sort of extraordinary and great thing it is that you promise me I can see there.' One of them answered me then and said, 'You will see, your majesty, if you traverse it, the two trees of the sun and moon speaking in Indic and in Greek. One of them is male, the tree of the sun, the other female, the tree of the

men þe hie frineð, hwæt godes oþðe yfles him becuman sceal.' Ða ne gelyfde ic him ac wende þæt hi mec on hyscte ond on bismer sægdon, ond ic swa cwæð to minum geferan: 'Min þrym is from eastewearde middan-gearde oþ þæt westanweardne, ond mec þas forealdodan el-reordegan nu her bysmergeað.'

"Mynte ic hie haton yflian; ða sworan hie swiðe þæt hie soð sægdon ond noht lugen þara þinga. Ða wolde ic gecunnian hwæþer hie mec soð sægdon, ond mec mine geferan bædon þæt hie swelcra merþo bescerede ne wæron, ac ðæt we his gecunnedon, hwæþer hit swelc wære, ða hit næs micel to geferanne. Genom þa mid mec þreo þusendo ond forlet mine fyrd elcor in Fasiacen under Pore þæm kyninge ond under minum gerefum ðær abidon. Ða foran we, ond usic þa lad-teowas læddon þurh þa wædlan stowe wætres ond þurh þa unarefndon lond wildeora ond wyrma, þa wæron wunderlicum nomum on Indisc geceged.

"Mid þy we þa nealehtan ðæm þeod-londe, þa gesawon we ægþer ge wif ge wæpned-men mid panthera fellum ond tigriscum þara deora hydum gegyryde ond nanes oðres brucon. Mid þy ic þa frægn hie ond ahsode hwelcre ðeode kynnes hie wæron, ða ondswarodon hie mec ond sægdon on hiora geþeode þæt hie wæran Indos. Wæs seo stow rum ond wynsumo, ond balzamum ond recels ðær wæs genihtsumnis, ond þæt eac of þæra treowa telgan weol, ond þa men þæs londes bi ðy lifdon ond þæt æton.

"Mid þy we ða geornlicor þa stowe sceawodon ond betwih þa bearwas eodon, ond ic ða wynsumnesse ond fægernesse þæs londes wundrade, ða cwom se bisceop þære stowe us togeanes. Wæs he se bisceop .x. fota upheah, ond eall him wæs

moon, and they tell whoever asks them what of good or bad will happen to them.' I did not believe them but supposed that they were speaking to me in derision and mockery, and so I said to my companions, 'My might extends from the East of the world to the West, and these old and decrepit gibberish-speakers here are now jeering.'

"I intended to order that they be done some harm; then they swore up and down that they were speaking the truth and were not fabricating these matters. I wanted to test whether they were telling me the truth, and my companions implored me that they not be deprived of the glory of such exploits, but that we try out whether it was so, now that it was not far to go. I took with me three thousand and left the rest of my army to wait in Fasiacen under King Porus and under my viceroys. Then we left, and the guides led us through the place poor in water and through the intolerable regions of wild animals and vermin, which were called by remarkable names in Indic.

"As we were nearing the inhabited region, we saw both women and men dressed in panther pelts and the hides of those animals called tigers, and they made do with nothing else. When I questioned them and asked what nationality they were, they answered me and said in their language that they were Indians. The place was spacious and pleasant, and there was an abundance of balsam and incense, and it also oozed from the branches of the trees, and the people of that region lived on it and ate it.

"While we were investigating the place in greater detail and walking among the groves, and I was marveling at the delightfulness and beauty of the region, the bishop of the place came toward us. The bishop was ten feet tall, and his

se lic-homa sweart buton þæm toþum, ða wæron hwite, ond þa earan him þurh þyrelode, ond ear-hringas onhongedon of mænigfealdan gim-cynne geworhte, ond he wæs mid wildeora fellum gegerwed. Þa he se bisceop to me cwom, ða grette he me sona ond halette his leod-þeawe. Frægn he eac me to hwon ic þider cwome ond hwæt ic þær wolde. Þa ondswarode ic him þæt mec lyste geseon þa halgan trio sunnan ond monan. Ða ondswarode he, 'Gif þine geferan beoð clæne from wif-gehrine, þonne moton hie gongan in þone godcundan bearo.' Wæs minra geferana mid me þrio hund monna. Þa het se bisceop mine geferan þæt hie hiora gescie ond ealne heora gerelan him of adyden, ond het ic æghwæt swa don swa he us bebead. Wæs hit þa sio endlefte tid dæges. Ða bad se socerd sunnan setl-gonges, forþon sunnan trio agefeð ondsware æt þæm up-gonge ond eft æt setl-gonge, ond þæt monan triow gelice swa on niht dyde.

"Ða ongon ic geornlicor þa stowe sceawigan ond geond þa bearwas ond treowu gongan. Þa geseah ic þær balzamum þæs betstan stences genoh of þæm treowum ut weallan. Þæt balzamum ægþer ge ic ge mine geferan þær betwih þæm rindum noman þæra trio. Þonne wæron ða halgan trio sunnan ond monan on middum þæm oðrum treowum; meahton hie beon hunteontiges fota upheah, ond eac þær wæron oþre treow wunderlicre heanisse ða hatað Indeos *bebronas.* Þara triowa heannisse ic wundrade ond cwæð þæt ic wende þæt hie for miclum wætan ond regnum swa hea geweoxon. Ða sægde se bisceop þæt þær næfre in þæm londum regnes dropa ne cwome ne fugel ne wildeor, ne nænig ætern wyrm, þæt her dorste gesecean ða halgan gemæro sunnan ond monan. Eac þonne he sægde se bisceop þonne þæt *eclypsis* wære, þæt is þonne ðæs sunnan asprungnis oðþe þære mo-

entire body was black except for the teeth, which were white, and his ears pierced through, and earrings made of various gemstones hung down, and he was clothed in the skins of wild animals. When the bishop came to me, he approached me at once and greeted me after the local custom. He asked me why I had come there and what I wanted there. I answered him that it would please me to see the sacred trees of the sun and moon. Then he answered, 'If your companions are undefiled by intimacy with women, they are permitted to go into the divine grove.' Of my comrades, three hundred of my men were with me. Then the bishop told my companions to take off their shoes and all their clothing, and I ordered that everything be done as he asked us. It was then the eleventh hour of the day. The priest then waited for the setting of the sun, because the tree of the sun gives answers at sunrise and again at sunset, and the tree of the moon likewise did so at night.

"I began then to explore the place more thoroughly and to walk among the groves and trees. Then I saw there plenty of balsam of the best fragrance oozing out of the trees. Both my companions and I gathered the balsam between the bark of the trees. The sacred trees of the sun and moon were amidst the other trees; they could have been a hundred feet tall, and also there were other trees of amazing height that Indians call *bebronas.* I marveled at the height of the trees and said that I supposed they grew so tall on account of plenty of moisture and rain. The bishop said then that in those regions there came not a drop of rain nor a bird or beast, nor any poisonous vermin, such that it dared visit the sacred precincts of the sun and moon. The bishop also said that when there was an eclipse, that is, extinction of the sun

nan, þæt ðe halgan triow swiðe weopen ond mid micle sare instyred wæron, forþon hie ondredon þæt hie hiora godmægne sceoldon beon benumene. Ða þohte ic," sægde Alexander, "þæt ic wolde onsægdnisse þær onsecgan, ac þa forbead me se bisceop ond sægde þæt ðæt nære alyfed ænigum men þæt he þær ænig nyten cwealde oþþe blod-gyte worhte, ac mec het þæt ic me to þara triowa fotum gebæde, þæt sunna ond mone me soþe ondswarege ondwyrdum þara þinga ðe ic frune sioððan þas þing þus gedon wæron. Þa gesawon we westan þone leoman sunnan, ond se leoma gehran þæm treowum ufonweardum. Ða cwæð se sacerd, 'Lociað nu ealle up, ond be swa hwylcum þingum swa ge willon frinan, þence on his heortan deagollice, ond nænig mon his geþoht openum wordum ut ne cyðe.'

"Mid þy we þa wel neah stodan þam bearwum ond þæm god-sprecum, þa ðohte ic on minum mode hwæþer ic meahte ealne middan-geard me on onweald geslean, ond þonne sioþþan mid þæm siogorum geweorþad, ic eft meahte becuman in Macedoniam to Olimphiade minre meder, ond minum geswustrum. Ða ondswarode me þæt triow Indiscum wordum ond þus cwæd: 'Ðu unoferswyðda Alexander in gefeohtum, þu weorðest cyning ond hlaford ealles middan-geardes, ac hwæþre ne cymst þu on þinne eþel ðonan þu ferdest ær, forþon ðin gesceaft hit swa be þinum heafde ond fore hafað aræded.' Ða wæs ic ungleaw þæs geþeodes þara Indiscra worda þe þæt triow me to spræc; ða rehte hit me se bisceop ond sægde. Mid þy hit mine geferan gehyrdon þæt ic eft cwic ne moste in minne eþel becuman, ða wæron hie swiðe unrote forþon. Þa wolde ic eft on þa æfen-tid ma ahsian, ac þa næs se mona þa gyt uppe. Mid þy we þa eft eodon in þone halgan bearo ond we þa eft be þæm treowum sto-

or of the moon, the sacred trees wept profusely and were moved by great pain, because they feared that they would be deprived of their divine power. Then I thought," said Alexander, "that I would offer a sacrifice there, but the bishop forbade me and said that it was not permitted anyone to kill any animal or cause bloodshed there, but he told me to pray at the foot of the trees, that the sun and moon would answer me truthfully with responses about the things I asked after these matters were done that way. We then saw the radiance of the sun in the west, and the radiance touched the tops of the trees. Then the priest said, 'Now everyone look up, and whatever matters that you wish to ask about, think about it privately in the heart, and let no one reveal his thoughts in open speech.'

"While we were standing quite near the groves and the oracles, I thought to myself whether I could force the entire world into subjugation to me, and then afterward, exalted by those victories, whether I could return to Macedonia to my mother Olimphias and my sisters. The tree then answered me with words in Indic and spoke thus: 'Alexander, undefeated in battles, you will be king and lord of the entire world, but still you will not come to your own country from which you first set out, because your fate has decreed it thus ahead of you and beforehand.' I was ignorant of the meaning of the words in Indic that the tree had spoken to me; the bishop then explained it and told me. When my companions heard that I would not be allowed to return alive to my own country, they were very disturbed about it. I wanted to ask yet more in the evening hours, but the moon was not up yet. When we re-entered the sacred grove and we stood again by the trees, we immediately made requests

dan, gebædon us þa sona to þæm treowum swa we ær dydon. Ond ic eac in mid mec gelædde mine þrie ða getreowestan frynd, ða wæron mine syndrige treow-geþoftan—þæt wæs ærest Perticam ond Clitomum ond Pilotan—forþon ic me ne ondred þæt me þæra ænig beswice, forþon þær næs riht on þære stowe ænigne to acwellanne for þære stowe weorþunge.

"Ða þohte ic on minum mode ond on minum geþohte on hwelcre stowe ic sweltan scolde. Mid þy ða ærest se mona upeode, þa gehran he mid his sciman þæm triowum ufeweardum ond þæt triow ondswarode þæm minum geþohte ond þus cwæð: 'Alexander, fulne ende þines lifes þu hæfst gelifd, ac þys æftran geare þu swyltst on Babilone on Maius monðe from þæm þu læst wenst from þæm þu bist beswicen.' Ða wæs ic swiðe sariges modes, ond þa mine frynd swa eac þa me þær mid wæron, ond hie weopon swiðe, forþon him wære min gesynto leofre þonne hiora seolfra hælo. Ða gewiton we to urum geferum eft, ond hie woldon to hiora swæsendum sittan, ond ic wolde for þæm bysegum mines modes me gerestan. Ac þa bædon mec mine geferan þæt ic on swa micelre modes unreto ond nearonisse mec selfne mid fæstenne ne swencte. Þigde ða tela medmicelne mete wið mines modes willan, ond þa tidlice to minre reste eode, forþon ic wolde beon gearo æt sunnan up-gonge þæt ic eft in geeode.

"Ða on morgne mid þy hit dagode, þa onbræd ic ond þa mine getreowestan frynd aweahte, þæt ic wolde in þa halgan stowe gan. Ac þa reste hine se bisceop þa giet, ond mid wildeora fellum wæs gegerwed ond bewrigen. Ond irenes ond leades þa men on þæm londum wædliað ond goldes genihtsumiað, ond be ðæm balzamum þa men in þæm londe lifgeað, ond of ðæm neah-munte wealleð hluter wæter ond

of the trees as we had done earlier. And I also took in with me my three truest friends, who were my particular loyal comrades—that was first Perticas and Clitomus and Pilotas—because I was not worried that any of them would betray me, since it was not lawful to kill anyone in that spot on account of respect for the place.

"I then thought to myself and in my mind in what place I should die. At the first rising of the moon, it touched the tops of the trees with its light, and the tree answered my thoughts and spoke thus: 'Alexander, you have lived your life to its full term, but this coming year in Babylon in the month of May you will die of what you least expect you will be overcome by.' Then I was in depressed spirits, and my friends likewise who were there with me, and they wept a great deal, because my security meant more to them than their own well-being. Then we returned to our comrades, and they wanted to sit down to their dinner, and I wanted to get some rest on account of the troubles on my mind. But my comrades asked me not to distress myself with fasting in so much disturbance and anxiety of mind. I partook of a very slender meal against my heart's desire, and then I went to bed early, since I wanted to be ready at sunrise to go in again.

"When it dawned the next day, I got up and wakened my truest friends, since I wanted to enter the sacred place. But the bishop was still in bed, and he was outfitted and covered with the skins of wild animals. And the people of that region lack iron and lead and have plenty of gold, and the people in that region live on the balsam, and from the neighboring mountain there flows water clear and fine and very sweet. The people are accustomed to drinking that and living on it.

fæger ond þæt swiðe swete. Þonne drincað þa men þæt ond by lifigeað. Ond þonne hie restað, þonne restað hie buton bedde ond bolstre, ac on wildeora fellum heora bedding bið. Ða awehte ic þone bisceop. Hæfde se bisceop þreo hund wintra on yldo.

"Mid þy he þa se bisceop aras, ða eode ic on þa godcundan stowe ond þa þriddan siðe þæt sunnan treow ongon frinan þurh hwelces monnes hond min ende wære getiod, oððe hwelcne ende-dæg min modor oþðe min geswuster nu gebidan scoldon. Þa ondswarode me þæt treow on grecisc ond þus cwæð: 'Gif ic þe þone syrere gesecge þines feores, yþelice þu ða wyrde oncyrrest ond his hond befehst. Ac soð ic þe secge þæt yb anes geares fyrst ond eahta monað þu swyltst in Babilone, nalles mid iserne acweald swa ðu wenst, ac mid atre. Ðin modor gewiteð of weorulde þurh scondlicne deað ond unarlicne, ond heo ligeð unbebyrged in wege fuglum to mete ond wildeorum. Þine sweostor beoð longe gesæliges lifes. Ðu þonne ðeah þu lytle hwile lifge, hweþre ðu geweorðest an cyning ond hlaford ealles middan-geardes. Ac ne frign ðu unc nohtes ma ne ne axa, forþon wit habbað oferhleoðred þæt gemære uncres leohtes, ac to Fasiacen ond Porre þæm cyninge eft gehworf þu.' Ond fer ðy þa weopon mine geferan, forþon ic swa lytle hwile lyfigan moste. Ac þa forbead hit se bisceop þæt hi ne weopon, þy læs þa halgan treow þurh heora wop ond tearas abulgen.

"Ond ne geherde ða ondsware þara treowa ma manna þonne þa mine getreowestan freond, ond hit nænig mon ut cyþan ne moste, þy læs þa el-reordegan kyningas ðe ic ær mid nede to hyrsumnesse gedyde, þæt hie on þæt fægon þæt ic swa lytle hwile lifgean moste. Ne hit eac ænig mon þære ferde ðon ma ut mæran moste, þy læs hie forðon ormode

And when they go to sleep, they lie down without bed or pillow, but their bedding is of the skins of wild animals. Then I wakened the bishop. The bishop was three hundred years of age.

"When the bishop got up, I entered the divine precinct and for the third time began to ask the tree of the sun through which man's hand my end was ordained, or what final day my mother or my sisters should now expect. Then the tree answered me in Greek and spoke thus: 'If I reveal to you the plotter against your life, you will easily turn aside that event and stay his hand. But I tell you the truth that in the space of one year and eight months you will die in Babylon, killed not by a weapon, as you expect, but by poison. Your mother will depart from the world by a humiliating and dishonorable death, and she will lie unburied on the road as a meal for birds and wild animals. Your sisters will live long and happy lives. You, then, although you will live just a little while, nonetheless will become sole king and lord of the entire world. But do not question us or ask us any more, for we have talked beyond the limit of our light, but turn back to Fasiacen and King Porus.' And therefore my comrades wept, because I should be allowed to live so short a while. But the bishop forbade it that they should weep, lest they offend the sacred trees with their cries and tears.

"And no one other than my truest friends heard the answer of the trees, and no one was permitted to reveal it, lest the barbarian kings I had brought into subjection by force should take heart that I should be allowed to live so short a while. Neither was anyone allowed to report it any more widely within the army, lest the men become despondent on

wæron ond þy sænran mines willan ond weorð-myndo, ðæs hie mid mec to fromscipe geferan scoldon. Ond me næs se hrædlica ende mines lifes swa miclum weorce swa me wæs þæt ic læs mærðo gefremed hæfde þonne min willa wære. Ðas þing ic write to þon, min se leofa *magister,* þæt þu ærest gefeo in þæm fromscipe mines lifes ond eac blissige in þæm weorð-myndum. Ond eac swelce ecelice min gemynd stonde ond hleouige oðrum eorð-cyningum to bysne, ðæt hie witen þy gearwor þæt min þrym ond min weorð-mynd maran wæron þonne ealra oþra kyninga þe in middan-gearde æfre wæron."

Finit.

that account and more negligent of my will and my honor, since they were expected to travel the route to success with me. And the approaching end of my life was not so very distressing to me as was the thought that I had achieved less glory than I had intended. I am writing these things, my dear teacher, so that you before all may rejoice in the success of my life and also revel in the honors. And likewise may my memory stand eternally and tower as an example to other earthly kings, so that they may know for certain that my glory and my honor were greater than those of all other kings who were ever on earth."

The end.

BEOWULF

Hwæt, we Gar-Dena   in gear-dagum,
þeod-cyninga   þrym gefrunon,
hu ða æþelingas   ellen fremedon.
Oft Scyld Scefing   sceaþena þreatum,
monegum mægþum   meodo-setla ofteah,
egsode eorlas,   syððan ærest wearð
fea-sceaft funden.   He þæs frofre gebad:
weox under wolcnum,   weorð-myndum þah,
oð þæt him æghwylc   þara ymb-sittendra
ofer hron-rade   hyran scolde,
gomban gyldan.   Þæt wæs god cyning.
Ðæm eafera wæs   æfter cenned
geong in geardum,   þone God sende
folce to frofre;   fyren-ðearfe ongeat—
þæt hie ær drugon   aldorlease
lange hwile.   Him þæs Lif-Frea,
wuldres wealdend   worold-are forgeaf:
Beow wæs breme   —blæd wide sprang—
Scyldes eafera   Scede-landum in.
Swa sceal geong guma   gode gewyrcean,
fromum feoh-giftum   on fæder bearme,
þæt hine on ylde   eft gewunigen
wil-gesiþas,   þonne wig cume,
leode gelæsten;   lof-dædum sceal
in mægþa gehwære   man geþeon.

Yes, we have heard of the greatness of the Spear-Danes' high
kings in days long past, how those nobles practiced bravery.
Often Scyld, son of Scef, expelled opponents' hosts, many 4
peoples, from mead-seats, made men fear him, after he was
first discovered destitute. He lived to see remedy for that:
grew up under the heavens, prospered in marks of distinc-
tion, until every neighbor across the whale-road had to an-
swer to him, pay tribute. That was a good king. A son was 11
born in succession to him, a young one among manors,
whom God sent as a comfort to his people; he had perceived
their dire need, what they had suffered, lordless, for a great
while. For that the Lord of life, wielder of glory, granted
them that worldly favor: Beow was renowned—his fame
sprang wide—the heir of Scyld, in Scania. So ought a young 20
man to ensure by his liberality, by ready largess, while in his
father's care, that close companions will in turn stand by
him in his later years, his men be true when war comes; from
praiseworthy deeds comes success in every nation.

Him ða Scyld gewat   to gescæp-hwile
fela-hror feran   on Frean wære.
Hi hyne þa ætbæron   to brimes faroðe,
swæse gesiþas,   swa he selfa bæd
þenden wordum weold.   Wine Scyldinga,
leof land-fruma   lange ahte—
þær æt hyðe stod,   hringed-stefna
isig ond ut-fus—   æþelinges fær;
aledon þa   leofne þeoden,
beaga bryttan   on bearm scipes,
mærne be mæste.   Þær wæs madma fela
of feor-wegum   frætwa gelæded.
Ne hyrde ic cymlicor   ceol gegyrwan
hilde-wæpnum   ond heaðo-wædum,
billum ond byrnum;   him on bearme læg
madma mænigo,   þa him mid scoldon
on flodes æht   feor gewitan.
Nalæs hi hine læssan   lacum teodan,
þeod-gestreonum,   þonne þa dydon
þe hine æt frum-sceafte   forð onsendon
ænne ofer yðe   umbor-wesende.
Þa gyt hie him asetton   segen gyldenne
heah ofer heafod,   leton holm beran,
geafon on garsecg;   him wæs geomor sefa,
murnende mod.   Men ne cunnon
secgan to soðe,   sele-rædende,
hæleð under heofenum,   hwa þæm hlæste onfeng.

I

Ða wæs on burgum   Beow Scyldinga,
leof leod-cyning   longe þrage
folcum gefræge   —fæder ellor hwearf,

Then at the appointed time Scyld, very elderly, set out to 26
pass into the keeping of the Lord. They bore him then to
the ocean's shore, his close confederates, as he himself had
requested while he had command of words. The friend of 30
the Scyldings, beloved leader of that race, had long owned—
it stood there in the harbor, a ring-prowed one, icy and set
to depart—a prince's vessel; then they laid their well-loved
lord, disburser of rings, in the ship's bosom, the renowned
man by the mast. A trove of treasures and trappings was
brought there from far ways. I have never heard of a ferry
more finely decked with war-weapons and battle-garments,
blades and chain-mail; in his lap lay a mass of riches, which
were to go far with him into the possession of the flood.
They equipped him with offerings, treasures of the commu- 43
nity by no means humbler than the ones they had provided
who sent him forth at the start, alone over the wave in his
infancy. And now they raised high over his head a golden
standard, let the sea take him, gave him over to the deep;
their spirits were brooding, their mood full of mourning.
No one can say for a fact, counselors in halls, heroes under
heaven, who received that cargo.

I

Then among the strongholds Beow of the Scyldings, be- 53
loved king of that folk, was celebrated by peoples for long
years—his father had passed elsewhere, that elder from the

aldor of earde— oþ þæt him eft onwoc
heah Healfdene; heold þenden lifde
gamol ond guð-reouw glæde Scyldingas.
Đæm feower bearn forð-gerimed
in worold wocun, weoroda ræswan,
Heorogar ond Hroðgar ond Halga til;
hyrde ic þæt [.] wæs Onelan cwen,
Heaðo-Scilfingas heals-gebedda.
Þa wæs Hroðgare here-sped gyfen,
wiges weorð-mynd, þæt him his wine-magas
georne hyrdon, oðð þæt seo geogoð geweox,
mago-driht micel. Him on mod bearn
þæt heal-reced hatan wolde,
medo-ærn micel men gewyrcean
þonne yldo bearn æfre gefrunon,
ond þær on innan eall gedælan
geongum ond ealdum swylc him God sealde,
buton folc-scare ond feorum gumena.
Đa ic wide gefrægn weorc gebannan
manigre mægþe geond þisne middan-geard,
folc-stede frætwan. Him on fyrste gelomp,
ædre mid yldum, þæt hit wearð eal gearo,
heal-ærna mæst; scop him Heort naman
se þe his wordes geweald wide hæfde.
He beot ne aleh: beagas dælde,
sinc æt symle. Sele hlifade
heah ond horn-geap; heaðo-wylma bad,
laðan liges— ne wæs hit lenge þa gen
þæt se ecg-hete aþum-sweoran
æfter wæl-niðe wæcnan scolde.
Đa se ellen-gæst earfoðlice

earth—until to him in turn high Healfdene awoke; he held sway as long as he lived, old and battle-fierce, over the gracious Scyldings. To him four children in sum awoke in the world, to that leader of armies, Heorogar and Hrothgar and Halga the good; I have heard that [. . . . . .] was Onela's queen, cherished bedfellow of the War-Scylfing.

Then to Hrothgar was given war-success, distinction in 64
battle, so that his friends and kinsmen were willingly ruled by him, until the cadre of new recruits grew to a large force of young men. It became fixed in his mind that he would direct men to construct a hall-structure, a mead-mansion larger than the offspring of the ancients had ever heard of, and there inside he would hand over to young and old all such as God had granted him, aside from the state itself and
human lives. Then, I have heard, the work was imposed far 74
and wide on many a folk throughout this middle-earth, the public place furnished. By and by it came to pass for them, not long among humankind, that it was all finished, the greatest of hall-houses; he whose word had wide authority crafted for it the name Heorot. He did not neglect his promise: he distributed rings, a fortune at feast. The hall towered, tall and wide-gabled; it awaited battle-surges, dreaded flame; it was sooner yet that the blade-hostility should be roused for father- and son-in-law after deadly violence.

Then the powerful demon endured the time with effort, 86

þrage geþolode,   se þe in þystrum bad,
þæt he dogora gehwam   dream gehyrde
hludne in healle.   Þær wæs hearpan sweg,
swutol sang scopes.   Sægde se þe cuþe
frum-sceaft fira   feorran reccan,
cwæð þæt se ælmihtiga   eorðan worhte,
wlite-beorhtne wang,   swa wæter bebugeð,
gesette sige-hreþig   sunnan ond monan,
leoman to leohte   land-buendum,
ond gefrætwade   foldan sceatas
leomum ond leafum,   lif eac gesceop
cynna gehwylcum   þara ðe cwice hwyrfaþ.
Swa ða driht-guman   dreamum lifdon,
eadiglice,   oð ðæt an ongan
fyrene fremman   feond on helle;
wæs se grimma gæst   Grendel haten,
mære mearc-stapa,   se þe moras heold,
fen ond fæsten;   fifel-cynnes eard
won-sæli wer   weardode hwile,
siþðan him scyppen   forscrifen hæfde
in Caines cynne—   þone cwealm gewræc
ece Drihten,   þæs þe he Abel slog;
ne gefeah he þære fæhðe,   ac he hine feor forwræc,
Metod for þy mane   man-cynne fram.
Þanon untydras   ealle onwocon,
eotenas ond ylfe   ond orc-neas,
swylce gigantas,   þa wið Gode wunnon
lange þrage;   he him ðæs lean forgeald.

II

Gewat ða neosian,   syþðan niht becom,
hean huses,   hu hit Hring-Dene

he who waited in the shadows, that every day he heard noisy
pleasures in the hall. There was the music of the harp, the
clear song of the performer. He who could reckon the ori-
gins of mortals from distant times said that the Almighty
created the earth, a resplendent world, as far as contained
by water—positioned, triumphant, sun and moon, lamps as
illumination to landsmen, and embellished the surface of
the earth with branches and leaves, likewise generated life
in all the species that actively move about. Thus the troop- 99
men lived agreeably, at ease, until a certain one began to per-
petrate crimes, a hellish foe; the unyielding demon was
named Grendel, a well-known wanderer in the wastes, who
ruled the heath, fen, and fastnesses; the ill-starred man had
occupied for some time the habitat of monstrosities, after
the Creator had cursed him among the race of Cain—the
eternal Lord was avenging the murder after he killed Abel;
he derived no satisfaction from that feud, but Providence
banished him far away from humankind on account of that
crime. Thence awoke all deformed races, ogres and elves and 111
lumbering brutes, likewise giants, who struggled against
God for a long while; he gave them their deserts for that.

II
He set out then after night fell to examine the tall build- 115
ing, how the Ring-Danes had settled in after the drinking

æfter beorþege gebun hæfdon.
Fand þa ðær inne æþelinga gedriht
swefan æfter symble; sorge ne cuðon,
won-sceaft wera. Wiht unhælo,
grim ond grædig, gearo sona wæs,
reoc ond reþe, ond on ræste genam
þritig þegna; þanon eft gewat
huðe hremig to ham faran,
mid þære wæl-fylle wica neosan.
Ða wæs on uhtan mid ær-dæge
Grendles guð-cræft gumum undyrne;
þa wæs æfter wiste wop up ahafen,
micel morgen-sweg. Mære þeoden,
æþeling ær-god, unbliðe sæt,
þolode ðryð-swyð, þegn-sorge dreah,
syðþan hie þæs laðan last sceawedon,
wergan gastes; wæs þæt gewin to strang,
lað ond longsum. Næs hit lengra fyrst,
ac ymb ane niht eft gefremede
morð-beala mare, ond no mearn fore,
fæhðe ond fyrene; wæs to fæst on þam.
Þa wæs eað-fynde þe him elles hwær
gerumlicor ræste sohte,
bed æfter burum, ða him gebeacnod wæs,
gesægd soðlice sweotolan tacne
heal-ðegnes hete; heold hyne syðþan
fyr ond fæstor se þæm feonde ætwand.
Swa rixode ond wið rihte wan,
ana wið eallum, oð þæt idel stod
husa selest. Wæs seo hwil micel:
twelf wintra tid torn geþolode

rounds. He found therein a band of nobles sleeping after the
feast; they knew no cares, no human misfortune. The crea- 120
ture of malignity, unyielding and rapacious, was ready at
once, fierce and savage, and seized where they lay thirty men
of the court; from there he set out again, exulting in the
spoils, to go home, to visit his territory with his fill of the
slaughtered. Then in the early hours before dawn Grendel's
warfare was revealed to all; then after feasting, wailing was
lifted up, a loud morning-song. The renowned lord, a prince 129
good since old times, sat distraught; the mighty one suf-
fered, endured misery over his men, after they observed the
track of the despised one, the accursed demon; that afflic-
tion was too strong, repellent and enduring. There was little
delay, but after a single night he committed more murders,
feuding and crimes, and showed no remorse; he was too in-
tent on it. Then there was no dearth of those who found
themselves sleeping-quarters elsewhere, farther away, a bed
among the private chambers, when the hall-thane's malice
was demonstrated to them, truly expressed by clear signs;
whoever escaped the fiend lodged themselves farther away
and more securely after that. Thus he reigned and made war 144
on justice, alone against all, until the finest of buildings
stood idle. The period was long: for the space of twelve win-

wine Scyldinga, weana gehwelcne,
sidra sorga. Forðam gesyne wearð
ylda bearnum, undyrne cuð
gyddum geomore þætte Grendel wan
hwile wið Hroþgar, hete-niðas wæg,
fyrene ond fæhðe fela missera,
singale sæce; sibbe ne wolde
wið manna hwone mægenes Deniga,
feorh-bealo feorran, fea þingian,
ne þær nænig witena wenan þorfte
beorhtre bote to banan folmum,
ac se æglæca ehtende wæs,
deorc deaþ-scua, duguþe ond geogoþe,
seomade ond syrede; sin-nihte heold,
mistige moras; men ne cunnon
hwyder hel-runan hwyrftum scriþað.
Swa fela fyrena feond man-cynnes,
atol an-gengea oft gefremede,
heardra hynða; Heorot eardode,
sinc-fage sel sweartum nihtum.
No he þone gif-stol gretan moste,
maþðum for Metode, ne his myne wisse.
Þæt wæs wræc micel wine Scyldinga,
modes brecða. Monig oft gesæt,
rice to rune; ræd eahtedon,
hwæt swið-ferhðum selest wære
wið fær-gryrum to gefremmanne.
Hwilum hie geheton æt hærg-trafum
wig-weorþunga, wordum bædon
þæt him gast-bona geoce gefremede
wið þeod-þreaum. Swylc wæs þeaw hyra,

ters the friend of the Scyldings endured torment, every sort
of agony, sprawling miseries. On that account it was made 149
plain to the offspring of the ancients, disclosed and revealed
grievously in narratives, that Grendel had for some time
been in a struggle with Hrothgar, waged a war of aggression,
crimes and feuding for many a season, continual persecu-
tion; he wanted no truce with any of the men of the force
of the Danes, or to put aside all the killing, negotiate a set-
tlement, nor did any of the senior councilors need expect
gleaming compensation at the hands of the killer, but the
troublemaker, that dark death-shadow, persisted in perse-
cuting veterans as well as new recruits, lurked and plotted,
ruled the foggy heath in continual night; men do not know
where hell's intimates pass in their rambles.

Thus, the enemy of humankind, repulsive loner, often 164
committed a great many crimes, sharp humiliations; he oc-
cupied Heorot, the treasure-laden edifice, on gloomy nights.
He was not permitted to approach the throne or valuables
on account of Providence, nor did he gain satisfaction. That 170
was a great distress to the friend of the Scyldings, a cause
of broken spirits. Many an officer often sat in consultation,
deliberated alternatives as to what it would be best for the
firm-hearted to do about thc grisly peril. At times they
pledged honors to idols, prayed explicitly that a soul-slayer
would lend them assistance against that country-wide disas-
ter. Such was their way, the hope of heathens; they minded 178

hæþenra hyht; helle gemundon
in mod-sefan, Metod hie ne cuþon,
dæda demend, ne wiston hie Drihten God,
ne hie huru heofena helm herian ne cuþon,
wuldres waldend. Wa bið þæm ðe sceal
þurh sliðne nið sawle bescufan
in fyres fæþm, frofre ne wenan,
wihte gewendan; wel bið þæm þe mot
æfter deað-dæge Drihten secean
ond to fæder fæþmum freoðo wilnian.

III

Swa ða mæl-ceare maga Healfdenes
singala seað; ne mihte snotor hæleð
wean onwendan; wæs þæt gewin to swyð,
laþ ond longsum, þe on ða leode becom,
nyd-wracu niþ-grim, niht-bealwa mæst.
Þæt fram ham gefrægn Higelaces þegn
god mid Geatum, Grendles dæda;
se wæs mon-cynnes mægenes strengest
on þæm dæge þysses lifes,
æþele ond eacen. Het him yð-lidan
godne gegyrwan; cwæð, he guð-cyning
ofer swan-rade secean wolde,
mærne þeoden, þa him wæs manna þearf.
Đone siðfæt him snotere ceorlas
lythwon logon, þeah he him leof wære;
hwetton hige-rofne, hæl sceawedon.
Hæfde se goda Geata leoda
cempan gecorone, þara þe he cenoste
findan mihte. Fiftyna sum
sund-wudu sohte; secg wisade,

hell in their heart of hearts; they did not recognize Providence, the arbiter of all things done; they did not know the Lord God, nor did they even know to praise heaven's helm, the master of magnificence. Woe to one who has to thrust his soul through dire affliction into the fire's embrace, expect no comfort, experience no change at all; well to one who is permitted after his death-day to seek the Lord and sue for peace in the father's embrace.

III

So Healfdene's offspring continually brooded over his 189
time of troubles; the wise hero could not set aside his sorrow—that conflict was too forceful, ugly and enduring, which had been visited on that people, an inexorably malign oppression, the most tremendous of night-scourges.

At home, Hygelac's man, good among the Geats, heard 194
about that, Grendel's doings; of humans he was the mightiest in strength in that day of this mortal existence, noble and prodigious. He directed that a good wave-wanderer be readied for him; he said he intended to go see that war-king over the swan-road, that famous lord, now that he had need
of men. Wise men blamed him little for that undertaking, 202
though he was dear to them; they urged on the valiant one, read the auguries. The good one had selected fighters from among the men of the Geats, the boldest he could find. One of fifteen, he went to the sailing-wood; the champion, that

lagu-cræftig mon land-gemyrcu.
Fyrst forð gewat; flota wæs on yðum,
bat under beorge. Beornas gearwe
on stefn stigon. Streamas wundon,
sund wið sande. Secgas bæron
on bearm nacan beorhte frætwe,
guð-searo geatolic; guman ut scufon,
weras on wil-sið wudu bundenne.
Gewat þa ofer wæg-holm winde gefysed
flota fami-heals fugle gelicost,
oð þæt ymb an-tid oþres dogores
wunden-stefna gewaden hæfde,
þæt ða liðende land gesawon,
brim-clifu blican, beorgas steape,
side sæ-næssas; þa wæs sund liden,
eoletes æt ende. Þanon up hraðe
Wedera leode on wang stigon,
sæ-wudu sældon, syrcan hrysedon,
guð-gewædo; Gode þancedon
þæs þe him yþ-lade eaðe wurdon.
  Þa of wealle geseah weard Scildinga,
se þe holm-clifu healdan scolde,
beran ofer bolcan beorhte randas,
fyrd-searu fuslicu; hine fyrwyt bræc
mod-gehygdum hwæt þa men wæron.
Gewat him þa to waroðe wicge ridan
þegn Hroðgares, þrymmum cwehte
mægen-wudu mundum, meþel-wordum frægn:
  "Hwæt syndon ge searo-hæbbendra,
byrnum werede, þe þus brontne ceol
ofer lagu-stræte lædan cwomon,

sea-crafty man, showed the way to the land's end. The time 210
arrived; the vessel was on the waves, the boat under the
headland. Ready men climbed onto the prow. Currents ed-
died, sea against sand. Champions hauled into the bosom
of the craft gleaming equipment, stately battle-gear; the
heroes, men on a mission, pushed off the vessel of joined
planks. Driven by the wind, the foamy-necked ship then
passed over the sea-waves most like a bird, until after the
lapse of a normal space of time, on the following day the
ring-prowed craft had reached the point where the travelers
saw land, ocean-cliffs standing out, steep headlands, broad
sea-scarps; then the journey had concluded at the far end
of the voyage. From there the men of the Geats instantly 224
stepped up onto solid ground, moored the sea-wood, shook
their shirts of mail, war-garments; they thanked God that
their passage over the waves had been easy.

Then from the heights the sentinel of the Scyldings, who 229
kept a lookout over the ocean's edge, saw gleaming bosses,
ready war-tackle borne over the gunwales; it piqued his in-
most curiosity what sort of people these might be. Hroth-
gar's officer set off for the beach riding a mount, forcefully
brandished a mighty wooden spear in his hands, questioned
them formally:

"What kind of arms-bearers are you, outfitted in mail- 237
shirts, who have come steering so lofty a vessel over the sea-

hider ofer holmas? Ic hwile wæs
ende-sæta, æg-wearde heold,
þe on land Dena laðra nænig
mid scip-herge sceðþan ne meahte.
No her cuðlicor cuman ongunnon
lind-hæbbende, ne ge leafnes-word
guð-fremmendra gearwe ne wisson,
maga gemedu. Næfre ic maran geseah
eorla ofer eorþan ðonne is eower sum,
secg on searwum; nis þæt seld-guma,
wæpnum geweorðad, næfne him his wlite leoge,
ænlic ansyn. Nu ic eower sceal
frum-cyn witan, ær ge fyr heonan
leas-sceaweras on land Dena
furþur feran. Nu ge feor-buend,
mere-liðende, minne gehyrað
anfealdne geþoht: ofost is selest
to gecyðanne hwanan eowre cyme syndon."

IIII

Him se yldesta andswarode,
werodes wisa, word-hord onleac:
"We synt gum-cynnes Geata leode
ond Higelaces heorð-geneatas.
Wæs min fæder folcum gecyþed,
æþele ord-fruma, Ecgþeow haten;
gebad wintra worn, ær he on weg hwurfe,
gamol of geardum; hine gearwe geman
witena welhwylc wide geond eorþan.
We þurh holdne hige hlaford þinne,
sunu Healfdenes secean cwomon,
leod-gebyrgean. Wes þu us larena god.

street, here over the water? For some time I have held the frontier, have kept surveillance of the sea, so that no enemy could do harm with a fleet in the land of the Danes. Shield-bearers have not ventured to land more casually, nor were you certain of the permission of war-makers, the consent of kinsmen. I have never in the world seen a larger man than is one of you, a champion in his equipment; ennobled by weapons, that is no mere hall-man, unless his looks play him false,
his unique appearance. Now I will know your background, 251
rather than your proceeding as spies past this point, farther into the land of the Danes. Now you strangers from far off, seafarers, mark my simple point: promptness is best for revealing where you have come from."

IIII
The most senior answered him, the leader of the troop, 258
unlocked a hoard of words: "We are men of the nation of the Geats and bound in loyalty to Hygelac. My father was widely known, a noble leader named Ecgtheo; he survived scores of winters before he turned on his way, aged, from among the households. Every knowledgeable person the world over remembers him readily. We have come looking for your lord, the son of Healfdene, shield of the nation, with amicable in-

Habbað we to þæm mæran micel ærende
Deniga frean. Ne sceal þær dyrne sum
wesan, þæs ic wene: þu wast, gif hit is
swa we soþlice secgan hyrdon,
þæt mid Scyldingum sceaðona ic nat hwylc,
deogol dæd-hata deorcum nihtum
eaweð þurh egsan uncuðne nið,
hynðu ond hra-fyl. Ic þæs Hroðgar mæg
þurh rumne sefan ræd gelæran
hu he frod ond god feond oferswyðeþ—
gyf him edwenden æfre scolde
bealuwa bisigu, bot eft cuman—
ond þa cear-wylmas colran wurðaþ;
oððe a syþðan earfoð-þrage,
þrea-nyd þolað þenden þær wunað
on heah-stede husa selest."

Weard maþelode ðær on wicge sæt,
ombeht unforht: "Æghwæþres sceal
scearp scyld-wiga gescad witan,
worda ond worca, se þe wel þenceð.
Ic þæt gehyre, þæt þis is hold weorod
frean Scyldinga. Gewitaþ forð beran
wæpen ond gewædu; ic eow wisige.
Swylce ic magu-þegnas mine hate
wið feonda gehwone flotan eowerne,
niw-tyrwydne nacan on sande
arum healdan, oþ ðæt eft byreð
ofer lagu-streamas leofne mannan
wudu wunden-hals to Weder-mearce,
god-fremmendra swylcum gifeþe bið
þæt þone hilde-ræs hal gedigeð."

tent. Be good to us by way of instruction. We have an impor- 270
tant errand to the famous lord of the Danes. A certain thing
ought not to be concealed in that quarter, to my way of
thinking: you will know if it is so, as we have certainly heard
tell, that among the Scyldings who knows what marauder, a
mysterious persecutor in the dark of night, shows through
his terror inexplicable malice, abasement and carnage. With 277
candid intentions I can offer Hrothgar advice about that,
how he, sage and good, will overcome his enemy, if change
and relief should ever come to him in turn for the troubles
of his suffering—and his surging cares will grow cooler, or
ever afterward he will suffer a time of trouble, sore affliction
for as long as the finest of buildings remains there on high
ground."

The watchman made a speech where he sat on horseback, 286
that dauntless officer: "A sharp shield-warrior who considers carefully ought to recognize the difference between the two—between words and deeds. I hear that this band is true to the lord of the Scyldings. Proceed bearing weapons and armor; I shall guide you. Likewise I will direct my lieutenants to hold your ship honorably, your new-tarred craft on the sand, against every enemy, until the ring-necked wood carries back over the ocean-currents to Weder-land whichever friend among these benefactors is fortunate enough to survive whole the storm of battle."

Gewiton him þa feran;   flota stille bad,
seomode on sale   sid-fæþmed scip,
on ancre fæst;   eofor-lic scionon
ofer hleor-bergan   gehroden golde,
fah ond fyr-heard;   ferh-wearde heold
guþ-mod grim-mon.   Guman onetton,
sigon ætsomne,   oþ þæt hy sæl timbred
geatolic ond gold-fah   ongyton mihton;
þæt wæs fore-mærost   fold-buendum
receda under roderum,   on þæm se rica bad;
lixte se leoma   ofer landa fela.
Him þa hilde-deor   hof modigra
torht getæhte,   þæt hie him to mihton
gegnum gangan;   guð-beorna sum
wicg gewende,   word æfter cwæð:
"Mæl is me to feran;   fæder alwalda
mid ar-stafum   eowic gehealde
siða gesunde.   Ic to sæ wille,
wið wrað werod   wearde healdan."

V

Stræt wæs stan-fah,   stig wisode
gumum ætgædere.   Guð-byrne scan
heard hond-locen;   hring-iren scir
song in searwum.   Þa hie to sele furðum
in hyra gryre-geatwum   gangan cwomon,
setton sæ-meþe   side scyldas,
rondas regn-hearde   wið þæs recedes weal;
bugon þa to bence.   Byrnan hringdon,
guð-searo gumena;   garas stodon,
sæ-manna searo   samod ætgædere,
æsc-holt ufan græg;   wæs se iren-þreat

They set out traveling then; the vessel remained still, a 301
wide-girthed ship tied to a rope, fastened to an anchor; boar-
images gleamed, covered with gold, over cheek-guards, pat-
terned and fire-hardened; the warlike, helmeted man ac-
corded them safe conduct. The men moved along quickly,
marched together, until they could make out a timbered
hall, stately and gold-trimmed; of halls, that was the single
best-known under the heavens to the inhabitants of earth,
in which the powerful one waited; its brilliance shone over
many regions. The battle-brave man directed them then to 312
the resplendent court of the courageous, so that they could
go directly to it; one of the war-makers turned his steed and
thereupon spoke a few words:

"It is time for me to leave; may the all-powerful father 316
with generosity keep you safe in your travels. I will go to the
sea, to keep guard against hostile bands."

V

The road was cobbled; the path guided the men as a 320
group. A war-shirt gleamed, hard and linked by hand; bright
ring-iron sang in the armor. Just when they arrived, com-
ing to the hall in their intimidating gear, the sea-weary men
set their broad shields, wonderfully strong bosses against
the wall of the building; they retired then to benches. Their
mail-shirts rang, the men's war-devices; spears stood, the
seafarers' gear, together in a group, an ash-grove gray from
above; the iron-troop was distinguished by its weapons.

wæpnum gewurþad.
Þa ðær wlonc hæleð
oret-mecgas æfter æþelum frægn:
"Hwanon ferigeað ge fætte scyldas,
græge syrcan, ond grim-helmas,
here-sceafta heap? Ic eom Hroðgares
ar ond ombiht. Ne seah ic el-þeodige
þus manige men modiglicran.
Wen' ic þæt ge for wlenco, nalles for wræc-siðum
ac for hige-þrymmum, Hroðgar sohton."
Him þa ellen-rof andswarode,
wlanc Wedera leod, word æfter spræc
heard under helme: "We synt Higelaces
beod-geneatas; Beowulf is min nama.
Wille ic asecgan sunu Healfdenes,
mærum þeodne min ærende,
aldre þinum, gif he us geunnan wile
þæt we hine swa godne gretan moton."
Wulfgar maþelode; þæt wæs Wendla leod;
wæs his mod-sefa manegum gecyðed,
wig ond wisdom: "Ic þæs wine Deniga,
frean Scildinga frinan wille,
beaga bryttan, swa þu bena eart,
þeoden mærne ymb þinne sið,
ond þe þa andsware ædre gecyðan
ðe me se goda agifan þenceð."
Hwearf þa hrædlice þær Hroðgar sæt
eald ond anhar mid his eorla gedriht;
eode ellen-rof, þæt he for eaxlum gestod
Deniga frean; cuþe he duguðe þeaw.
Wulfgar maðelode to his wine-drihtne:

Then a proud hero there asked the battle-challengers 331
about their background: "From where are you bringing plated shields, gray shirts, and masked helmets, a host of army-shafts? I am Hrothgar's herald and officer. I have not seen more vigorous outlanders in such numbers. I expect you have come to see Hrothgar out of daring, not on account of exile but out of determination."

The man of mettle then answered him, proud hero of the 340
Geats, thereupon spoke some words, hardy under helmet: "We are Hygelac's loyal retainers; Beowulf is my name. I will tell my business to the son of Healfdene, the renowned lord, your leader, if he will be so good as to allow us to approach him."

Wulfgar made a speech; that was a man of the Wendels; 348
his character was known to many, his valor and wisdom: "About that I will ask the friend of the Danes, lord of the Scyldings, the bestower of rings, as you are requesting, the renowned lord about your mission, and inform you at once about the answer that the good one thinks to give me."

He turned then quickly to where Hrothgar sat, old and 356
very hoary with his troop of men, walked boldly till he stood before the shoulders of the lord of the Danes; he knew the custom of the court. Wulfgar made a speech to his benign

"Her syndon geferede, feorran cumene
ofer geofenes begang Geata leode;
þone yldestan oret-mecgas
Beowulf nemnað. Hy benan synt
þæt hie, þeoden min, wið þe moton
wordum wrixlan. No ðu him wearne geteoh
ðinra gegn-cwida, glæd-man Hroðgar.
Hy on wig-getawum wyrðe þinceað
eorla geæhtlan; huru se aldor deah,
se þæm heaðo-rincum hider wisade."

VI

Hroðgar maþelode, helm Scyldinga:
"Ic hine cuðe cniht-wesende;
wæs his eald-fæder Ecgþeo haten,
ðæm to ham forgeaf Hreþel Geata
angan dohtor; is his eafora nu
heard her cumen, sohte holdne wine.
Ðonne sægdon þæt sæ-liþende,
þa ðe gif-sceattas Geata fyredon
þyder to þance, þæt he þritiges
manna mægen-cræft on his mund-gripe
heaþo-rof hæbbe. Hine halig God
for ar-stafum us onsende,
to West-Denum, þæs ic wen hæbbe,
wið Grendles gryre. Ic þæm godan sceal
for his mod-þræce madmas beodan.
Beo ðu on ofeste, hat in gan
seon sibbe-gedriht samod ætgædere;
gesaga him eac wordum, þæt hie sint wil-cuman
Deniga leodum."

lord: "Here have arrived, come from afar over the expanse of ocean, men of the Geats, the most senior of whom the battle-challengers call Beowulf. They are petitioning that they, my lord, be permitted to exchange words with you. Do not offer them refusal of your audience, gracious Hrothgar. In their war-dress they seem worthy of the esteem of men; indeed, the leader is outstanding who led the militia here."

VI

Hrothgar made a speech, helm of the Scyldings: "I knew 371
him when he was a child; his father was called Ecgtheo, to
whom Hrethel of the Geats gave his only daughter; his hardy
heir has now come here to visit a loyal friend. Seafarers who
ferried the gifts of the Geats here to our satisfaction used to
say that he, brave in war, had the strength of thirty men in
his hand-grip. The blessed Lord in his mercy has sent him to
us, to the West-Danes, I think, against the terror of Gren-
del. I shall offer the good one riches for his daring. Be quick 386
about it, direct the band of brothers to appear together in a
group; tell them also in a few words that they are welcome
to the nation of the Danes."

Wedera leodum word inne abead:
"Eow het secgan sige-drihten min,
aldor East-Dena, þæt he eower æþelu can,
ond ge him syndon ofer sæ-wylmas
heard-hicgende hider wil-cuman.
Nu ge moton gangan in eowrum guð-getawum
under here-griman Hroðgar geseon;
lætað hilde-bord her onbidan,
wudu wæl-sceaftas worda geþinges."
Aras þa se rica, ymb hine rinc manig,
þryðlic þegna heap; sume þær bidon,
heaðo-reaf heoldon, swa him se hearda bebead.
Snyredon ætsomne, þa secg wisode,
under Heorotes hrof; eode hilde-deor
heard under helme, þæt he on heorðe gestod.
Beowulf maðelode; on him byrne scan,
searo-net seowed smiþes orþancum:
"Wæs þu, Hroðgar, hal! Ic eom Higelaces
mæg ond mago-ðegn; hæbbe ic mærða fela
ongunnen on geogoþe. Me wearð Grendles þing
on minre eþel-tyrf undyrne cuð;
secgað sæ-liðend þæt þæs sele stande,
reced selesta rinca gehwylcum
idel ond unnyt, siððan æfen-leoht
under heofenes haðor beholen weorþeð.
Þa me þæt gelærdon leode mine
þa selestan, snotere ceorlas,
þeoden Hroðgar, þæt ic þe sohte,
forþan hie mægenes cræft minne cuþon;
selfe ofersawon ða ic of searwum cwom
fah from feondum, þær ic fife geband,

. . . offered the men of the Geats a word inside: "My victo- 390
rious lord, leader of East-Danes, has directed me to tell you
that he knows your background, and you brave-minded ones
are welcome to him here over the surging sea. Now you may
go in your war-gear under masked helmets to see Hrothgar;
let your battle-boards await here, with your wooden
slaughter-shafts, the result of your discussions."

The powerful man arose then, around him many a war- 399
rior, a mighty company of confederates. Some remained
there and safeguarded the war-loot, as the hardy one re-
quested of them. They made haste together, when the man
led the way, under Heorot's roof; the battle-brave one, hardy
under helmet, went till he stood on the hearth.

Beowulf made a speech; on him a mail-shirt gleamed, a 405
crafty net sewn by the ingenuity of the smith. "Be well,
Hrothgar! I am Hygelac's relative and young follower. I have
undertaken many accomplishments in my youth. The affair
of Grendel was openly reported to me in my native country;
seafarers say that this hall, the finest building, stands empty
and unused by any warriors after the evening light goes into
hiding under the confinement of heaven. Then the best of 415
my people, wise citizens, instructed me, lord Hrothgar, that
I should come to see you, since they knew the power of my
strength; they themselves had seen when I emerged from

yðde eotena cyn, ond on yðum slog
niceras nihtes, nearo-þearfe dreah,
wræc Wedera nið —wean ahsodon—
forgrand gramum; ond nu wið Grendel sceal,
wið þam aglæcan ana gehegan
ðing wið þyrse. Ic þe nuða,
brego Beorht-Dena, biddan wille,
eodor Scyldinga, anre bene,
þæt ðu me ne forwyrne, wigendra hleo,
freo-wine folca, nu ic þus feorran com,
þæt ic mote ana, minra eorla gedryht,
ond þes hearda heap Heorot fælsian.
Hæbbe ic eac geahsod þæt se æglæca
for his won-hydum wæpna ne recceð;
ic þæt þonne forhicge, swa me Higelac sie,
min mon-drihten modes bliðe,
þæt ic sweord bere oþðe sidne scyld,
geolo-rand to guþe, ac ic mid grape sceal
fon wið feonde ond ymb feorh sacan,
lað wið laþum; ðær gelyfan sceal
Dryhtnes dome se þe hine deað nimeð.
Wen' ic þæt he wille, gif he wealdan mot,
in þæm guð-sele Geatena leode
etan unforhte, swa he oft dyde
mægen-hreð manna. Na þu minne þearft
hafalan hydan, ac he me habban wile
dreore fahne, gif mec deað nimeð:
byreð blodig wæl, byrgean þenceð,
eteð an-genga unmurnlice,
mearcað mor-hopu— no ðu ymb mines ne þearft
lices feorme leng sorgian.

ambushes stained with the blood of enemies, where I tied
up five, laid waste a family of ogres, and on the waves killed
sea-serpents by night, endured dire straits, avenged aggres-
sion against the Weders—they were asking for trouble—
crushed those fierce ones; and now against Grendel, against
that troublemaker, I shall alone prosecute the case against
that ghoul. Now I want to ask you, sovereign of Bright- 426
Danes, defense of the Scyldings, one request, that you, pro-
tector of fighters, noble friend of nations, not refuse me,
now that I have come thus far, that I myself, the troop of my
men and this company of hardy ones be permitted to purge
Heorot. I have also learned that the troublemaker in his
heedless way disdains weapons; then I, so that my lord
Hygelac may be pleased with me in his heart, scorn that I
should bear a sword or a broad shield, a pale buckler to bat-
tle, but with my grasp I will grapple with the enemy and
compete for survival, foe against foe; there he whom death
takes will have to trust in the Lord's judgment. I expect that 442
he wants, if he can manage, in this war-hall to eat men of the
Geats with impunity, as he has often done the mighty flower
of humanity. You will have no need to hide my head, but he
will have me covered with gore, if death takes me; he will
bear off the bloody corpse, will plan to consume it; the loner
will eat without remorse, stain the solitudes of the moor—
you will need trouble no further about provisions for my

Onsend Higelace,   gif mec hild nime,
beadu-scruda betst   þæt mine breost wereð,
hrægla selest;   þæt is Hrædlan laf,
Welandes geweorc.   Gæð a wyrd swa hio scel."

VII

Hroðgar maþelode,   helm Scyldinga:
"Fore fyhtum þu,   wine min Beowulf,
ond for ar-stafum   usic sohtest.
Gesloh þin fæder   fæhðe mæste;
wearþ he Heaþolafe   to hand-bonan
mid Wilfingum;   ða hine Wedera cyn
for here-brogan   habban ne mihte.
Þanon he gesohte   Suð-Dena folc
ofer yða gewealc,   Ar-Scyldinga;
ða ic furþum weold   folce Deniga
ond on geogoðe heold   ginne rice,
hord-burh hæleþa,   ða wæs Heregar dead,
min yldra mæg   unlifigende,
bearn Healfdenes;   se wæs betera ðonne ic.
Siððan þa fæhðe   feo þingode:
sende ic Wylfingum   ofer wæteres hrycg
ealde madmas;   he me aþas swor.
Sorh is me to secganne   on sefan minum
gumena ængum   hwæt me Grendel hafað
hynðo on Heorote   mid his hete-þancum,
fær-niða gefremed;   is min flet-werod,
wig-heap gewanod;   hie wyrd forsweop
on Grendles gryre.   God eaþe mæg
þone dol-scaðan   dæda getwæfan!
Ful oft gebeotedon   beore druncne
ofer ealo-wæge   oret-mecgas

body. Send to Hygelac, if battle takes me, this best of war-garments that I wear on my chest, the finest of clothing; that is a legacy of Hrethel, the work of Wayland. Things always go as they must."

VII

Hrothgar made a speech, helm of the Scyldings: "For 456
fighting, my friend Beowulf, and out of generosity you have come to see us. Your father caused the greatest vendetta; he came to be the killer of Heatholaf among the Wylfings; then for fear of war the nation of Weders could not keep him. From there he came to see the people of the South-Danes over the tumult of waves, the Honor-Scyldings; I had then just assumed rule of the Danish people, and in my youth I governed a vast realm, the treasure-stronghold of heroes, now that Heorogar was dead, my elder kinsman no longer living, the son of Healfdene; he was better born than I. Afterward I settled that feud with payment: I sent the Wylfings over the water's back old valuables; he swore me oaths. It is an anguish for me to tell any man what humiliations in my heart, violent wrongs Grendel has done with his antagonism; my hall-band, my war-troop is decimated; events swept them into Grendel's terror. God can easily hinder the mad ravager from these deeds! Very often war-challengers

þæt hie in beor-sele   bidan woldon
Grendles guþe   mid gryrum ecga.
Đonne wæs þeos medo-heal   on morgen-tid,
driht-sele dreor-fah   þonne dæg lixte,
eal benc-þelu   blode bestymed,
heall heoru-dreore;   ahte ic holdra þy læs,
deorre duguðe,   þe þa deað fornam.
Site nu to symle   ond onsæl meoto,
sige-hreð secgum,   swa þin sefa hwette."
   Þa wæs Geat-mæcgum   geador ætsomne
on beor-sele   benc gerymed;
þær swið-ferhþe   sittan eodon,
þryðum dealle.   Þegn nytte beheold,
se þe on handa bær   hroden ealo-wæge,
scencte scir wered.   Scop hwilum sang
hador on Heorote.   Þær wæs hæleða dream,
duguð unlytel   Dena ond Wedera.

VIII

Unferð maþelode,   Ecglafes bearn,
þe æt fotum sæt   frean Scyldinga,
onband beadu-rune.   Wæs him Beowulfes sið,
modges mere-faran,   micel æfþunca,
forþon þe he ne uþe   þæt ænig oðer man
æfre mærða þon ma   middan-geardes
gehedde under heofenum   þonne he sylfa:
"Eart þu se Beowulf,   se þe wið Brecan wunne
on sidne sæ,   ymb sund flite,
ðær git for wlence   wada cunnedon
ond for dol-gilpe   on deop wæter
aldrum neþdon?   Ne inc ænig mon,
ne leof ne lað,   belean mihte

flush with drink have vowed over ale-cups that they would await Grendel's warfare in the drink-hall with the ferocity of blades. Then this mead-hall in the morning-time, the court-building, was painted with gore when the day dawned, all the bench-planks spattered with blood, the hall sword-reddened; I had the fewer loyal men, valued veterans, in proportion as death carried them off. Sit down now to the banquet and unmoor your thoughts, your renowned victories for these warriors, as the spirit moves you."

Then there was cleared a bench for the Geatish fellows 491
all together in a group in the drinking-hall; there the resolute ones went to sit, magnificent in their might. A courtier attended to his duty, who bore in hand an embellished ale-vessel, dispensed clear, sweet drink. Now and then the performer sang brightly in Heorot. There was heroes' enjoyment there, no small host of Danes and Weders.

VIII

Unferth made a speech, Ecglaf's offspring, who sat at the 499
feet of the lord of the Scyldings, unbound concealed hostility. The mission of Beowulf, that brave sailor, was to him a severe irritation, since he would not allow that any other man of middle-earth should attend more to glory under the heavens than he himself: "Are you the Beowulf who vied with Breca on the open sea, competed at swimming, where you for pride tested the waters and for foolish boasting ventured your lives in deep water? No man, friend or foe, could

sorhfullne sið, þa git on sund reon.
Þær git eagor-stream earmum þehton,
mæton mere-stræta, mundum brugdon,
glidon ofer garsecg; geofon yþum weol,
wintrys wylmum. Git on wæteres æht
seofon-niht swuncon; he þe æt sunde oferflat,
hæfde mare mægen. Þa hine on morgen-tid
on Heaþo-Ræmes holm up ætbær;
ðonon he gesohte swæsne eþel,
leof his leodum, lond Brondinga,
freoðo-burh fægere, þær he folc ahte,
burh ond beagas. Beot eal wið þe
sunu Beanstanes soðe gelæste.
Ðonne wene ic to þe wyrsan geþingea,
ðeah þu heaðo-ræsa gehwær dohte,
grimre guðe, gif þu Grendles dearst
niht-longne fyrst nean bidan."
Beowulf maþelode, bearn Ecgþeowes:
"Hwæt, þu worn fela, wine min Unferð,
beore druncen ymb Brecan spræce,
sægdest from his siðe. Soð ic talige,
þæt ic mere-strengo maran ahte,
eafeþo on yþum, ðonne ænig oþer man.
Wit þæt gecwædon cniht-wesende
ond gebeotedon —wæron begen þa git
on geogoð-feore— þæt wit on garsecg ut
aldrum neðdon, ond þæt geæfndon swa.
Hæfdon swurd nacod, þa wit on sund reon,
heard on handa; wit unc wið hron-fixas
werian þohton. No he wiht fram me
flod-yþum feor fleotan meahte,

dissuade you two from that dismal undertaking when you
rowed at sea. There you covered the ocean-current with
your arms, measured the sea-street, wove with your hands,
glided over the flood. The ocean heaved with swells, with
the turbulence of winter. Seven nights you labored in the 516
possession of the water; he overmatched you at swimming,
had greater strength. Then in the morning hours the break-
ers brought him up among the Heatho-Reams. From there
he went to his own country, that man loved by his people,
the land of the Brandings, the beautiful fortress of tranquil-
lity, where he had his people, stronghold, and rings. The son
of Beanstan in truth completely fulfilled his vow with you.
Then I expect worse results for you, even if you have acquit-
ted yourself in the rush of battle everywhere, in grim war-
fare, should you dare experience Grendel close up for the
space of a night."

Beowulf made a speech, the offspring of Ecgtheo: "Well, 529
my friend Unferth, drunk with grog you have said quite a lot
about Breca, told about his exploit. I consider it the truth
that I had greater sea-strength, sturdiness on the waves,
than any other person. We two, being boys—we were both
then still in our early youth—declared and vowed that we
would venture our lives out on the ocean, and that we did.
We had bare swords hard in hand when we rowed on the sea;
we thought to defend ourselves against whale-fishes. He was 541

hraþor on holme,   no ic fram him wolde.
Ða wit ætsomne   on sæ wæron
fif-nihta fyrst,   oþ þæt unc flod todraf,
wado weallende,   wedera cealdost,
nipende niht,   ond norþan wind
heaðo-grim ondhwearf;   hreo wæron yþa.
Wæs mere-fixa   mod onhrered;
þær me wið laðum   lic-syrce min
heard hond-locen   helpe gefremede;
beado-hrægl broden   on breostum læg
golde gegyrwed.   Me to grunde teah
fah feond-scaða,   fæste hæfde
grim on grape;   hwæþre me gyfeþe wearð
þæt ic aglæcan   orde geræhte,
hilde-bille;   heaþo-ræs fornam
mihtig mere-deor   þurh mine hand.

VIIII

"Swa mec gelome   lað-geteonan
þreatedon þearle.   Ic him þenode
deoran sweorde,   swa hit gedefe wæs.
Næs hie ðære fylle   gefean hæfdon,
man-fordædlan,   þæt hie me þegon,
symbel ymbsæton   sæ-grunde neah,
ac on mergenne   mecum wunde
be yð-lafe   uppe lægon,
sweordum aswefede,   þæt syðþan na
ymb brontne ford   brim-liðende
lade ne letton.   Leoht eastan com,
beorht beacen Godes,   brimu swaþredon,
þæt ic sæ-næssas   geseon mihte,
windige weallas.   Wyrd oft nereð

not able to float far at all from me on the waves of the flood,
faster in the swells, nor did I care to leave him. Then we
were together on the sea the space of five nights, until the
current drove us apart, the surging water, coldest of storms,
darkening night, and the battle-grim wind turned from the
north; the whitecaps were fierce. The courage of the sea-fish
was stirred up; there my body-shirt, hard and linked by
hand, provided me help against the adversaries; the woven
war-garment chased with gold lay on my chest. A hostile at- 553
tacker dragged me to the bottom, unyielding, had me fast in
its grasp. Yet I was so fortunate as to get to the troublemaker
with a blade, a war-sword; the storm of combat bore off the
mighty sea-beast through my hand.

VIIII

"Thus, ugly villains continually pressed me hard. I served 559
them with a costly sword, as was fitting. By no means did
they have the satisfaction of their fill, those evildoers, that
they made a meal of me, sat around a banquet on the sea
floor, but in the morning, wounded by arms they lay up
among the waves' leavings, put to sleep by swords, so that
never again on the high water-way would they prevent
ocean-goers from passing. Light came from the east, God's 569
bright beacon; the seas subsided, so that I could make out
headlands, windy escarpments. Events often spare a man

unfægne eorl, þonne his ellen deah!
Hwæþere me gesælde þæt ic mid sweorde ofsloh
niceras nigene. No ic on niht gefrægn
under heofones hwealf heardran feohtan,
ne on eg-streamum earmran mannon;
hwæþere ic fara feng feore gedigde,
siþes werig. Đa mec sæ oþbær,
flod æfter faroðe on Finna land,
wadu weallendu. No ic wiht fram þe
swylcra searo-niða secgan hyrde,
billa brogan. Breca næfre git
æt heaðo-lace, ne gehwæþer incer,
swa deorlice dæd gefremede
fagum sweordum —no ic þæs fela gylpe—
þeah ðu þinum broðrum to banan wurde,
heafod-mægum; þæs þu in helle scealt
werhðo dreogan, þeah þin wit duge.
Secge ic þe to soðe, sunu Ecglafes,
þæt næfre Grendel swa fela gryra gefremede,
atol æglæca, ealdre þinum,
hynðo on Heorote, gif þin hige wære,
sefa swa searo-grim swa þu self talast;
ac he hafað onfunden þæt he þa fæhðe ne þearf,
atole ecg-þræce eower leode
swiðe onsittan, Sige-Scyldinga;
nymeð nyd-bade, nænegum arað
leode Deniga, ac he lust wigeð,
swefeð, ondsendeþ, secce ne weneþ
to Gar-Denum. Ac ic him Geata sceal
eafoð ond ellen ungeara nu,
guþe gebeodan. Gæþ eft se þe mot

who is not doomed, when his courage is up to it! Whatever
the case, it happened to me that with my sword I killed nine
sea-monsters. I have never heard of a harder fight at night
under heaven's vault, nor a more pitiable man on the ocean-
currents; nonetheless I escaped with my life from the grasp
of foes, exhausted by the exploit. Then the sea carried me 579
away, the flood along the currents into the land of the Finns,
the swelling waves. I have not heard anything at all by way
of comparable treacherous contests, terror of weapons, said
about you. Breca has never yet at sword-play, nor either of
you, accomplished so daring a deed with chased swords—
I boast little about it—though you turned out to be your
brothers' killer, your closest kinsmen's, for which you will
suffer damnation in hell, clever as you are. I tell you for a 590
fact, son of Ecglaf, that Grendel would never have caused so
much alarm, the terrifying troublemaker, to your ruler, hu-
miliation in Heorot, if your mind, your spirit were as reso-
lute as you yourself regard it; but he has discovered that he
need not fear much the vengeance, the blade-fury of your
kind, the Triumph-Scyldings; he exacts forced tribute,
spares no one of the nation of Danes, but he takes his plea-
sure, puts to sleep and dispatches, expects no struggle from
the Spear-Danes. But I shall tender him the strength and 601
courage of the Geats, combat before long now. He who can,

to medo modig,   siþþan morgen-leoht
ofer ylda bearn   oþres dogores,
sunne swegl-wered   suþan scineð."
    Þa wæs on salum   sinces brytta
gamol-feax ond guð-rof;   geoce gelyfde
brego Beorht-Dena;   gehyrde on Beowulfe
folces hyrde   fæst-rædne geþoht.
    Ðær wæs hæleþa hleahtor,   hlyn swynsode,
word wæron wynsume.   Eode Wealhþeo forð,
cwen Hroðgares   cynna gemyndig,
grette gold-hroden   guman on healle,
ond þa freolic wif   ful gesealde
ærest East-Dena   eþel-wearde,
bæd hine bliðne   æt þære beor-þege,
leodum leofne;   he on lust geþeah
symbel ond sele-ful,   sige-rof kyning.
Ymbeode þa   ides Helminga
duguþe ond geogoþe   dæl æghwylcne,
sinc-fato sealde,   oþ þæt sæl alamp
þæt hio Beowulfe,   beag-hroden cwen
mode geþungen   medo-ful ætbær;
grette Geata leod,   Gode þancode
wisfæst wordum   þæs ðe hire se willa gelamp
þæt heo on ænigne   eorl gelyfde
fyrena frofre.   He þæt ful geþeah,
wæl-reow wiga   æt Wealhþeon,
ond þa gyddode   guþe gefysed.
    Beowulf maþelode,   bearn Ecgþeowes:
"Ic þæt hogode,   þa ic on holm gestah,
sæ-bat gesæt   mid minra secga gedriht,
þæt ic anunga   eowra leoda

will go proud to his mead after the morning light of another day over the descendants of the elders, the sun clothed in radiance, shines from the south."

Then the disperser of rings, gray-haired and vigorous 607
in battle, was content; the sovereign of the Bright-Danes trusted in assistance; the people's caretaker had heard a resolute intent in Beowulf.

There was laughter of heroes, the noise resonated, con- 611
versation was cheery. Wealhtheo made an entrance, Hroth-
gar's queen versed in courtesies, covered in gold, greeted the
men in the hall, and then the noble woman gave a cup first
to the guardian of the homeland of the East-Danes, told him
to be happy at the drinking-rounds, beloved by his men; he
partook of the banquet and the hall-cup with pleasure, a
king renowned for victories. Then the lady of the Helmings 620
moved among every part of the company of soldiers old and new, distributed ornate vessels, until the occasion arose that she, ring-covered queen excellent of character, brought a mead-cup to Beowulf, greeted the man of the Geats and, astute in her words, thanked God that her wish had come to pass that she could trust in any man for relief from her sufferings. Fierce warrior, he took the cup from Wealhtheo and then made a formal statement, primed for combat.

Beowulf made a speech, offspring of Ecgtheo: "I in- 631
tended, when I ventured on the waves, rode in a sea-boat with my company of men, that I would by all means accom-

willan geworhte oþðe on wæl crunge
feond-grapum fæst. Ic gefremman sceal
eorlic ellen, oþðe ende-dæg
on þisse meodu-healle minne gebidan."
Ðam wife þa word wel licodon,
gilp-cwide Geates; eode gold-hroden
freolicu folc-cwen to hire frean sittan.
Þa wæs eft swa ær inne on healle
þryð-word sprecen, ðeod on sælum,
sige-folca sweg, oþ þæt semninga
sunu Healfdenes secean wolde
æfen-ræste; wiste þæm ahlæcan
to þæm heah-sele hilde geþinged,
siððan hie sunnan leoht geseon meahton
oþ ðe nipende niht ofer ealle,
scadu-helma gesceapu scriðan cwoman
wan under wolcnum. Werod eall aras.
Gegrette þa guma oþerne,
Hroðgar Beowulf, ond him hæl abead,
win-ærnes geweald, ond þæt word acwæð:
"Næfre ic ænegum men ær alyfde,
siþðan ic hond ond rond hebban mihte,
ðryþ-ærn Dena buton þe nuða.
Hafa nu ond geheald husa selest,
gemyne mærþo, mægen-ellen cyð,
waca wið wraþum! Ne bið þe wilna gad
gif þu þæt ellen-weorc aldre gedigest."

x

Ða him Hroþgar gewat mid his hæleþa gedryht,
eodur Scyldinga ut of healle;
wolde wig-fruma Wealhþeo secan,

plish the desire of your people or succumb to slaughter fast in the enemy's grasp. I shall achieve a manly feat or meet my final day in this mead-hall."

These words pleased the woman well, the boastful decla- 639
ration of the Geat. The noble queen of the nation went, covered in gold, to sit by her husband.

Then again as before brave words were spoken in the hall, 642
the folk in contentment, the noise of triumphant people, until all at once the son of Healfdene wished to seek his evening's rest; he knew that combat at the high hall had been settled on for the troublemaker from the time that they could see the light of the sun until deepening night, shapes of covering shadows, came creeping dark under the clouds. The company all arose. Then one man addressed the other, Hrothgar Beowulf, and wished him luck, domination of the wine-building, and made this declaration:

"Never before, since I could lift hand and shield, have I 655
entrusted the mighty hall of the Danes to any man except now to you. Have now and keep the best of buildings, hold glory in mind, prove your valorous strength, keep vigil against the angry one! There will be no lack of desirable things for you if you pass through that courageous accomplishment with your life."

X

Then Hrothgar went with his company of heroes, ruler 662
of Scyldings out of the hall; the war-leader wished to visit

cwen to gebeddan. Hæfde kyning-wuldor
Grendle togeanes, swa guman gefrungon,
sele-weard aseted; sundor-nytte beheold
ymb aldor Dena, eoton-weard' abead.
Huru Geata leod georne truwode
modgan mægnes, metodes hyldo.
Đa he him of dyde isern-byrnan,
helm of hafelan, sealde his hyrsted sweord,
irena cyst, ombiht-þegne,
ond gehealdan het hilde-geatwe.
Gespræc þa se goda gylp-worda sum,
Beowulf Geata, ær he on bed stige:
"No ic me an here-wæsmun hnagran talige
guþ-geweorca þonne Grendel hine;
forþan ic hine sweorde swebban nelle,
aldre beneotan, þeah ic eal mæge.
Nat he þara goda þæt he me ongean slea,
rand geheawe, þeah ðe he rof sie
niþ-geweorca; ac wit on niht sculon
secge ofersittan gif he gesecean dear
wig ofer wæpen, ond siþðan witig God
on swa hwæþere hond, halig Dryhten
mærðo deme, swa him gemet þince."
Hylde hine þa heaþo-deor, hleor-bolster onfeng
eorles andwlitan, ond hine ymb monig
snellic sæ-rinc sele-reste gebeah.
Nænig heora þohte þæt he þanon scolde
eft eard-lufan æfre gesecean,
folc oþðe freo-burh þær he afeded wæs;
ac hie hæfdon gefrunen þæt hie ær to fela micles
in þæm win-sele wæl-deað fornam,

Wealhtheo, the queen as his bed-fellow. The king of glory
had, as men learned, appointed a hall-guard against Gren-
del; he paid a special service to the chief of the Danes, of-
fered protection against ogres. Certainly, the man of the
Geats trusted deeply in his prideful strength, the favor of
Providence. Then he stripped off his iron mail-shirt, the 671
helmet from his head, gave his inlaid sword, the best of met-
als, to an attending officer, and directed him to take charge
of that war-equipment.

The good man then pronounced a certain vaunting 675
speech, Beowulf of the Geats, before he climbed into bed:
"I do not account myself less liberal of the fruits of war in
martial deeds than Grendel does himself; therefore I will
not put him to rest with a sword, deprive him of life, though
I am fully capable. He does not know the advantages such
that he could strike against me, cleave a shield, no matter
how skilled he is at violent acts; but in the night we two shall
forgo swords if he dares to look for combat without weap-
ons, and afterward let God in his wisdom, the holy Lord as-
sign glory on whichever hand he sees fit."

Then the battle-brave one bent down, the cheek-cushion 688
met the man's face, and around him many a ready sea-warrior
inclined to his bed in the hall. None of them thought that
he should ever go from there to see his sweet homeland
again, his people or the noble stronghold where he was
reared; but they had learned that carrion death had carried
off far too many of them in that wine-hall, people of the

Denigea leode. Ac him Dryhten forgeaf
wig-speda gewiofu, Wedera leodum,
frofor ond fultum, þæt hie feond heora
ðurh anes cræft ealle ofercomon,
selfes mihtum. Soð is gecyþed
þæt mihtig God manna cynnes
weold wideferhð.
Com on wanre niht
scriðan sceadu-genga. Sceotend swæfon,
þa þæt horn-reced healdan scoldon,
ealle buton anum —þæt wæs yldum cuþ
þæt hie ne moste, þa Metod nolde,
se scyn-scaþa under sceadu bregdan—
ac he wæccende wraþum on andan
bad bolgen-mod beadwa geþinges.

XI

Ða com of more under mist-hleoþum
Grendel gongan, Godes yrre bær;
mynte se man-scaða manna cynnes
sumne besyrwan in sele þam hean.
Wod under wolcnum to þæs þe he win-reced,
gold-sele gumena gearwost wisse
fætum fahne; ne wæs þæt forma sið
þæt he Hroþgares ham gesohte;
næfre he on aldor-dagum ær ne siþðan
heardran hæle, heal-ðegnas fand.
Com þa to recede rinc siðian
dreamum bedæled. Duru sona onarn
fyr-bendum fæst, syþðan he hire folmum æthran;
onbræd þa bealo-hydig, ða he gebolgen wæs,
recedes muþan. Raþe æfter þon

Danes. But the Lord granted them weavings of war-success, men of the Weders, comfort and aid, so that they would all overcome their enemy through the skill of one, the might of the man himself. The truth is plain that mighty God has always ruled the human race.

There came in the gloomy night a shadow-walker creep- 702
ing. The shooters slept who were to guard that horned hall,
all but one—that was plain to all that the phantom marauder
could not drag them under the shadows when Providence
refused—but he, keeping vigil in enmity to the angry one,
awaited enraged the settlement of the conflict.

XI

Then under misty bluffs came Grendel walking from the 710
moor, bearing God's wrath; the villainous raider meant to
entrap a certain human being in the tall building. He came
forward under the clouds to where he well knew the wine-
house was, the golden hall of men, garnished with trim—
that was not the first time he had come looking for Hroth-
gar's home. Never before or after in the days of his life did
he encounter harder luck, hardier hall-thanes. The warrior 720
came roving to the building, cut off from contentment. The
door opened at once, reinforced by forged bands, when he
touched it with his hands; then, intent on harm, now that he
was enraged, he swung open the hall's entryway. Rapidly af-

on fagne flor feond treddode,
eode yrre-mod; him of eagum stod
ligge gelicost leoht unfæger.
Geseah he in recede rinca manige,
swefan sibbe-gedriht samod ætgædere,
mago-rinca heap. Þa his mod ahlog;
mynte þæt he gedælde, ær þon dæg cwome,
atol aglæca anra gehwylces
lif wið lice, þa him alumpen wæs
wist-fylle wen. Ne wæs þæt wyrd þa gen
þæt he ma moste manna cynnes
ðicgean ofer þa niht. Þryð-swyð beheold
mæg Higelaces hu se man-scaða
under fær-gripum gefaran wolde.
Ne þæt se aglæca yldan þohte,
ac he gefeng hraðe forman siðe
slæpendne rinc, slat unwearnum,
bat ban-locan, blod edrum dranc,
syn-snædum swealh; sona hæfde
unlyfigendes eal gefeormod,
fet ond folma. Forð near ætstop,
nam þa mid handa hige-þihtigne
rinc on ræste. He him ræhte ongean,
feond mid folme; he onfeng hraþe
inwit-þancum ond wið earm gesæt.
Sona þæt onfunde fyrena hyrde,
þæt he ne mette middan-geardes,
eorþan sceata on elran men
mund-gripe maran. He on mode wearð
forht on ferhðe; no þy ær fram meahte.
Hyge wæs him hin-fus, wolde on heolster fleon,

ter that the fiend trod the patterned floor, walked in an an-
gry mood. From his eyes emanated an unlovely light very
like a flame. In the building he saw many warriors, a band
of brothers sleeping all together in a group, a company of
young men. Then his heart laughed; he intended before day 730
came, the terrible troublemaker, to part body from soul of
every one of them, now that he had the expectation of his
fill of rations. That was no longer to be the case, that he
would be able to feed on more of the human race beyond
that night. The forceful kinsman of Hygelac observed how
the criminal attacker wished to proceed with his sudden
snatchings. The troublemaker had no mind to delay, but at 739
the first opportunity he quickly grabbed a sleeping soldier
and without hindrance split him, bit into the body, drank
the arterial blood, swallowed huge mouthfuls; in no time
he had devoured the lifeless man, feet, hands, and all. He
stepped up nearer, then seized with his hand the strong-
willed warrior at rest. He reached toward him, the enemy,
with his hand; he quickly seized it with a belligerent aim
and sat up supporting himself on his arm. Immediately that 750
herder of crimes discovered that he had not encountered in
middle-earth, in the corners of the world, a greater hand-
grip in another human. In his heart he grew frightened to
his soul; none the sooner could he get away. He was anxious
in his intent to escape, wanted to flee into the darkness, go

secan deofla gedræg; ne wæs his drohtoð þær
swylce he on ealder-dagum ær gemette.
Gemunde þa se goda, mæg Higelaces,
æfen-spræce, uplang astod
ond him fæste wiðfeng; fingras burston;
eoten wæs utweard, eorl furþur stop.
Mynte se mæra hwær he meahte swa
widre gewindan ond on weg þanon
fleon on fen-hopu; wiste his fingra geweald
on grames grapum. Þæt wæs geocor sið
þæt se hearm-scaþa to Heorute ateah.
Dryht-sele dynede; Denum eallum wearð,
ceaster-buendum, cenra gehwylcum,
eorlum ealu-scerwen. Yrre wæron begen,
reþe ren-weardas. Reced hlynsode.
Þa wæs wundor micel þæt se win-sele
wiðhæfde heaþo-deorum, þæt he on hrusan ne feol,
fæger fold-bold; ac he þæs fæste wæs
innan ond utan iren-bendum
searo-þoncum besmiþod. Þær fram sylle abeag
medu-benc monig, mine gefræge,
golde geregnad, þær þa graman wunnon.
Þæs ne wendon ær witan Scyldinga
þæt hit a mid gemete manna ænig
betlic ond ban-fag tobrecan meahte,
listum tolucan, nymþe liges fæþm
swulge on swaþule. Sweg up astag
niwe geneahhe; Norð-Denum stod
atelic egesa, anra gehwylcum
þara þe of wealle wop gehyrdon,
gryre-leoð galan Godes andsacan,

join the confederacy of devils; his condition there was not
such as he had before experienced in all the days of his life.
Then the good man, Hygelac's kinsman, remembered his
declaration of that evening, stood upright and laid firm hold
of him; fingers broke; the ogre was aiming for the exit, the
man stepped further on. The famous one meant to turn 762
wherever he could get farther away and fly off from there
into the solitude of the fen; he knew the control of his fin-
gers was in the grasp of the fierce one. That was a bitter visit
that the harm-doer paid to Heorot. Noise filled the noble
hall. For all of the Danes, townsmen, for all the bold men, it
was an ale-service. They were both infuriated, the seething
hall-guards. The building resounded. It was a considerable 771
surprise, then, that the wine-palace withstood the battle-
brave ones, that it did not fall to the ground, that lovely
earth-edifice; but it was firmly enough constructed inside
and out, ingeniously with iron bands. There many a mead-
bench started from the floor, according to what I have
heard, trimmed with gold, where the fierce ones grappled.
The elders of the Scyldings had not imagined that any per-
son could by ordinary means break it down, grand and ivo-
ried, cunningly pull it apart, unless the embrace of fire swal-
lowed it in a conflagration. The volume mounted again and 782
again; there arose in the North-Danes an acute horror, in
everyone who heard the wailing through the wall, God's ad-

sigeleasne sang, sar wanigean
helle hæfton. Heold hine fæste
se þe manna wæs mægene strengest
on þæm dæge þysses lifes.

XII

Nolde eorla hleo ænige þinga
þone cwealm-cuman cwicne forlætan,
ne his lif-dagas leoda ængum
nytte tealde. Þær genehost brægd
eorl Beowulfes ealde lafe,
wolde frea-drihtnes feorh ealgian,
mæres þeodnes, ðær hie meahton swa.
Hie þæt ne wiston, þa hie gewin drugon,
heard-hicgende hilde-mecgas,
ond on healfa gehwone heawan þohton,
sawle secan: þone syn-scaðan
ænig ofer eorþan irenna cyst,
guð-billa nan, gretan nolde,
ac he sige-wæpnum forsworen hæfde,
ecga gehwylcre. Scolde his aldor-gedal
on ðæm dæge þysses lifes
earmlic wurðan, ond se ellor-gast
on feonda geweald feor siðian.
Ða þæt onfunde se þe fela æror
modes myrðe manna cynne,
fyrene gefremede —he wæs fag wið God—
þæt him se lic-homa læstan nolde,
ac hine se modega mæg Hygelaces
hæfde be honda; wæs gehwæþer oðrum
lifigende lað. Lic-sar gebad
atol æglæca; him on eaxle wearð

versary singing a grisly lay, a triumphless tune, the captive of hell keening over his pain. He held him firmly who of humans was the strongest of might in that day of this mortal existence.

XII
The safeguard of men did not want by any means for the 791
deadly visitor to depart alive, nor did he consider the days of
his life of use to anyone. There many a comrade of Beowulf's
frequently drew an old heirloom, wanted to defend their
liege's life, the renowned lord's, if they could. They did not 798
know when they took up the struggle, firm-willed war-
makers, and thought to strike on each side, aim for his soul:
no paragon of irons over the earth, of war-swords, would af-
fect the criminal marauder, but he had rendered victory-
weapons useless by a spell, every blade. His parting from life
on that day of this mortal existence was bound to be miser-
able, and the alien demon was to pass far into the power
of fiends. Then he discovered, who had earlier perpetrated 809
many an offense, a blow to the spirits of the human race—
he was a foe of God—that his body would not endure, but
the courageous kinsman of Hygelac had him by the hand;
each alive was intolerable to the other. The awful trouble-
maker felt bodily pain; on his shoulder an immense wound

syn-dolh sweotol,   seonowe onsprungon,
burston ban-locan.   Beowulfe wearð
guð-hreð gyfeþe.   Scolde Grendel þonan
feorh-seoc fleon   under fen-hleoðu,
secean wynleas wic;   wiste þe geornor
þæt his aldres wæs   ende gegongen,
dogera dæg-rim.   Denum eallum wearð
æfter þam wæl-ræse   willa gelumpen:
hæfde þa gefælsod   se þe ær feorran com,
snotor ond swyð-ferhð,   sele Hroðgares,
genered wið niðe.   Niht-weorce gefeh,
ellen-mærþum.   Hæfde East-Denum
Geat-mecga leod   gilp gelæsted,
swylce oncyþðe   ealle gebette,
inwid-sorge   þe hie ær drugon
ond for þrea-nydum   þolian scoldon,
torn unlytel.   Þæt wæs tacen sweotol
syþðan hilde-deor   hond alegde,
earm ond eaxle   —þær wæs eal geador
Grendles grape—   under geapne hrof.

XIII

Ða wæs on morgen   mine gefræge
ymb þa gif-healle   guð-rinc monig;
ferdon folc-togan   feorran ond nean
geond wid-wegas   wundor sceawian,
laþes lastas.   No his lif-gedal
sarlic þuhte   secga ænegum
þara þe tirleases   trode sceawode,
hu he werig-mod   on weg þanon,
niða ofercumen,   on nicera mere
fæge ond geflymed   feorh-lastas bær.

came into evidence, the muscles sprang asunder, the joints
burst. War-glory was allotted to Beowulf. Grendel had to 819
flee sick unto death from there under the fen-bluffs, go in
search of a comfortless lair; he knew all the more certainly
that the end of his life had been reached, the count of his
days. After that deadly confrontation the desire of all Danes
had come to pass: he who had come from afar, wise and in-
domitable, had then cleansed Hrothgar's hall, redeemed it
from the violence. He took satisfaction in that night's work,
in his glorious accomplishments. The man of the sons of 828
the Geats had fulfilled his boast to the East-Danes, likewise
remedied all the suffering, the anguish that they had expe-
rienced and had to endure for a tormented time, no little
trouble. It was a public indication when the battle-brave
one set hand, arm, and shoulder—all of Grendel's grasp was
assembled there—under the vaulted roof.

XIII

Then in the morning, according to what I have heard, 837
there was many a war-maker around the gift-hall; chieftains
traveled from far and near across long distances to see that
marvel, the remains of the antagonist. The loss of his life
did not seem lamentable to any of those who examined the
track of the glory-deprived one, how he, with exhausted
spirits, overwhelmed by the violence, doomed and in flight,
dragged the remains of his existence away from there into a

Đær wæs on blode brim weallende;
atol yða geswing eal gemenged
haton heolfre heoro-dreore weol.
Deað-fæge deog siððan dreama leas
in fen-freoðo feorh alegde,
hæþene sawle; þær him hel onfeng.
Þanon eft gewiton eald-gesiðas
swylce geong manig of gomen-waþe
fram mere modge mearum ridan,
beornas on blancum. Đær wæs Beowulfes
mærðo mæned; monig oft gecwæð
þætte suð ne norð be sæm tweonum
ofer eormen-grund oþer nænig
under swegles begong selra nære
rond-hæbbendra, rices wyrðra.
Ne hie huru wine-drihten wiht ne logon,
glædne Hroðgar, ac þæt wæs god cyning.
Hwilum heaþo-rofe hleapan leton,
on geflit faran fealwe mearas,
ðær him fold-wegas fægere þuhton,
cystum cuðe. Hwilum cyninges þegn,
guma gilp-hlæden, gidda gemyndig,
se ðe eal fela eald-gesegena
worn gemunde, word oþer fand
soðe gebunden; secg eft ongan
sið Beowulfes snyttrum styrian
ond on sped wrecan spel gerade,
wordum wrixlan; welhwylc gecwæð
þæt he fram Sigemundes secgan hyrde
ellen-dædum, uncuþes fela,
Wælsinges gewin, wide siðas,

pool of water-monsters. There the water boiled with blood; 847
the dreary roll of waves all suffused with hot gore heaved
with battle-butchery. Doomed to death, he disappeared af-
ter he laid aside his life, his heathen soul void of content-
ment in his fen-sanctuary; there hell received him.

Then old officers set out in return from there, likewise 853
many a young one, from their diverting jaunt, brave ones
riding mounts from the pool, men on white horses. There
Beowulf's glory was proclaimed; many frequently said that
neither north nor south between the seas over the entire
earth was there any other, better shield-wielder under the
expanse of the firmament, worthier of rule. Neither, cer-
tainly, did they criticize their benevolent lord, gracious
Hrothgar, but that was a good king. At times the battle-firm
ones let their pale steeds gallop, go in a race, where the trails
seemed appealing to them, known for their excellence. At 867
times an attendant of the king, a man laden with glorious
words, with a memory for stories, who remembered all the
many multitudes of tales of old, came up with other words
accurately assembled; the man in turn began sagely to recite
Beowulf's exploit, to deliver successfully a skillful account,
to make variations with words; he related everything that he
had heard said about Sigemund's feats of courage, a great
deal unfamiliar, the struggles of the son of Wæls, wide trav-

þara þe gumena bearn gearwe ne wiston,
fæhðe ond fyrena, buton Fitela mid hine,
þonne he swulces hwæt secgan wolde,
eam his nefan, swa hie a wæron
æt niða gehwam nyd-gesteallan;
hæfdon eal fela eotena cynnes
sweordum gesæged. Sigemunde gesprong
æfter deað-dæge dom unlytel
syþðan wiges heard wyrm acwealde,
hordes hyrde. He under harne stan,
æþelinges bearn, ana geneðde
frecne dæde, ne wæs him Fitela mid;
hwæþre him gesælde ðæt þæt swurd þurhwod
wrætlicne wyrm, þæt hit on wealle ætstod,
dryhtlic iren; draca morðre swealt.
Hæfde aglæca elne gegongen
þæt he beah-hordes brucan moste
selfes dome; sæ-bat gehleod,
bær on bearm scipes beorhte frætwa
Wælses eafera; wyrm hat gemealt.
Se wæs wreccena wide mærost
ofer wer-þeode, wigendra hleo,
ellen-dædum —he þæs ær onðah—
siððan Heremodes hild sweðrode,
eafoð ond ellen. He mid Eotenum wearð
on feonda geweald forð forlacen,
snude forsended. Hine sorh-wylmas
lemedon to lange; he his leodum wearð,
eallum æþellingum to aldor-ceare;
swylce oft bemearn ærran mælum
swið-ferhþes sið snotor ceorl monig,

els, which the offspring of humanity did not readily know,
feuds and suffering, except for Fitela by his side, when he
cared to say anything of such a kind, uncle to his nephew,
as they were always companions in need at every difficulty;
they had laid low with swords an entire multitude of the race
of ogres. For Sigemund after the day of his death there 884
sprang up no little renown after he, hardy in war, killed a ser-
pent, the tender of a hoard. A noble's offspring, he ventured
a dangerous task alone under hoary stone; not even Fitela
was with him; still, he had the good fortune that the sword
passed through the scaly serpent, so that it stood in the wall,
that lordly iron; the dragon perished in that killing. The
troublemaker had accomplished a heroic act such that he
could partake of the hoard ad libitum; he laded a sea-boat;
the heir of Wæls loaded the gleaming equipment in the
bosom of the ship; the serpent, being hot, melted.

He was the exile most widely famed throughout the na- 898
tions, that defender of warriors, for his heroic acts—he had
prospered from that—after Heremod's fighting subsided,
his strength and heroism. Among the Jutes he was betrayed
into the hands of enemies, quickly dispatched. Seething dis-
content hobbled him for too long; he grew to be a mortal
affliction to his nation, all his nobles; likewise, many a clear-
headed citizen in those earlier times often regretted the
stout-hearted one's course, who had hoped in him as a rem-

se þe him bealwa to   bote gelyfde,
þæt þæt ðeodnes bearn   geþeon scolde,
fæder-æþelum onfon,   folc gehealdan,
hord ond hleo-burh,   hæleþa rice,
eþel Scyldinga.   He þær eallum wearð,
mæg Higelaces,   manna cynne,
freondum gefægra;   hine fyren onwod.
  Hwilum flitende   fealwe stræte
mearum mæton.   Ða wæs morgen-leoht
scofen ond scynded.   Eode scealc monig
swið-hicgende   to sele þam hean
searo-wundor seon;   swylce self cyning
of bryd-bure,   beah-horda weard,
tryddode tirfæst   getrume micle,
cystum gecyþed,   ond his cwen mid him
medo-stigge mæt   mægþa hose.

XIIII
Hroðgar maþelode—   he to healle geong,
stod on stapole,   geseah steapne hrof
golde fahne,   ond Grendles hond:
"Ðisse ansyne   alwealdan þanc
lungre gelimpe.   Fela ic laþes gebad,
grynna æt Grendle;   a mæg God wyrcan
wunder æfter wundre,   wuldres hyrde.
Ðæt wæs ungeara   þæt ic ænigra me
weana ne wende   to widan feore
bote gebidan,   þonne blode fah
husa selest   heoro-dreorig stod,
wea wid-scofen   witena gehwylcum,
ðara þe ne wendon   þæt hie wideferhð
leoda land-geweorc   laþum beweredon

edy for their ills, that that child of a chieftain should be successful, assume his father's rank, take charge of the people, the wealth, and the sheltering stronghold, the nation of heroes, the homeland of the Scyldings. He, the kinsman of Hygelac, grew more cherished by the entire human race, by his friends; violence found a home in *him.*

At times contenders measured the pale road on their 916
horses. By then the morning light was advanced and heightened. Many a firm-willed young man went to the high hall to see the curious wonder; likewise the king himself, defender of the ring-hoard, stepped full of glory from the women's apartments with a large following, known for his excellent qualities, and his queen with him measured the mead-path with a retinue of young women.

XIIII

Hrothgar made a speech—he walked to the hall, stood on 925
the steps, looked at the steep roof decorated with gold and Grendel's hand: "For this sight let thanks be raised at once to the all-wielder. I have suffered much grief, misfortunes at the hands of Grendel; God can ever work miracle after miracle, herder of glory. It was not long ago that I did not expect in all my life to survive to see remedy for any of my sufferings, when the best of buildings stood painted with blood, sword-gory, misery reaching wide to each of my councilors, who had not supposed that they would ever in their lives have been defending a stronghold of the nation against

scuccum ond scinnum. Nu scealc hafað
þurh Drihtnes miht dæd gefremede
ðe we ealle ær ne meahton
snyttrum besyrwan. Hwæt, þæt secgan mæg
efne swa hwylc mægþa swa ðone magan cende
æfter gum-cynnum, gyf heo gyt lyfað,
þæt hyre Eald-metod este wære
bearn-gebyrdo. Nu ic, Beowulf, þec,
secg betesta, me for sunu wylle
freogan on ferhþe; heald forð tela
niwe sibbe. Ne bið þe nænigre gad
worolde wilna þe ic geweald hæbbe.
Ful oft ic for læssan lean teohhode,
hord-weorþunge hnahran rince,
sæmran æt sæcce. Þu þe self hafast
dædum gefremed þæt þin dom lyfað
awa to aldre. Alwalda þec
gode forgylde, swa he nu gyt dyde!"
Beowulf maþelode, bearn Ecþeowes:
"We þæt ellen-weorc estum miclum,
feohtan fremedon, frecne geneðdon
eafoð uncuþes. Uþe ic swiþor
þæt ðu hine selfne geseon moste,
feond on frætewum fyl-werigne.
Ic hine hrædlice heardan clammum
on wæl-bedde wriþan þohte,
þæt he for mund-gripe minum scolde
licgean lif-bysig, butan his lic swice;
ic hine ne mihte, þa Metod nolde,
ganges getwæman, no ic him þæs georne ætfealh,
feorh-geniðlan; wæs to fore-mihtig

loathsome demons and ghouls. Now a youngster has through 939
the power of the Lord accomplished a deed that we all in
our cleverness had not been able to contrive. Yes, whatso-
ever woman among the human race gave birth to this son, if
she is still living, can say that Providence was gracious to her
in her child-bearing. Now, Beowulf, noblest hero, I will cher-
ish you in my heart as a son; henceforth observe well this
new kinship. For you there will be no lack of anything desir- 949
able in the world that I have at my command. Quite often I
have appointed a reward for less, a mark of distinction from
the treasury to a lowlier warrior, inferior in a fight. You your-
self have ensured that your glory will live for ever and ever.
May the all-wielder reward you with good, as he has already
done."

Beowulf made a speech, the offspring of Ecgtheo: "We 957
undertook this feat of arms, this fight, with the best of
intentions, dared to chance the strength of the stranger. I
would rather you had been able to see the enemy himself
in his glory, fall-weary. I intended to tie him at once to his
death-bed with a hard embrace, so that he should lie strug-
gling for life in the grasp of my hand, unless his body gave
out; I could not, when Providence did not wish, prevent him
from going, no matter how resolutely I clung to him, that

feond on feþe. Hwæþere he his folme forlet
to lif-wraþe last weardian,
earm ond eaxle. No þær ænige swa þeah
fea-sceaft guma frofre gebohte:
no þy leng leofað lað-geteona
synnum geswenced, ac hyne sar hafað
in nið-gripe nearwe befongen,
balwon bendum; ðær abidan sceal
maga mane fah miclan domes,
hu him scir Metod scrifan wille."
Ða wæs swigra secg, sunu Eclafes,
on gylp-spræce guð-geweorca,
siþðan æþelingas eorles cræfte
ofer heanne hrof hand sceawedon,
feondes fingras; foran æghwylc wæs,
steda nægla gehwylc style gelicost,
hæþenes hand-sporu, hilde-rinces,
egl' unheoru. Æghwylc gecwæð
þæt him heardra nan hrinan wolde
iren ær-god þæt ðæs ahlæcan
blodge beadu-folme onberan wolde.

XV

Ða wæs haten hreþe Heort innanweard
folmum gefrætwod; fela þæra wæs,
wera ond wifa þe þæt win-reced,
gest-sele gyredon. Gold-fag scinon
web æfter wagum, wundor-siona fela
secga gehwylcum þara þe on swylc starað.
Wæs þæt beorhte bold tobrocen swiðe,
eal inneweard iren-bendum fæst,
heorras tohlidene; hrof ana genæs

mortal enemy; the fiend was too overbearing in flight. Nonetheless, to save his life he left his hand guarding his retreat, arm and shoulder. Still, the wretch of a man did not buy himself any relief that way: the hostile attacker is living no longer afflicted by his crimes, but pain has wrapped him tight in its insidious grasp, in deadly restraints; there the young man stained with guilt shall await the great judgment, how radiant Providence will prescribe for him."

The man was then quieter, the son of Ecglaf, in boasting of martial deeds after the nobles observed the hand over the high roof by the man's doing, the enemy's fingers. At the end each was, all the places of the nails, very like steel, the horrible, disagreeable hand-vestiges of the heathen combatant. Everyone said that no iron of hardy ones, good from old, would touch him in such a way that it would weaken the troublemaker's bloody battle-hand.

XV

Then, by command, the inside of Heorot was decorated quickly by hand; there were many men and women who prepared the wine-hall, the guest-house. Gold-patterned textiles gleamed along the walls, a collection of wonderful sights for any who gaze on the like. That bright building was extensively damaged, reinforced on the entire inside with iron stays, the hinges pried open; the roof alone survived ev-

ealles ansund, þe se aglæca
fyren-dædum fag on fleam gewand,
aldres orwena. No þæt yðe byð
to befleonne —fremme se þe wille—
ac gesecan sceal sawl-berendra
nyde genydde, niþða bearna,
grund-buendra gearwe stowe,
þær his lic-homa leger-bedde fæst
swefeþ æfter symle.
Þa wæs sæl ond mæl
þæt to healle gang Healfdenes sunu;
wolde self cyning symbel þicgan.
Ne gefrægen ic þa mægþe maran weorode
ymb hyra sinc-gyfan sel gebæran.
Bugon þa to bence blæd-agande,
fylle gefægon; fægere geþægon
medo-ful manig magas þara
swið-hicgende on sele þam hean,
Hroðgar ond Hroþulf. Heorot innan wæs
freondum afylled; nalles facen-stafas
Þeod-Scyldingas þenden fremedon.
Forgeaf þa Beowulfe brand Healfdenes,
segen gyldenne sigores to leane,
hroden hilde-cumbor, helm ond byrnan.
Mære maðþum-sweord manige gesawon
beforan beorn beran. Beowulf geþah
ful on flette; no he þære feoh-gyfte
for sceotendum scamigan ðorfte.
Ne gefrægn ic freondlicor feower madmas
golde gegyrede gum-manna fela
in ealo-bence oðrum gesellan.

erything intact, since the troublemaker tainted by terrible
doings had turned in flight, despairing of life. That is not 1002
easy to flee—do it who will—but constrained by necessity,
he shall go in search of a place ready for soul-bearers, the
children of mortals, settlers on the earth, where his body,
fixed in a place to lie down, slumbers after the feast.

Then it was due time that Healfdene's son came walking 1008
to the hall; the king himself chose to sample the banquet. I
have not heard that that nation conducted themselves bet-
ter in a larger cohort around their wealth-giver. Men of
repute seated themselves then on the bench, enjoyed their
fill; their resolute kinsmen ceremoniously quaffed many a
mead-cup in the high hall, Hrothgar and Hrothulf. Heorot's
interior was filled with friends; at that time the Nation-
Scyldings did not at all practice treachery. Then he gave 1020
Healfdene's sword to Beowulf, a golden standard of victory
as reward, an ornamented war-banner, helmet and mail-
shirt. Many saw the famous precious sword brought before
the man. Beowulf had a cupful in the hall; he had no need
to be ashamed of that bestowal of valuables in front of the
shooters. I have not heard of many men giving four trea-
sures made with gold to another more lovingly on an

Ymb þæs helmes hrof   heafod-beorge
wirum bewunden   walu utan heold,
þæt him feola laf   frecne ne meahte
scur-heard sceþðan,   þonne scyld-freca
ongean gramum   gangan scolde.
Heht ða eorla hleo   eahta mearas
fæted-hleore   on flet teon,
in under eoderas;   þara anum stod
sadol searwum fah,   since gewurþad;
þæt wæs hilde-setl   heah-cyninges
ðonne sweorda gelac   sunu Healfdenes
efnan wolde—   næfre on ore læg
wid-cuþes wig   ðonne walu feollon.
Ond ða Beowulfe   bega gehwæþres
eodor Ing-wina   onweald geteah,
wicga ond wæpna;   het hine wel brucan.
Swa manlice   mære þeoden,
hord-weard hæleþa,   heaþo-ræsas geald
mearum ond madmum,   swa hy næfre man lyhð,
se þe secgan wile   soð æfter rihte.

XVI

Ða gyt æghwylcum   eorla drihten
þara þe mid Beowulfe   brim-lade teah
on þære medu-bence   maþðum gesealde,
yrfe-lafe,   ond þone ænne heht
golde forgyldan,   þone ðe Grendel ær
mane acwealde—   swa he hyra ma wolde,
nefne him witig God   wyrd forstode
ond ðæs mannes mod.   Metod eallum weold
gumena cynnes,   swa he nu git deð.
Forþan bið andgit   æghwær selest,

ale-bench. Around the top of the helmet outside, a ridge 1030
wrapped in wires offered head-protection, so that the
shower-hard leaving of files could not harm him gravely
when a shield-brave one should go against an adversary.
Then the men's defender directed that eight horses with
cheek-guards be led onto the hall-floor, in under shelter. On
one of them sat a saddle ingeniously patterned, made pre-
cious with jewels; that was the war-seat of the high king
when Healfdene's son would engage in sword-play—his
widely known war-making never failed in the vanguard when
the slain fell. And then the shelter of the friends of Ing be- 1043
stowed each of the two on Beowulf, horses and weapons,
told him to make good use of them. Thus, that famous lord,
guardian of heroes' riches, paid manfully for pitched battles,
with horses and valuables, so that no one will find fault with
them who intends rightly to tell the truth.

XVI

Further yet, the lord of men gave valuables, heirlooms to 1050
each of those on the mead-bench who had made the sea-
journey with Beowulf, and he directed that that one be paid
for with gold whom Grendel had criminally killed—as he
would have done to more, if God in his wisdom and that
man's courage had not prevented that occurrence. Provi-
dence governed all of the human race, as it still does. There-
fore understanding is best in all circumstances, forethought

ferhðes fore-þanc: fela sceal gebidan
leofes ond laþes se þe longe her
on ðyssum win-dagum worolde bruceð.
Þær wæs sang ond sweg samod ætgædere
fore Healfdenes hilde-wisan,
gomen-wudu greted, gid oft wrecen,
ðonne Healgamen, Hroþgares scop
æfter medo-bence mænan scolde
Finnes eaferan; ða hie se fær begeat,
hæleð Healf-Dena, Hnæf Scyldinga
in Fres-wæle feallan scolde.
Ne huru Hildeburh herian þorfte
Eotena treowe; unsynnum wearð
beloren leofum æt þam lind-plegan
bearnum ond broðrum; hie on gebyrd hruron
gare wunde; þæt wæs geomuru ides!
Nalles holinga Hoces dohtor
Meotod-sceaft bemearn syþðan morgen com,
ða heo under swegle geseon meahte
morþor-bealo maga, þær heo ær mæste heold
worolde wynne. Wig ealle fornam
Finnes þegnas nemne feaum anum,
þæt he ne mehte on þæm meðel-stede
wig Hengeste wiht gefeohtan,
ne þa wea-lafe wige forþringan,
þeodnes ðegne; ac hig him geþingo budon,
þæt hie him oðer flet eal gerymdon,
healle ond heah-setl, þæt hie healfre geweald
wið Eotena bearn agan moston,
ond æt feoh-gyftum Folcwaldan sunu
dogra gehwylce Dene weorþode,

of heart: anyone who enjoys this world for long in these days of struggle has to experience much that is to be liked and disliked.

There was singing joined with music in the presence of 1063
Healfdene's battle-leader, entertainment-wood touched, a narrative often related, when Healgamen, Hrothgar's singer, was to tell from the mead-bench of Finn's son; when the calamity overcame them, heroes of the Half-Danes, Hnæf of the Scyldings was to fall in the Frisian slaughter.

Certainly, Hildeburh had no need to praise the good faith 1071
of the Jutes; at the shield-sport she came to be bereft of her
guiltless loved ones, sons and brothers; they succumbed to
destiny, pierced by a spear; that was a rueful lady! Not at
all without reason did Hoc's daughter regret the dictates of
Providence after morning arrived, when under the eye of
heaven she could see the extermination of kinsmen, where
she had formerly counted on her greatest happiness in the
world. Battle had borne off all Finn's men-at-court but an 1080
isolated few, so that he could not in the place of assembly at
all fight out a war against Hengest, that lord's thane, nor dis-
lodge the bitter survivors by warfare; but they offered them
terms, that they would clear for them the entire half of a
hall, edifice and high-seat, so that they would be allowed to
maintain control of one side against the descendants of the
Jutes, and at the distribution of valuables the son of Folc-
walda would daily honor the Danes with wealthy gifts, ac-

Hengestes heap hringum wenede
efne swa swiðe sinc-gestreonum
fættan goldes swa he Fresena cyn
on beor-sele byldan wolde.
Đa hie getruwedon on twa healfa
fæste frioðu-wære. Fin Hengeste
elne unflitme aðum benemde
þæt he þa wea-lafe weotena dome
arum heolde, þæt ðær ænig mon
wordum ne worcum wære ne bræce,
ne þurh inwit-searo æfre gemænden,
ðeah hie hira beag-gyfan banan folgedon
ðeodenlease, þa him swa geþearfod wæs;
gyf þonne Frysna hwylc frecnen spræce
ðæs morþor-hetes myndgiend wære,
þonne hit sweordes ecg syððan scede.
Ad wæs geæfned ond icge gold
ahæfen of horde; Here-Scyldinga
betst beado-rinca wæs on bæl gearu.
Æt þæm ade wæs eþ-gesyne
swat-fah syrce, swyn eal gylden,
eofer iren-heard, æþeling manig
wundum awyrded; sume on wæle crungon.
Het ða Hildeburh æt Hnæfes ade
hire selfre sunu sweoloðe befæstan,
ban-fatu bærnan, ond on bæl don
eame on eaxle. Ides gnornode,
geomrode giddum. Guð-rec astah,
wand to wolcnum; wæl-fyra mæst
hlynode for hlawe. Hafelan multon,
ben-geato burston ðonne blod ætspranc,

custom Hengest's band to rings just as much as he intended
to encourage the people of the Frisians in the drink-hall with
treasured heirlooms of plated gold. Then they concluded on 1095
both sides a firm peace treaty. Finn confirmed to Hengest
by oaths magnanimously and without quibbling that on
the advice of councilors he would govern the survivors of
the calamity honorably, that no one there by word or deed
should violate the truce, nor should they ever make mention
through cunning malice that they, lordless, followed the
killer of their ring-giver, now that the necessity was imposed
on them; if, then, any of the Frisians with provoking words
should continue to call to mind deadly animosity over the
killing, then the point of a sword should settle it after that.
A pyre was prepared and resplendent gold selected from the 1107
treasury; the best of warriors of the Army-Scyldings was
ready on the bier. At the pyre there was in evidence a mail-
shirt painted with battle-sweat, a swine made completely of
gold, an iron-hard boar, many a noble undone by wounds;
certain ones succumbed to slaughter. Then Hildeburh di-
rected that her own son be committed to the blaze at Hnæf's
pyre, the bone-vessels be burned, placed on the funeral pile
at the shoulder of the uncle. The lady lamented, mourned 1117
with dirges. War-smoke went up, spiraled to the sky; the
largest of slaughter-fires crackled in front of the burial
mound. Heads melted, wound-openings broke asunder
when blood burst out, hostile bites in the body. The flame,

lað-bite lices;   lig ealle forswealg,
gæsta gifrost,   þara ðe þær guð fornam
bega folces.   Wæs hira blæd scacen.

XVII

Gewiton him ða wigend   wica neosian
freondum befeallen,   Frys-land geseon,
hamas ond hea-burh.   Hengest ða gyt
wæl-fagne winter   wunode mid Finne;
he unhlitme   eard gemunde,
þeah þe ne meahte   on mere drifan
hringed-stefnan   —holm storme weol,
won wið winde,   winter yþe beleac
is-gebinde—   oþ ðæt oþer com
gear in geardas,   swa nu gyt deð,
þa ðe syngales   sele bewitiað,
wuldor-torhtan weder.   Ða wæs winter scacen,
fæger foldan bearm.   Fundode wrecca,
gist of geardum;   he to gyrn-wræce
swiðor þohte   þonne to sæ-lade,
gif he torn-gemot   þurhteon mihte,
þæt he Eotena bearn   inne gemunde—
swa he ne forwyrnde   worold-rædenne—
þonne him Hunlafing   hilde-leoman,
billa selest   on bearm dyde,
þæs wæron mid Eotenum   ecge cuðe.
Swylce ferhð-frecan   Fin eft begeat
sweord-bealo sliðen   æt his selfes ham,
siþðan grimne gripe   Guðlaf ond Oslaf
æfter sæ-siðe   sorge mændon,
ætwiton weana dæl;   ne meahte wæfre mod
forhabban in hreþre.   Ða wæs heal roden

most ravenous of spirits, swallowed all of those of both nations whom war had carried off there. Their glory was departed.

XVII

The fighters deprived of friends then set out to find their 1125
homes, to visit Friesland, residences and tall fortress.
Hengest still remained with Finn a slaughter-stained winter;
he fondly remembered his homeland, though he could not
drive a ring-prow on the sea—the deep surged with storms,
contended with the wind, winter locked the waves in icy
bonds—until another year arrived among the households, as
now still happens, those which continually observe the time,
gloriously bright weathers. Then winter had fled, the bosom 1136
of the earth was lovely. The exile was anxious to go, the guest
out of the homesteads; he thought rather about revenge for
injury than about seafaring, whether he could bring about a
hostile encounter, so that he might inwardly call to mind the
children of the Jutes—since he had not refused leadership—
when Hunlafing should place in his lap a battle-light, the
best of blades, whose edges were familiar to the Jutes. Like- 1146
wise, in turn, dire sword-destruction overtook bold-spirited
Finn at his own home, after Guthlaf and Oslaf spoke of the
tenacious grasp of grief after the sea-voyage, laid blame for
their share of troubles; a restless heart could not forbear in
the breast. Then the building was reddened with the lives of

feonda feorum, swilce Fin slægen,
cyning on corþre, ond seo cwen numen.
Sceotend Scyldinga to scypon feredon
eal in-gesteald eorð-cyninges,
swylce hie æt Finnes ham findan meahton
sigla searo-gimma. Hie on sæ-lade
drihtlice wif to Denum feredon,
læddon to leodum.
Leoð wæs asungen,
gleo-mannes gyd. Gamen eft astah,
beorhtode benc-sweg; byrelas sealdon
win of wunder-fatum. Þa cwom Wealhþeo forð
gan under gyldnum beage þær þa godan twegen
sæton suhterge-fæderan; þa gyt wæs hiera sib ætgædere,
æghwylc oðrum trywe. Swylce þær Unferþ þyle
æt fotum sæt frean Scyldinga; gehwylc hiora his ferhþe treowde,
þæt he hæfde mod micel, þeah þe he his magum nære
arfæst æt ecga gelacum. Spræc ða ides Scyldinga:
"Onfoh þissum fulle, freo-drihten min,
sinces brytta. Þu on sælum wes,
gold-wine gumena, ond to Geatum spræc
mildum wordum, swa sceal man don.
Beo wið Geatas glæd, geofena gemyndig,
nean ond feorran þa þu nu hafast.
Me man sægde þæt þu ðe for sunu wolde
here-rinc habban. Heorot is gefælsod,
beah-sele beorhta; bruc þenden þu mote
manigra medo, ond þinum magum læf
folc ond rice þonne ðu forð scyle,
Metod-Sceaft seon. Ic minne can

enemies, likewise Finn slain, the king among his corps, and the queen taken. The shooters of the Scyldings ferried to ships all the property of that earth-king, whatever brooches and jewels they could find at Finn's home. They took the noble woman on a sea-passage to the Danes, brought her to her people.

The lay was sung through, the entertainer's account. 1159
Amusement arose again, bench-noise brightened; serving-boys distributed wine from wonderful vessels. Then Wealhtheo came forward walking under a golden collar where the two good men sat, nephew and paternal uncle; they were still joined in friendship, each true to the other. Likewise the spokesman Unferth sat at the feet of the lord of the Scyldings; each of them trusted his soul, that he had great courage, though he had not been honorable to his kin at the sport of swords. Then the lady of the Scyldings spoke:

"Accept this cup, my noble lord, disperser of jewels. Be in 1169
good spirits, gold-friend of men, and speak to the Geats with benevolent words, as ought to be done. Be well-disposed toward the Geats, attentive about the gifts from near and far that you now have. I have been informed that you wished to take the warrior as your son. Heorot is purged, the bright ring-hall; make use, while you are permitted, of your many blessings, and leave to your family the nation and the rule when you shall go forth to witness the decree of
Providence. I know my gracious Hrothulf, that he will treat 1180

glædne Hroþulf,   þæt he þa geogoðe wile
arum healdan   gyf þu ær þonne he,
wine Scildinga,   worold oflætest;
wene ic þæt he mid gode   gyldan wille
uncran eaferan   gif he þæt eal gemon,
hwæt wit to willan   ond to worð-myndum
umbor-wesendum ær   arna gefremedon."
  Hwearf þa bi bence,   þær hyre byre wæron,
Hreðric ond Hroðmund,   ond hæleþa bearn,
giogoð ætgædere;   þær se goda sæt,
Beowulf Geata   be þæm gebroðrum twæm.

XVIII

Him wæs ful boren,   ond freond-laþu
wordum bewægned,   ond wunden gold
estum geeawed,   earm-reade twa,
hrægl ond hringas,   heals-beaga mæst
þara þe ic on foldan   gefrægen hæbbe.
Nænigne ic under swegle   selran hyrde
hord-maððum hæleþa   syþðan Hama ætwæg
to þære byrhtan byrig   Brosinga mene,
sigle ond sinc-fæt—   searo-niðas fleah
Eormenrices,   geceas ecne ræd.
Þone hring hæfde   Higelac Geata,
nefa Swertinges   nyhstan siðe,
siðþan he under segne   sinc ealgode,
wæl-reaf werede;   hyne wyrd fornam
syþðan he for wlenco   wean ahsode,
fæhðe to Frysum.   He þa frætwe wæg,
eorclan-stanas   ofer yða ful,
rice þeoden;   he under rande gecranc.
Gehwearf þa in Francna fæþm   feorh cyninges,

the young warriors honorably if you, friend of Scyldings, depart the world before he; I expect he will repay our sons with good if he remembers everything, what favors we did to his contentment and to his dignity before, when he was a child."

She turned then along the bench, where her boys were, 1188
Hrethric and Hrothmund, and the children of heroes, the
young men together; there the good one sat, Beowulf of the
Geats, beside the two brothers.

XVIII

A cup was brought to him and friendship offered ex- 1192
pressly, and wrought gold presented with good will, two
armlets, a garment and rings, the largest collar on earth that
I have knowledge of. I have never heard of a finer hoard-
treasure of heroes under the heavens since Hama carried
off to his radiant stronghold the necklace of the Brosings,
jewels and precious settings—he was fleeing the treacher-
ies of Eormenric, chose a permanent course. Hygelac of the
Geats, Swerting's nephew, had that ring for the last time
when he defended the treasure under a banner, guarded the
spoils of battle; the course of events carried him off after he
for pride went looking for trouble, a feud with Frisians. He 1207
bore those trappings, gemstones over the cup of waves, that
powerful lord; he succumbed under his shield. There passed
then into the embrace of the Franks the life of the king, his

breost-gewædu, ond se beah somod.
Wyrsan wig-frecan wæl reafeden
æfter guð-sceare; Geata leode
hrea-wic heoldon. Heal swege onfeng.
Wealhðeo maþelode; heo fore þæm werede spræc:
"Bruc ðisses beages, Beowulf leofa,
hyse, mid hæle, ond þisses hrægles neot,
þeod-gestreona, ond geþeoh tela,
cen þec mid cræfte, ond þyssum cnyhtum wes
lara liðe. Ic þe þæs lean geman.
Hafast þu gefered þæt ðe feor ond neah
ealne wide-ferhþ weras ehtigað,
efne swa side swa sæ bebugeð,
wind-geard, weallas. Wes þenden þu lifige,
æþeling, eadig. Ic þe an tela
sinc-gestreona. Beo þu suna minum
dædum gedefe, dream-healdende.
Her is æghwylc eorl oþrum getrywe,
modes milde, man-drihtne hold;
þegnas syndon geþwære, þeod eal gearo;
druncne dryht-guman doð swa ic bidde."
Eode þa to setle. Þær wæs symbla cyst,
druncon win weras. Wyrd ne cuþon,
geo-sceaft grimme, swa hit agangen wearð
eorla manegum, syþðan æfen cwom,
ond him Hroþgar gewat to hofe sinum,
rice to ræste. Reced weardode
unrim eorla, swa hie oft ær dydon.
Benc-þelu beredon; hit geondbræded wearð
beddum ond bolstrum. Beor-scealca sum
fus ond fæge flet-ræste gebeag.

breast-garments, and the ring together. Lowlier war-makers looted the corpses after the carnage; the men of the Geats occupied a camp of cadavers. The hall took up the sound.

Wealhtheo made an address; she spoke before the host: 1215
"Enjoy this ring, dear Beowulf, young man, in well-being, and make use of this garment, this people's treasures, and get on well, show that you have skill, and instruct these boys kindly. For that I shall bear in mind a repayment for you. You have accomplished it that far and wide, for all eternity men will esteem you, even as far as the sea, home of the winds, encompasses headlands. Be, as long as you live, prince, blessed. I shall liberally confer on you precious legacies. Be just in your actions toward my sons, you who are key to our contentment. Here every man is true to the other, kindly of heart, loyal to his lord; the thanes are in harmony, the people completely ready; the reveling men of the corps do as I ask."

She went then to her seat. It was the choicest of banquets 1232
there; the men drank wine. They did not know the course of events, relentless destiny, such as had come to pass for many men, after evening came and Hrothgar departed to his chambers, the powerful one to his rest. Countless men guarded the hall, as they had often done. They cleared the floor of benches; it was overspread with beds and pillows. A certain one of the drinking lads, ready and doomed, bent

Setton him to heafdon   hilde-randas,
bord-wudu beorhtan;   þær on bence wæs
ofer æþelinge   yþ-gesene
heaþo-steapa helm,   hringed byrne,
þrec-wudu þrymlic.   Wæs þeaw hyra
þæt hie oft wæron   anwig-gearwe,
ge æt ham ge on herge,   ge gehwæþer þara
efne swylce mæla   swylce hira man-dryhtne
þearf gesælde;   wæs seo þeod tilu.

XVIIII

Sigon þa to slæpe.   Sum sare angeald
æfen-ræste,   swa him ful oft gelamp
siþðan gold-sele   Grendel warode,
unriht æfnde,   oþ þæt ende becwom,
swylt æfter synnum.   Þæt gesyne wearþ,
wid-cuþ werum,   þætte wrecend þa gyt
lifde æfter laþum,   lange þrage,
æfter guð-ceare;   Grendles modor,
ides aglæc-wif   yrmþe gemunde,
se þe wæter-egesan   wunian scolde,
cealde streamas,   siþðan Cain wearð
to ecg-banan   angan breþer,
fæderen-mæge;   he þa fag gewat,
morþre gemearcod   man-dream fleon,
westen warode.   Þanon woc fela
geo-sceaft-gasta;   wæs þæra Grendel sum,
heoro-wearh hetelic,   se æt Heorote fand
wæccendne wer   wiges bidan.
Þær him aglæca   ætgræpe wearð;
hwæþre he gemunde   mægenes strenge,
gimfæste gife   ðe him God sealde,

to his floor-bed. They set war-spears at their heads, bright 1242
wooden boards; there on the bench over a noble it was easy
to find a battle-tall helmet, a ringed mail-shirt, a mighty
force-timber. It was their practice that they were often pre-
pared against attack, both at home and on campaign, and in
either case at just such a time as the need arose for their
mortal lord; that nation was excellent.

XVIIII

They sank into sleep then. One paid dearly for his eve- 1251
ning's rest, as had happened very often to them after Gren-
del had occupied the gold-hall, perpetrated injustice, until
the end came, extinction after his offenses. It became ap-
parent, widely known to men, that an avenger was still living
after the detested one, for a long time after the war-distress;
Grendel's mother, lady, female troublemaker, kept in mind
her misery, who was accustomed to inhabiting dreadful wa-
ters, cold currents, after Cain turned out to be the murderer
of his only brother, his father's son. He departed outlawed,
then, marked by murder, fleeing human society, occupied
the wastes. From that arose many fated spirits; one of them 1265
was Grendel, hateful war-outlaw, who found at Heorot a
waking man waiting for combat. There the troublemaker
laid hold of him; nonetheless, he kept in mind the force of
his strength, the ample gift that God had granted him, and

ond him to anwaldan are gelyfde,
frofre ond fultum; ðy he þone feond ofercwom,
gehnægde helle gast. Þa he hean gewat,
dreame bedæled deaþ-wic seon,
man-cynnes feond, ond his modor þa gyt
gifre ond galg-mod gegan wolde
sorhfulne sið, sunu deoð wrecan.
Com þa to Heorote, ðær Hring-Dene
geond þæt sæld swæfun. Þa ðær sona wearð
edhwyrft eorlum, siþðan inne fealh
Grendles modor. Wæs se gryre læssa
efne swa micle swa bið mægþa cræft,
wig-gryre wifes be wæpned-men,
þonne heoru bunden, hamere geþruen,
sweord swate fah swin ofer helme
ecgum dyhttig andweard scireð.
Þa wæs on healle heard-ecg togen
sweord ofer setlum, sid-rand manig
hafen handa fæst; helm ne gemunde,
byrnan side, þa hine se broga angeat.
Heo wæs on ofste, wolde ut þanon,
feore beorgan, þa heo onfunden wæs;
hraðe heo æþelinga anne hæfde
fæste befangen, þa heo to fenne gang.
Se wæs Hroþgare hæleþa leofost
on gesiðes had be sæm tweonum,
rice rand-wiga, þone ðe heo on ræste abreat,
blædfæstne beorn. Næs Beowulf ðær,
ac wæs oþer in ær geteohhod
æfter maþðum-gife mærum Geate.
Hream wearð on Heorote; heo under heolfre genam

trusted in the ruler's favor for him, his support and aid;
thereby he overcame the enemy, subdued the creature of
hell. Then he set out humbled, bereft of comfort, looking
for his place of death, humankind's enemy, and his mother
still, ravenous and gallows-minded, intended to mount a
grievous undertaking, to avenge her son's death.

She came then to Heorot, where the Ring-Danes slept 1279
throughout the building. Immediately, then, there was a re-
versal of fortune for the men there, after Grendel's mother
penetrated indoors. The terror was less by just so much as
the strength of females, the battle-intimidation of women,
is in comparison to males, when a bound weapon shaped by
hammers, a sword painted with battle-sweat, keen of edge,
cuts against a boar on top of a helmet. Then in the hall a
hard-edged sword was drawn over the seats, many a broad
shield raised firmly in hand; he did not consider a helmet, a
broad mail-shirt, when the horror seized him. She was in 1292
haste, wanted to get out of there, preserve her life, now that
she had been discovered; quickly she had one of the nobles
firmly in her grasp, when she went to the fen. To Hrothgar
he was the most valued hero in the status of a king's man
between the seas, a powerful spear-warrior, whom she oblit-
erated in his bed, a man of confirmed reputation. Beowulf
was not present, but other accommodations had been ap-
pointed after the bestowal of treasures on the renowned
Geat. A tumult arose in Heorot; she took the familiar hand

cuþe folme; cearu wæs geniwod,
geworden in wicun. Ne wæs þæt gewrixle til,
þæt hie on ba healfa bicgan scoldon
freonda feorum.
Þa wæs frod cyning,
har hilde-rinc on hreon mode
syðþan he aldor-þegn unlyfigendne,
þone deorestan deadne wisse.
Hraþe wæs to bure Beowulf fetod,
sigor-eadig secg. Samod ær-dæge
eode eorla sum, æþele cempa
self mid gesiðum þær se snotera bad
hwæþer him alwalda æfre wille
æfter wea-spelle wyrpe gefremman.
Gang ða æfter flore fyrd-wyrðe man
mid his hand-scale —heal-wudu dynede—
þæt he þone wisan wordum nægde
frean Ing-wina, frægn gif him wære
æfter neod-laðum niht getæse.

XX

Hroðgar maþelode, helm Scyldinga:
"Ne frin þu æfter sælum! Sorh is geniwod
Denigea leodum: dead is Æschere,
Yrmenlafes yldra broþor,
min run-wita ond min ræd-bora,
eaxl-gestealla ðonne we on orlege
hafelan weredon, þonne hniton feþan,
eoferas cnysedan. Swylc scolde eorl wesan,
æþeling ær-god, swylc Æschere wæs.
Wearð him on Heorote to hand-banan
wæl-gæst wæfre; ic ne wat hwæder

covered in blood; anguish was renewed, risen up among the manors. That was not a good exchange, that they should pay for the lives of loved ones on both sides.

Then the wise old king, the hoary war-maker, was in a 1306
rueful mood, after he knew that his lordly thane was lifeless, his dearest dead. Beowulf was quickly summoned to the king's bedchamber, that man blessed by victories. Before daybreak a certain man went, the noble champion himself with his companions, to where the sage awaited whether the all-wielder would ever effect a change for him after that period of affliction. The man distinguished in war then walked across the floor with his group of comrades—the hall-wood thundered—so that he addressed words to the wise lord of the friends of Ing, asked whether he had found the night as agreeable as he might desire.

XX

Hrothgar made a speech, helm of the Scyldings: "Do not 1321
ask about happiness! Grief is renewed for the Danish people: Æschere is dead, Yrmenlaf's elder brother, my privy councilor and my aide-de-camp, an intimate when we defended heads in combat, when infantry clashed, dashed against boars. Such should a man be, a noble tried and true, as Æschere was. A restless, slaughtering spirit was his killer in Heorot; I do not know where the monster exulting in car-

atol æse wlanc   eft-siðas teah,
fylle gefrecnod.   Heo þa fæhðe wræc
þe þu gystran niht   Grendel cwealdest
þurh hæstne had   heardum clammum,
forþan he to lange   leode mine
wanode ond wyrde.   He æt wige gecrang
ealdres scyldig,   ond nu oþer cwom
mihtig man-scaða,   wolde hyre mæg wrecan,
ge feor hafað   fæhðe gestæled—
þæs þe þincean mæg   þegne monegum,
se þe æfter sinc-gyfan   on sefan greoteþ—
hreþer-bealo hearde;   nu seo hand ligeð,
se þe eow welhwylcra   wilna dohte.
"Ic þæt lond-buend,   leode mine,
sele-rædende   secgan hyrde
þæt hie gesawon   swylce twegen
micle mearc-stapan   moras healdan,
ellor-gæstas.   Ðæra oðer wæs,
þæs þe hie gewislicost   gewitan meahton,
idese onlicnæs;   oðer earm-sceapen
on weres wæstmum   wræc-lastas træd,
næfne he wæs mara   þonne ænig man oðer;
þone on gear-dagum   Grendel nemdon
fold-buende;   no hie fæder cunnon,
hwæþer him ænig wæs   ær acenned
dyrnra gasta.   Hie dygel lond
warigeað, wulf-hleoþu,   windige næssas,
frecne fen-gelad,   ðær fyrgen-stream
under næssa genipu   niþer gewiteð,
flod under foldan.   Nis þæt feor heonon
mil-gemearces   þæt se mere standeð;

rion went on her return, emboldened by that feast. She took
vengeance in the feud in which you the other night killed
Grendel in a violent manner in your hard clutches, since
he had for too long decimated and destroyed my people.
He succumbed in combat, answerable with his life, and now 1337
another powerful criminal attacker has come, wanted to
avenge her kin, and to be sure, has gone far toward avenging
the offense—as it must seem to many a thane who weeps in
his soul for his treasure-giver—the hard heart-harm; now
the hand lies still that was generous to you of every desirable
thing.

"I have heard countrymen say, my people, hall-councilors, 1345
that they have seen two similar large heath-roamers ruling
the moors, alien spirits. One of them was, as plainly as they
could tell, the likeness of a lady; the other misshapen thing
trod paths of exile in the form of a man, except that he was
larger than any other human, whom mortals in days of old
named Grendel; they knew of no father, whether any mys-
terious creatures had been born before him. They inhabit 1357
hidden country, wolf-hills, windy crags, a dangerous passage
through fen, where a cascading river passes down under
the gloom of cliffs, a watercourse under the earth. It is not
far in miles from here that the pool stands; over it hang

ofer þæm hongiað hrinde bearwas,
wudu wyrtum fæst wæter oferhelmað.
Þær mæg nihta gehwæm nið-wundor seon,
fyr on flode. No þæs frod leofað
gumena bearna þæt þone grund wite.
Ðeah þe hæð-stapa hundum geswenced,
heorot hornum trum holt-wudu sece,
feorran geflymed, ær he feorh seleð,
aldor on ofre, ær he in wille,
hafelan beorgan; nis þæt heoru stow.
Þonon yð-geblond up astigeð
won to wolcnum þonne wind styreþ
lað gewidru, oð þæt lyft ðrysmaþ,
roderas reotað. Nu is se ræd gelang
eft æt þe anum. Eard git ne const,
frecne stowe, ðær þu findan miht
sinnigne secg; sec gif þu dyrre!
Ic þe þa fæhðe feo leanige,
eald-gestreonum, swa ic ær dyde,
wundnan golde, gyf þu on weg cymest."

XXI

Beowulf maþelode, bearn Ecgþeowes:
"Ne sorga, snotor guma. Selre bið æghwæm
þæt he his freond wrece þonne he fela murne.
Ure æghwylc sceal ende gebidan
worolde lifes; wyrce se þe mote
domes ær deaþe; þæt bið driht-guman
unlifgendum æfter selest.
Aris, rices weard, uton hraþe feran,
Grendles magan gang sceawigan.
Ic hit þe gehate, no he on helm losaþ,

frost-covered groves, firmly rooted woods overshadow the
water. There every night a dire portent can be seen, fire on
the flood. There lives no offspring of men so well informed 1366
that he knows the bottom. Even if a heath-roamer beset by
hounds, a hart firm of antlers, makes for the forest, driven
far in flight, it will sooner give up the ghost, its life on the
bank, than enter and save its head; that is not a pleasant
place. There the tossing waves mount up dark to the clouds
when the wind stirs up ugly storms, until they choke the air
and the heavens weep. Now the course of action is again de- 1376
pendent on you alone. You are not yet acquainted with the
region, that dangerous place where you can find the one who
is the offender; go look if you dare! I will reward you for the
feud with valuables, heirlooms, as I have already done with
wrought gold, if you get away."

XXI

Beowulf made a speech, Ecgtheo's offspring: "Do not 1383
grieve, wise warrior. It is better for each that he avenge his
friend than that he lament much. Each of us shall face the
end of his life in this world; let him achieve glory who is per-
mitted before his death; for a warrior no longer living that
will be best afterward. Stand up, guardian of the realm, let
us go at once to scout out the route of Grendel's kinswoman.
I swear to you, she will not escape under cover, neither in

ne on foldan fæþm   ne on fyrgen-holt
ne on gyfenes grund,   ga þær he wille.
Ðys dogor þu   geþyld hafa
weana gehwylces,   swa ic þe wene to."
Ahleop ða se gomela,   Gode þancode,
mihtigan Drihtne,   þæs se man gespræc.
Þa wæs Hroðgare   hors gebæted,
wicg wunden-feax.   Wisa fengel
geatolic gende;   gum-feþa stop
lind-hæbbendra.   Lastas wæron
æfter wald-swaþum   wide gesyne,
gang ofer grundas,   þær gegnum for
ofer myrcan mor,   mago-þegna bær
þone selestan   sawolleasne
þara þe mid Hroðgare   ham ealgode.
Ofereode þa   æþelinga bearn
steap stan-hliðo,   stige nearwe,
enge an-paðas,   uncuð gelad,
neowle næssas,   nicor-husa fela;
he feara sum   beforan gengde
wisra monna   wong sceawian,
oþ þæt he færinga   fyrgen-beamas
ofer harne stan   hleonian funde,
wynleasne wudu;   wæter under stod
dreorig ond gedrefed.   Denum eallum wæs,
winum Scyldinga,   weorce on mode
to geþolianne,   ðegne monegum,
oncyð eorla gehwæm,   syðþan Æscheres
on þam holm-clife   hafelan metton.
Flod blode weol   —folc to sægon—
hatan heolfre.   Horn stundum song

the bosom of the earth nor in mountain forests nor on the ocean floor, go where she will. Have patience this day with all suffering, just as I should expect of you."

Then the old man leapt up, thanked God, the mighty 1397
Lord, for what the man had said.

A horse was then bridled for Hrothgar, a steed with a 1399
wavy mane. The wise sovereign went richly equipped; a band
of shield-bearers proceeded on foot. Footprints were in
wide evidence along the forest paths, a route over the ground
where she had gone forward over the gloomy moor, had
borne lifeless the best young thane who had defended their
home with Hrothgar. The children of nobles moved then 1408
over steep stone-slopes, narrow defiles, straitened single-file
paths, a strange passage, precipitous bluffs, many lairs of
sea-monsters. He went ahead with a small group of knowl-
edgeable men to scout the area, until all at once he encoun-
tered mountain-trees leaning over hoary stone, a joyless
wood; water stood beneath, bloody and troubled. For all the
Danes, friends of Scyldings, it was painful to endure in their
hearts, for many a thane, a distress to each of the men, when
on the water-cliff they encountered Æschere's head. The 1422
flood seethed with blood—the people looked on—with hot
gore. Time and again a horn sounded an eager martial note.

fuslic fyrd-leoð.   Feþa eal gesæt.
Gesawon ða æfter wætere   wyrm-cynnes fcla,
sellice sæ-dracan   sund cunnian,
swylce on næs-hleoðum   nicras licgean,
ða on undern-mæl   oft bewitigað
sorhfulne sið   on segl-rade,
wyrmas ond wildeor.   Hie on weg hruron,
bitere ond gebolgne;   bearhtm ongeaton,
guð-horn galan.   Sumne Geata leod
of flan-bogan   feores getwæfde,
yð-gewinnes,   þæt him on aldre stod
here-stræl hearda;   he on holme wæs
sundes þe sænra   ðe hyne swylt fornam.
Hræþe wearð on yðum   mid eofer-spreotum
heoro-hocyhtum   hearde genearwod,
niða genæged,   ond on næs togen,
wundorlic wæg-bora;   weras sceawedon
gryrelicne gist.
                    Gyrede hine Beowulf
eorl-gewædum,   nalles for ealdre mearn;
scolde here-byrne   hondum gebroden,
sid ond searo-fah,   sund cunnian,
seo ðe ban-cofan   beorgan cuþe,
þæt him hilde-grap   hreþre ne mihte,
eorres inwit-feng,   aldre gesceþðan;
ac se hwita helm   hafelan werede,
se þe mere-grundas   mengan scolde,
secan sund-gebland   since geweorðad,
befongen frea-wrasnum,   swa hine fyrn-dagum
worhte wæpna smið,   wundrum teode,
besette swin-licum,   þæt hine syðþan no

The soldiers all sat. Then they observed throughout the wa-
ter many species of serpents, strange sea-dragons testing the
waters, likewise water-monsters lying on cliff-ledges, such as
often in the forenoon scrutinize a lamentable voyage on the
sail-road, serpents and wild beasts. They rushed away, bitter
and enraged; they perceived the clamor, the war-horn sound-
ing. With an arrow from a bow a man of the Geats sundered 1432
a certain one from its life, from its struggling in the water, so
that the hard war-missile stood in its vitals; it was the more
sluggish at swimming in the water for death's bearing it off.
Quickly, on the waves it was firmly constrained with barbed
boar-javelins, assailed violently, and dragged onto the cliff,
that amazing wave-roamer; the men examined the grisly
guest.

Beowulf readied himself with a man's garments, did not 1441
care about his life at all; his mail-shirt woven by hand, wide
and ingeniously trimmed, was to try its swimming ability;
it knew how to protect the bone-chamber, so that war-
grasping, the hostile grip of an angry one, could not harm
his chest, his life; but the bright helmet, which was to stir
up the pool bed, explore the mingled waters, preserved the
head distinguished by jewels, encompassed by a fringe of
chain mail, just as the armorer had constructed it in days
long gone, formed it amazingly, studded it with boar-images,

brond ne beado-mecas bitan ne meahton.
Næs þæt þonne mætost mægen-fultuma
þæt him on ðearfe lah ðyle Hroðgares;
wæs þæm hæft-mece Hrunting nama;
þæt wæs an foran eald-gestreona;
ecg wæs iren, ater-tanum fah,
ahyrded heaþo-swate; næfre hit æt hilde ne swac
manna ængum þara þe hit mid mundum bewand,
se ðe gryre-siðas gegan dorste,
folc-stede fara; næs þæt forma sið
þæt hit ellen-weorc æfnan scolde.
Huru ne gemunde mago Ecglafes,
eafoþes cræftig, þæt he ær gespræc
wine druncen, þa he þæs wæpnes onlah
selran sweord-frecan; selfa ne dorste
under yða gewin aldre geneþan,
drihtscype dreogan; þær he dome forleas,
ellen-mærðum. Ne wæs þæm oðrum swa
syðþan he hine to guðe gegyred hæfde.

XXII

Beowulf maðelode, bearn Ecgþeowes:
"Geþenc nu, se mæra maga Healfdenes,
snottra fengel, nu ic eom siðes fus,
gold-wine gumena, hwæt wit geo spræcon,
gif ic æt þearfe þinre scolde
aldre linnan, þæt ðu me a wære
forðgewitenum on fæder stæle.
Wes þu mund-bora minum mago-þegnum,
hond-gesellum, gif mec hild nime;
swylce þu ða madmas þe þu me sealdest,
Hroðgar leofa, Higelace onsend.

so that afterward no blade or battle-sword could bite into it. It was not the most insignificant aid to his might that Hrothgar's spokesman then lent him in his need; the name of that hilted sword was Hrunting; it was uniquely foremost of heirlooms; the blade was iron, painted with poison-twigs, hardened in battle-sweat; in warfare it had never failed anyone who had wrapped his hands around it, who dared to venture on terrifying exploits, the home ground of foes; that was not the first time that it should accomplish a heroic feat. Certainly, the son of Ecglaf, skillful in his strength, did not recall what he had said, intoxicated with wine, when he lent that weapon to the better swordsman; for his own part, he did not dare to venture his life under the tumult of waves, engage in bravery; there he gave up glory, fame from valor. It was not so for the other after he had readied himself for battle.

XXII

Beowulf made a speech, offspring of Ecgtheo: "Think 1473
now, renowned son of Healfdene, wise sovereign, now that I am on the verge of this exploit, gold-friend of men, about what we two discussed earlier, if in your service I should part with my life, that you would always occupy for me, once departed, the place of a father. Be the patron of my young thanes, my close comrades, if war takes me; likewise, cherished Hrothgar, send to Hygelac the treasures you have

Mæg þonne on þæm golde ongitan Geata dryhten,
geseon sunu Hrædles, þonne he on þæt sinc starað,
þæt ic gum-cystum godne funde
beaga bryttan, breac þonne moste.
Ond þu Unferð læt ealde lafe,
wrætlic wæg-sweord wid-cuðne man
heard-ecg habban; ic me mid Hruntinge
dom gewyrce, oþðe mec deað nimeð."
Æfter þæm wordum Weder-Geata leod
efste mid elne, nalas andsware
bidan wolde; brim-wylm onfeng
hilde-rince. Ða wæs hwil dæges
ær he þone grund-wong ongytan mehte.
Sona þæt onfunde se ðe floda begong
heoro-gifre beheold hund missera,
grim ond grædig, þæt þær gumena sum
æl-wihta eard ufan cunnode.
Grap þa togeanes, guð-rinc gefeng
atolan clommum; no þy ær in gescod
halan lice; hring utan ymbbearh,
þæt heo þone fyrd-hom ðurhfon ne mihte,
locene leoðo-syrcan laþan fingrum.
Bær þa seo brim-wylf, þa heo to botme com,
hringa þengel to hofe sinum,
swa he ne mihte —no he þæs modig wæs—
wæpna gewealdan, ac hine wundra þæs fela
swencte on sunde, sæ-deor monig
hilde-tuxum here-syrcan bræc,
ehton aglæcan. Ða se eorl ongeat
þæt he in nið-sele nathwylcum wæs,
þær him nænig wæter wihte ne sceþede,

given me. Then the lord of the Geats will be able to discern 1484
from that gold, Hrethel's son be able to see, when he looks
on that fortune, that I found a distributor of rings, excellent
in the qualities of a man; I did well while I was permitted.
And let Unferth, that widely known man, have the old in-
heritance, splendid, hard-edged wave-sword; I shall get my-
self glory with Hrunting, or death will take me."

After these words the man of the Weder-Geats moved 1492
briskly, would hardly wait for an answer; the surging water
took possession of the war-maker. It was then a good part of
the day before he could make out the level bottom. The one
who had ruled the expanse of the flood for a hundred sea-
sons, bloodthirsty, unyielding and greedy, detected at once
that a certain man from above was exploring the realm of
alien creatures. She reached out toward him then, seized the 1501
warrior in her horrible clutches; none the sooner did she
break into the hale body; the ring gave surrounding pro-
tection on the outside, so that she could not pierce the
battle-garment, the interlocked limb-shirt, with her mali-
cious fingers. When she came to the bottom, the sea-wolf
carried the prince of rings to her court, so that he could not,
no matter how courageous he was, wield weapons, but such
a multitude of prodigies assailed him as he swam, many a
sea-beast attempted to break into the war-shirt with battle-
tusks, afflicted the troublemaker. Then the man made out 1512
that he was in some sort of oppressive hall where no water

ne him for hrof-sele hrinan ne mehte
fær-gripe flodes; fyr-leoht geseah,
blacne leoman beorhte scinan.
  Ongeat þa se goda grund-wyrgenne,
mere-wif mihtig; mægen-ræs forgeaf
hilde-bille, hond sweng ne ofteah,
þæt hire on hafelan hring-mæl agol
grædig guð-leoð. Ða se gist onfand
þæt se beado-leoma bitan nolde,
aldre sceþðan, ac seo ecg geswac
ðeodne æt þearfe; ðolode ær fela
hond-gemota, helm oft gescær,
fæges fyrd-hrægl; ða wæs forma sið
deorum madme þæt his dom alæg.
  Eft wæs anræd, nalas elnes læt,
mærða gemyndig mæg Hylaces:
wearp ða wunden-mæl wrættum gebunden
yrre oretta, þæt hit on eorðan læg,
stið ond styl-ecg; strenge getruwode,
mund-gripe mægenes. Swa sceal man don
þonne he æt guðe gegan þenceð
longsumne lof, na ymb his lif cearað.
Gefeng þa be feaxe —nalas for fæhðe mearn—
Guð-Geata leod Grendles modor;
brægd þa beadwe heard, þa he gebolgen wæs,
feorh-geniðlan, þæt heo on flet gebeah.
Heo him eft hraþe andlean forgeald
grimman grapum ond him togeanes feng;
oferwearp þa werig-mod wigena strengest,
feþe-cempa, þæt he on fylle wearð.
Ofsæt þa þone sele-gyst, ond hyre seax geteah

could harm them, nor could the perilous grasp of the flood
touch them on account of the roofed structure; he saw fire-
light, radiant illumination shining brightly.

Then the good man made out the outcast of the deep, the 1518
mighty lake-woman; he gave a powerful thrust to his war-
sword—his hand did not spare the blow—so that the ring-
weapon sang a hungry war-song on her head. The visitor
then discovered that the battle-light would not bite, do
harm to her life, but the implement failed its lord at his
need; it had endured many hand-meetings, often cleft a hel-
met, the battle-dress of a doomed man; that was the first
time for the precious treasure that its glory dimmed.

Again Hygelac's kinsman was determined, not at all slow 1529
to heroism, keeping fame in mind: the angry soldier then
threw the wavy weapon knit with ornaments, so that it lay
on the earth, stiff and steel-edged; he put his trust in his
strength, the hand-grip of the mighty man. So ought a man
to do when he intends to gain long-lived praise in warfare,
does not care at all about his life. Then—he did not shrink
from violence—the man of the War-Geats seized Grendel's
mother by the hair; then the man hard in battle, now that he
was enraged, flung the deadly foe so that she sank to the
floor. In turn, she promptly paid him in kind with her re- 1541
lentless grasp and reached toward him; then she overturned
the weary-hearted strongest of fighters, of foot-soldiers, so
that he came for a fall. Then she held down the hall-visitor

brad ond brun-ecg;   wolde hire bearn wrecan,
angan eaferan.   Him on eaxle læg
breost-net broden;   þæt gebearh feore
wið ord ond wið ecge,   ingang forstod.
Hæfde ða forsiðod   sunu Ecgþeowes
under gynne grund,   Geata cempa,
nemne him heaðo-byrne   helpe gefremede,
here-net hearde,   ond halig God.
Geweold wig-sigor   witig Drihten,
rodera rædend;   hit on ryht gesced
yðelice,   syþðan he eft astod.

XXIII

Geseah ða on searwum   sige-eadig bil,
eald-sweord eotenisc   ecgum þyhtig,
wigena weorð-mynd;   þæt wæs wæpna cyst,—
buton hit wæs mare   ðonne ænig mon oðer
to beadu-lace   ætberan meahte,
god ond geatolic,   giganta geweorc.
He gefeng þa fetel-hilt,   freca Scyldinga
hreoh ond heoro-grim,   hring-mæl gebrægd
aldres orwena,   yrringa sloh,
þæt hire wið halse   heard grapode,
ban-hringas bræc;   bil eal ðurhwod
fægne flæsc-homan,   heo on flet gecrong;
sweord wæs swatig,   secg weorce gefeh.
   Lixte se leoma,   leoht inne stod,
efne swa of hefene   hadre scineð
rodores candel.   He æfter recede wlat;
hwearf þa be wealle,   wæpen hafenade
heard be hiltum   Higelaces ðegn,
yrre ond anræd.   Næs seo ecg fracod

and drew her long-knife, broad and bright-edged; she
wanted to avenge her child, her sole heir. On his shoulder
lay his woven breast-net; that defended his life against point
and against edge, denied entry. Ecgtheo's son would have
gone missing then under the cavernous ground, champion
of the Geats, if his war-armor had not given him help, the
hard combat-net, and holy God. The Lord in his wisdom, ar- 1554
chitect of the skies, held in his power victory in battle; he
settled it with justice, effortlessly, after he stood again.

XXIII

Then he saw among the arms a victory-blessed weapon, 1557
an ancient ogreish sword firm in its edges, a badge of dis-
tinction for warriors; that was the choicest weapon—except
that it was larger than any other man could bear into battle-
play, good and richly equipped, the work of giants. He seized
the linked hilt then, champion of the Scyldings, fierce and
unyielding at arms, drew the ring-sword without hope of
surviving, struck angrily, so that the hard weapon groped for
her neck, broke the bone-rings; the sword went all the way
through the doomed covering of flesh, so that she sank to
the floor; the sword was sweaty, the man exulted in his
work.

The radiance beamed, a light stood within, just as the 1570
candle of heaven shines brilliantly from the firmament. He
looked through the hall, turned then along the wall, lifted
a hard weapon by the hilt, Hygelac's thane, angry and reso-
lute. The edge was not useless to the war-maker; he wanted

hilde-rince, ac he hraþe wolde
Grendle forgyldan guð-ræsa fela
ðara þe he geworhte to West-Denum
oftor micle ðonne on ænne sið,
þonne he Hroðgares heorð-geneatas
sloh on sweofote, slæpende fræt
folces Denigea fyftyne men
ond oðer swylc ut offerede,
laðlicu lac. He him þæs lean forgeald,
reþe cempa, ðæs þe he on ræste geseah
guð-werigne Grendel licgan,
aldorleasne, swa him ær gescod
hild æt Heorote —hra wide sprong
syþðan he æfter deaðe drepe þrowade,
heoro-sweng heardne— ond hine þa heafde becearf.
Sona þæt gesawon snottre ceorlas,
þa ðe mid Hroðgare on holm wliton,
þæt wæs yð-geblond eal gemenged,
brim blode fah. Blonden-feaxe,
gomele ymb godne ongeador spræcon
þæt hig þæs æðelinges eft ne wendon,
þæt he sige-hreðig secean come
mærne þeoden; þa ðæs monige gewearð
þæt hine seo brim-wylf abroten hæfde.
Ða com non dæges. Næs ofgeafon
hwate Scyldingas; gewat him ham þonon
gold-wine gumena. Gistas setan
modes seoce ond on mere staredon;
wiston ond ne wendon þæt hie heora wine-drihten
selfne gesawon.
Þa þæt sweord ongan

to repay Grendel at once for the many war-assaults he had
inflicted on the West-Danes much more often than on a sin-
gle occasion, when he struck at Hrothgar's inner circle in
their sleep, ate fifteen men of the Danish nation at rest and
carried off a like number, horrifying loot. He gave him his 1584
deserts for that, the fierce champion, after he saw Gren-
del lying in repose, war-exhausted, lifeless, as combat had
maimed him at Heorot—the corpse sprang wide asunder
when it suffered a blow after death, a hard sword-stroke—
and he cut the head from him.

Right away the observant men who were gazing with 1591
Hrothgar at the water saw that the muddled waves were all
tainted, the seawater stained with blood. Gray-haired men,
old ones around the good man, declared by consensus that
they had no expectation of the prince again, that he would
come exulting in victory to see that famous lord; then many
agreed in thinking that the sea-wolf had destroyed him.
Mid-afternoon arrived. The valiant Scyldings abandoned
the cliff; the men's gold-friend set out from there for home.
The visitors sat sick at heart and stared at the pool; they
wished and did not expect that they would see their friend
and lord himself.

Then the sword began on account of the battle-sweat, 1605

æfter heaþo-swate hilde-gicelum,
wig-bil wanian; þæt wæs wundra sum
þæt hit eal gemealt ise gelicost,
ðonne forstes bend Fæder onlæteð,
onwindeð wæl-rapas, se geweald hafað
sæla ond mæla; þæt is soð Metod.
Ne nom he in þæm wicum, Weder-Geata leod,
maðm-æhta ma, þeh he þær monige geseah,
buton þone hafelan ond þa hilt somod
since fage; sweord ær gemealt,
forbarn broden-mæl; wæs þæt blod to þæs hat,
ættren ellor-gæst se þær inne swealt.
Sona wæs on sunde se þe ær æt sæcce gebad
wig-hryre wraðra, wæter up þurhdeaf;
wæron yð-gebland eal gefælsod,
eacne eardas, þa se ellor-gast
oflet lif-dagas ond þas lænan gesceaft.
    Com þa to lande lid-manna helm
swið-mod swymman; sæ-laca gefeah
mægen-byrþenne þara þe he him mid hæfde.
Eodon him þa togeanes, Gode þancodon,
ðryðlic þegna heap, þeodnes gefegon,
þæs þe hi hyne gesundne geseon moston.
Ða wæs of þæm hroran helm ond byrne
lungre alysed. Lagu drusade,
wæter under wolcnum, wæl-dreore fag.
Ferdon forð þonon feþe-lastum
ferhþum fægne, fold-weg mæton,
cuþe stræte; cyning-balde men
from þæm holm-clife hafelan bæron
earfoðlice heora æghwæþrum

the war-weapon, to be reduced to combat-icicles; that was
some miracle that it melted completely, just like ice when
the Father slackens frost's fetters, unties the cords binding
springs, who has the governance of hours and seasons; that
is the true Providence. The man of the Geats did not col-
lect more valuables in that household, though he saw many
there, only the head and the hilt together ornamented with
jewels; the sword had melted, the patterned weapon had
burnt up; the blood was that hot, the alien spirit that poi-
sonous which died therein. At once the one who had lived to 1618
see the war-downfall of enemies in combat was swimming,
dived up through the water; the mingled waves were com-
pletely cleansed, the environment improved, now that the
alien spirit had let go of its life-days and this fleeting exis-
tence.

Then the strong-hearted helm of mariners came swim- 1623
ming to land, took pleasure in the ponderous burden of sea-
booty that he had with him. They came to meet him then,
thanked God, that powerful throng of thanes, rejoiced in
their lord, that they were permitted to see him again safe
and sound. Then helmet and mail-shirt were immediately
undone from the valorous man. The lagoon grew placid, wa-
ter under the clouds, tinged with battle-gore. Rejoicing in 1632
their hearts, they went forth from there by foot-paths, mea-
sured the earth-way, the familiar road; royally bold men car-
ried the head from the sea-cliff with difficulty for either pair

fela-modigra;   feower scoldon
on þæm wæl-stenge   weorcum geferian
to þæm gold-sele   Grendles heafod,
oþ ðæt semninga   to sele comon
frome fyrd-hwate   feowertyne
Geata gongan;   gum-dryhten mid
modig on gemonge   meodo-wongas træd.
Ða com in gan   ealdor ðegna,
dæd-cene mon   dome gewurþad,
hæle hilde-deor,   Hroðgar gretan.
Þa wæs be feaxe   on flet boren
Grendles heafod,   þær guman druncon,
egeslic for eorlum   ond þære idese mid,
wlite-seon wrætlic;   weras on sawon.

XXIIII

Beowulf maþelode,   bearn Ecgþeowes:
“Hwæt, we þe þas sæ-lac,   sunu Healfdenes,
leod Scyldinga,   lustum brohton
tires to tacne,   þe þu her to locast.
Ic þæt unsofte   ealdre gedigde
wigge under wætere,   weorc geneþde
earfoðlice;   ætrihte wæs
guð getwæfed,   nymðe mec God scylde.
Ne meahte ic æt hilde   mid Hruntinge
wiht gewyrcan,   þeah þæt wæpen duge;
ac me geuðe   ylda waldend
þæt ic on wage geseah   wlitig hangian
eald-sweord eacen;   ofost wisode
winigea leasum,   þæt ic ðy wæpne gebræd.
Ofsloh ða æt þære sæcce,   þa me sæl ageald,
huses hyrdas.   Þa þæt hilde-bil

of those very courageous men; it took four to carry Gren-
del's head with painful effort to the gold-hall on a battle-
shaft, until all at once the fourteen vigorous, war-strenuous
Geats came walking up to the building; their lord among
them, courageous in the company, trod the level meadows. 1644
The leader of the thanes, a man of decisive action, then
came walking in, bathed in glory, a battle-brave hero, to ap-
proach Hrothgar. Grendel's head was then carried by the
hair into the hall where men were drinking, gruesome for
the men and the lady among them, a beautiful, treasured
sight; the men looked on.

XXIIII

Beowulf made a speech, Ecgtheo's offspring: "So, with 1651
pleasure we have brought you this sea-loot which you are
looking at here, son of Healfdene, man of the Scyldings, as a
token of glory. With no small effort I safely passed through
it with my life, by underwater fighting, ventured the deed
with difficulty; the battle would have been cut off immedi-
ately if God had not shielded me. With Hrunting I could
not accomplish anything in the fight, though the weapon
is good; but the ruler of mortals granted me that I saw hang-
ing handsome on the wall an immense old sword; haste
guided the friendless man, so that I drew the weapon. Then 1665
in the conflict, when the opportunity presented itself to me,
I struck down the house's caretakers. The braid-patterned

forbarn brogden-mæl, swa þæt blod gesprang,
hatost heaþo-swata. Ic þæt hilt þanan
feondum ætferede, fyren-dæda wræc,
deað-cwealm Denigea, swa hit gedefe wæs.
Ic hit þe þonne gehate þæt þu on Heorote most
sorhleas swefan mid þinra secga gedryht
ond þegna gehwylc þinra leoda,
duguðe ond iogoþe, þæt þu him ondrædan ne þearft,
þeoden Scyldinga, on þa healfe,
aldor-bealu eorlum, swa þu ær dydest."
Ða wæs gylden hilt gamelum rince,
harum hild-fruman on hand gyfen,
enta ær-geweorc; hit on æht gehwearf
æfter deofla hryre Denigea frean,
wundor-smiþa geweorc; ond þa þas worold ofgeaf
grom-heort guma, Godes andsaca,
morðres scyldig, ond his modor eac,
on geweald gehwearf worold-cyninga
ðæm selestan be sæm tweonum
ðara þe on Sceden-igge sceattas dælde.
Hroðgar maðelode; hylt sceawode,
ealde lafe. On ðæm wæs or writen
fyrn-gewinnes; syðþan flod ofsloh,
gifen geotende giganta cyn,
frecne geferdon; þæt wæs fremde þeod
ecean Dryhtne; him þæs ende-lean
þurh wæteres wylm waldend sealde.
Swa wæs on ðæm scennum sciran goldes
þurh run-stafas rihte gemearcod,
geseted ond gesæd, hwam þæt sweord geworht,
irena cyst ærest wære,

war-weapon burned up then as the blood spurted, hottest of war-sweats. I brought the hilt from the enemies there, avenged their criminal doings, the murder of Danes, as was only right. Now then I promise you that you and every thane of your nation will be allowed to sleep care-free among the corps of your men in Heorot, young recruits and veterans, that you need not dread mortal danger to them, lord of Scyldings, from that quarter, for your men, as you did before."

The golden hilt was then given into the hand of the aged 1677
man, the hoary war-commander, the ancient work of giants; after the defeat of devils it passed into the keeping of the lord of Danes, the artifice of marvelous smiths; and when the cruel-hearted man gave up this world, God's opponent, guilty of murder, and his mother, too, it passed under the control of the best of earthly kings between the oceans, of those who dealt out wealth in Scania.

Hrothgar made a speech; he examined the hilt, the an- 1687
cient legacy. On it was incised the beginning of ancient strife; afterward the flood, the cascading ocean, struck down the race of giants; they fared terribly; that was a race foreign to the eternal Lord; the ruler gave them final retribution for that through the surging of water. Thus on the sword-guard of luminous gold it was rightly indicated through runic characters, set down and declared, for whom that sword had first been made, choicest of irons, with a

wreoþen-hilt ond wyrm-fah. Đa se wisa spræc
sunu Healfdenes; swigedon ealle:
"Þæt, la, mæg secgan se þe soð ond riht
fremeð on folce, feor eal gemon,
eald eþel-weard, þæt ðes eorl wære
geboren betera. Blæd is aræred
geond wid-wegas, wine min Beowulf,
ðin ofer þeoda gehwylce. Eal þu hit geþyldum healdest,
mægen mid modes snyttrum. Ic þe sceal mine gelæstan
freode, swa wit furðum spræcon. Đu scealt to frofre
weorþan
eal lang-twidig leodum þinum,
hæleðum to helpe.
"Ne wearð Heremod swa
eaforum Ecgwelan, Ar-Scyldingum;
ne geweox he him to willan ac to wæl-fealle
ond to deað-cwalum Deniga leodum;
breat bolgen-mod beod-geneatas,
eaxl-gesteallan, oþ þæt he ana hwearf,
mære þeoden mon-dreamum from.
Đeah þe hine mihtig God mægenes wynnum,
eafeþum stepte ofer ealle men,
forð gefremede, hwæþere him on ferhþe greow
breost-hord blod-reow, nallas beagas geaf
Denum æfter dome; dreamleas gebad
þæt he þæs gewinnes weorc þrowade,
leod-bealo longsum. Đu þe lær be þon,
gum-cyste ongit; ic þis gid be þe
awræc wintrum frod.
"Wundor is to secganne
hu mihtig God manna cynne

wrapped hilt and serpent-patterned. Then the sage son of Healfdene spoke; all were hushed:

"He who practices truth and right among his people, re- 1700
members all from far back, an old defender of the homeland, can well say that this man was born superior. Your glory is upraised, my friend Beowulf, through the world's wide ways over every nation. You will keep hold of all of it steadily, strength and discernment of intellect. I shall fulfill my friendship with you, as we two discussed a short time ago. You shall be a very long-lasting comfort to your people, a help to heroes.

"Heremod was not so to the heirs of Ecgwela, the Honor- 1709
Scyldings; he did not grow to please them but to the ruin and to the destruction of the Danish people; in a raging temper he cut down his table-companions, his intimates, until he passed alone, the famous lord, from human society. Though mighty God exalted him with the delights of power and strength over all, furthered him on his way, his breast-hoard nonetheless grew bloodthirsty in spirit, by no means gave rings to Danes for their glory; estranged from contentment, he lived to see it that he suffered the pain of that struggle, a long-lived bane to the people. Take a lesson from this, get to know virtue in a man; enlightened by winters, I have recited this tale for your sake.

"It is a wonder to say how mighty God in magnanimous 1724

þurh sidne sefan snyttru bryttað,
eard ond eorlscipe; he ah ealra geweald.
Hwilum he on lufan læteð hworfan
monnes mod-geþonc mæran cynnes,
seleð him on eþle eorþan wynne,
to healdanne hleo-burh wera,
gedeð him swa gewealdene worolde dælas,
side rice, þæt he his selfa ne mæg
for his unsnyttrum ende geþencean.
Wunað he on wiste; no hine wiht dweleð
adl ne yldo, ne him inwit-sorh
on sefan sweorceð, ne gesacu ohwær,
ecg-hete eoweð, ac him eal worold
wendeð on willan; he þæt wyrse ne con—

XXV

"oð þæt him on innan ofer-hygda dæl
weaxeð ond wridað; þonne se weard swefeð,
sawele hyrde; bið se slæp to fæst,
bisgum gebunden, bona swiðe neah,
se þe of flan-bogan fyrenum sceoteð.
Þonne bið on hreþre under helm drepen
biteran stræle —him bebeorgan ne con—
wom wundor-bebodum wergan gastes;
þinceð him to lytel þæt he lange heold,
gytsað grom-hydig, nallas on gylp seleð
fætte beagas, ond he þa forð-gesceaft
forgyteð ond forgymeð, þæs þe him ær God sealde,
wuldres waldend, weorð-mynda dæl.
Hit on ende-stæf eft gelimpeð
þæt se lic-homa læne gedreoseð,
fæge gefealleð; fehð oþer to,

spirit distributes wisdom to the human race, property and rank; he has control of everything. Sometimes he lets the designs of a man of good family wander in delight, gives him in his own country the pleasures of the earth, to rule the sheltering stronghold of men, makes portions of the world thus subject to him, a broad kingdom, so that he himself in
his ignorance cannot imagine an end. He lives in plenty; dis- 1735
ease and decrepitude do not hamper him at all, neither does treacherous trouble darken his disposition, nor does conflict, blade-hatred appear anywhere, but all the world bends to his will; he does not recognize the worse—

XXV

"until a measure of overconfidence sprouts and grows, 1740
when the watch sleeps, the soul's overseer; the slumber is too deep, tied up with cares, the killer very near, who shoots fiercely with his bow. He is then struck in the breast under helmet with a bitter dart—he does not know how to protect himself—with the perverse, astonishing directives of an accursed spirit; what he has held for long seems to him too little; bitter-minded, he is miserly, by no means gives plated rings with pomp, and he forgets and neglects his condition of life, what God had granted him, wielder of glory, his share
of honors. In the final chapter it in turn happens that the 1753
ephemeral body grows feeble—doomed, falls; another takes possession, who doles out the wealth without a scruple, a

se þe unmurnlice madmas dæleþ,
eorles ær-gestreon, egesan ne gymeð.
Bebeorh þe ðone bealo-nið, Beowulf leofa,
secg betesta, ond þe þæt selre geceos,
ece rædas; ofer-hyda ne gym,
mære cempa. Nu is þines mægnes blæd
ane hwile; eft sona bið
þæt þec adl oððe ecg eafoþes getwæfeð,
oððe fyres feng, oððe flodes wylm,
oððe gripe meces, oððe gares fliht,
oððe atol yldo; oððe eagena bearhtm
forsiteð ond forsworceð; semninga bið
þæt ðec, dryht-guma, deað oferswyðeð.
"Swa ic Hring-Dena hund missera
weold under wolcnum ond hig wigge beleac
manigum mægþa geond þysne middan-geard,
æscum ond ecgum, þæt ic me ænigne
under swegles begong gesacan ne tealde.
Hwæt, me þæs on eþle edwenden cwom,
gyrn æfter gomene, seoþðan Grendel wearð,
eald-gewinna, in-genga min;
ic þære socne singales wæg
mod-ceare micle. Þæs sig Metode þanc,
ecean Dryhtne, þæs ðe ic on aldre gebad
þæt ic on þone hafelan heoro-dreorigne
ofer eald gewin eagum starige.
Ga nu to setle, symbel-wynne dreoh
wig-geweorþad; unc sceal worn fela
maþma gemænra siþðan morgen bið."

man's inheritance from old, cares nothing about caution.
Safeguard yourself against that deadly affliction, beloved
Beowulf, finest warrior, and choose what is better for you,
lasting prudence; give no consideration to self-conceit, cel-
ebrated champion. Now is the glory of your strength for a 1761
single hour; in a moment it will be that disease or a blade
will part you from your power, or fire's embrace, or the
flood's flow, or the sword's grasp, or the spear's flight, or gro-
tesque senescence; or the eyes' brightness will fail and dim;
suddenly it will be, soldier, that death overpowers you.

"Thus, under the heavens I have governed the Ring- 1769
Danes for half a hundred years and by warfare held at bay
many nations throughout this middle-earth, by ash-spears
and blades, so that I reckoned on no adversary under the
vault of heaven. Well, in my own realm there came to me a
change of fortune, suffering after celebration, when Gren-
del, old adversary, became my invader; I continually felt the
immense mental suffering of that incursion. Thanks be to 1778
Providence for that, to the eternal Lord, that in my lifetime
I have experienced it that I can see with my own eyes this
sword-bloody head after an age-old struggle. Now go to your
seat, take pleasure in the feast, distinguished in battle; there
shall be a great many treasures shared between us after it is
morning."

Geat wæs glæd-mod,   geong sona to,
setles neosan,   swa se snottra heht.
Þa wæs eft swa ær   ellen-rofum,
flet-sittendum   fægere gereorded
niowan stefne.   Niht-helm geswearc
deorc ofer dryht-gumum.   Duguð eal aras;
wolde blonden-feax   beddes neosan,
gamela Scylding.   Geat unigmetes wel,
rofne rand-wigan,   restan lyste;
sona him sele-þegn   siðes wergum,
feorran-cundum   forð wisade,
se for andrysnum   ealle beweotede
þegnes þearfe,   swylce þy dogor
heaþo-liðende   habban scoldon.
Reste hine þa rum-heort;   reced hliuade
geap ond gold-fah;   gæst inne swæf,
oþ þæt hrefn blaca   heofones wynne
blið-heort bodode.   Ða com beorht leoma
ofer sceadwa scacan;   scaþan onetton,
wæron æþelingas   eft to leodum
fuse to farenne;   wolde feor þanon
cuma collen-ferhð,   ceoles neosan.
Heht þa se hearda   Hrunting beran
sunu Ecglafes,   heht his sweord niman,
leoflic iren;   sægde him þæs leanes þanc,
cwæð, he þone guð-wine   godne tealde,
wig-cræftigne,   nales wordum log
meces ecge;   þæt wæs modig secg.
Ond þa sið-frome,   searwum gearwe
wigend wæron;   eode weorð Denum

The Geat was cheerful, went off immediately to find his 1785
seat, as the sage had directed. Then again it was as before for the men vigorous in valor, a banquet handsomely prepared for the hall-occupants on a new occasion. The helm of night darkened black over the men of the court. The cohort all stood; the gray-haired man wished to go to bed, the aged Scylding. It pleased the Geat ever so much, the vigorous shield-warrior, to retire; at once a hall-officer led him away, the visitor from afar weary of his exploit; he reverently tended to all the thane's needs, such as battle-mariners should have in those days.

The great-hearted one took his rest then; the house tow- 1799
ered, vaulted and gold-trimmed; the guest slept inside, until the black raven, cheerful-hearted, heralded heaven's delight. Then the bright glow came gliding over the shadows; the raiders then made no delay, the nobles were eager to return to their people; the bold-hearted visitor wanted to be far from there, to go find his ship.

The hardy man directed that Hrunting be brought to the 1807
son of Ecglaf, told him to take his sword, the valued iron; he offered thanks to him for the loan, said, he regarded that war-friend as good, strong in battle, by no means explicitly found fault with the sword's edge; that was a magnanimous man.

And then the warriors were keen to set out, ready in their 1813
armor; the prince cherished by the Danes went to the dais

æþeling to yppan,   þær se oþer wæs,
hæle hilde-deor   Hroðgar grette.

XXVI

Beowulf maþelode,   bearn Ecgþeowes:
"Nu we sæ-liðend   secgan wyllað
feorran cumene   þæt we fundiaþ
Higelac secan.   Wæron her tela,
willum bewenede;   þu us wel dohtest.
Gif ic þonne on eorþan   owihte mæg
þinre mod-lufan   maran tilian,
gumena dryhten,   ðonne ic gyt dyde,
guð-geweorca,   ic beo gearo sona.
Gif ic þæt gefricge   ofer floda begang
þæt þec ymbsittend   egesan þywað,
swa þec hetende   hwilum dydon,
ic ðe þusenda   þegna bringe,
hæleþa to helpe.   Ic on Higelac wat,
Geata dryhten,   þeah ðe he geong sy,
folces hyrde,   þæt he mec fremman wile
wordum ond worcum,   þæt ic þe wel nerige
ond þe to geoce   gar-holt bere,
mægenes fultum,   þær ðe bið manna þearf.
Gif him þonne Hreþric   to hofum Geata
geþingeð þeodnes bearn,   he mæg þær fela
freonda findan;   feor-cyþðe beoð
selran gesohte   þæm þe him selfa deah."
  Hroðgar maþelode   him on andsware:
"Þe þa word-cwydas   wigtig Drihten
on sefan sende;   ne hyrde ic snotorlicor
on swa geongum feore   guman þingian.
Þu eart mægenes strang   ond on mode frod,

where the other was, the hero brave in battle approached Hrothgar.

XXVI

Beowulf made a speech, Ecgtheo's offspring: "Now we 1817
mariners come from afar want to say that we are setting out
to find Hygelac. Here we were hosted well and to our liking;
you have done well by us. If, then, I can cultivate any more
on earth of your affection, of martial deeds, lord of men,
than I have already done, I will be ready at once. If I hear
news over the expanse of the flood that neighbors threaten
you with danger, as enemies have at times done to you, I
shall bring you thousands of thanes in aid of heroes. I am 1830
confident of Hygelac, lord of Geats, though he is young, the
people's keeper, that he will offer me furtherance in word
and deed, so that I may redeem you and bring a forest of
spears to your assistance, the aid of a force, if you are in need
of men. Then if the lord's child Hrethric determines to go to
the court of the Geats, he will be able to find many friends
there; far countries are better visited by whoever will do
right for himself."

Hrothgar made a speech in reply to him: "God in his wis- 1840
dom put those remarks into your head. I have never heard a
man at such a young age conduct diplomacy more percep-
tively. You are physically strong and acute of mind, judicious

wis word-cwida. Wen ic talige,
gif þæt gegangeð þæt ðe gar nymeð,
hild heoru-grimme Hreþles eaferan,
adl oþðe iren ealdor ðinne,
folces hyrde, ond þu þin feorh hafast,
þæt þe Sæ-Geatas selran næbben
to geceosenne cyning ænigne,
hord-weard hæleþa, gyf þu healdan wylt
maga rice. Me þin mod-sefa
licað leng swa wel, leofa Beowulf.
Hafast þu gefered þæt þam folcum sceal,
Geata leodum ond Gar-Denum
sib gemænu, ond sacu restan,
inwit-niþas þe hie ær drugon,
wesan, þenden ic wealde widan rices,
maþmas gemæne, manig oþerne
godum gegretan ofer ganotes bæð;
sceal hring-naca ofer heafu bringan
lac ond luf-tacen. Ic þa leode wat
ge wið feond ge wið freond fæste geworhte,
æghwæs untæle ealde wisan."
Ða git him eorla hleo inne gesealde,
mago Healfdenes, maþmas twelfe;
het hine mid þæm lacum leode swæse
secean on gesyntum, snude eft cuman.
Gecyste þa cyning æþelum god,
þeoden Scyldinga ðegn betestan
ond be healse genam; hruron him tearas
blonden-feaxum. Him wæs bega wen
ealdum infrodum, oþres swiðor,
þæt hie seoððan no geseon moston,

of speech. I count it likely, if it will happen that a spear,
intractable bloody warfare, takes Hrethel's heir, disease or
iron, your ruler, the shepherd of the nation, and you have
your life, that the Sea-Geats would not have any better king
to choose, heroes' treasure-guard, if you will govern the
kinsmen's realm. Your character pleases me, the longer the 1852
better, dear Beowulf. You have brought it about that amity
will be shared by these peoples, men of the Geats and Spear-
Danes, and strife rest, malicious acts of violence in which
they formerly engaged; as long as I control a wide realm,
treasures will be shared, many a one will greet another with
goods across the gannet's bath; the ring-ship shall bring over
the ocean offerings and tokens of friendship. I know the
people to be firmly disposed toward both enemies and
friends, in every respect above reproach, in the old manner."

Then the shelter of men, Healfdene's son, gave him twelve 1866
further treasures indoors; he told him to go visit his own
people with those offerings in good health, to come again
soon. Then that king of noble lineage, lord of the Scyldings,
kissed the best thane and held him by the neck; the gray-
haired one dropped tears. Old and immensely wise, he had
two expectations—but one stronger, that they would not be
permitted to see each other again, brave men in meeting.

modige on meþle.   Wæs him se man to þon leof
þæt he þone breost-wylm   forberan ne mehte,
ac him on hreþre   hyge-bendum fæst
æfter deorum men   dyrne langað
born wið blode.   Him Beowulf þanan,
guð-rinc gold-wlanc   græs-moldan træd
since hremig;   sæ-genga bad
agend-frean,   se þe on ancre rad.
Þa wæs on gange   gifu Hroðgares
oft geæhted;   þæt wæs an cyning
æghwæs orleahtre,   oþ þæt hine yldo benam
mægenes wynnum,   se þe oft manegum scod.

XXVII

Cwom þa to flode   fela-modigra,
hæg-stealdra heap,   hring-net bæron,
locene leoðo-syrcan.   Land-weard onfand
eft-sið eorla,   swa he ær dyde;
no he mid hearme   of hliðes nosan
gæstas grette,   ac him togeanes rad,
cwæð þæt wil-cuman   Wedera leodum
scaþan scir-hame   to scipe foron.
Þa wæs on sande   sæ-geap naca
hladen here-wædum,   hringed-stefna
mearum ond maðmum;   mæst hlifade
ofer Hroðgares   hord-gestreonum.
He þæm bat-wearde   bunden golde
swurd gesealde,   þæt he syðþan wæs
on meodu-bence   maþme þy weorþra,
yrfe-lafe.   Gewat him on naca
drefan deop wæter,   Dena land ofgeaf.
Þa wæs be mæste   mere-hrægla sum,

The man was so dear to him that he could not suppress the turmoil in his breast, but in his heart, fixed in the manacles of his mind, a close-held yearning for the beloved man
burned in his blood. Beowulf, gold-stately warrior, trod the 1880
grassy earth away from him there, reveling in his rewards; the sea-goer awaited its lord and owner, which rode at anchor. Then on the way Hrothgar's gift was often praised; that was a unique king in all respects without fault, until old age, which has often robbed many, deprived him of the satisfactions of strength.

XXVII

The most courageous band of enterprising young men 1888
came then to the flood bearing ring-nets, linked limb-mail. The land-watch took note of the men's return, as he had before; by no means with insult did he address the visitors from the top of the palisades, but he rode toward them, announced that raiders in gleaming garb, welcome to the people of the Weders, were going to the ship. Then on the sand the sea-vaulted craft was laded with army-gear, the ring-prowed vessel with horses and heirlooms; the mast towered
over Hrothgar's treasury. He gave the boat-watch a sword 1900
bound with gold, so that after that on the mead-bench he was the worthier for that precious thing, that rich legacy. The ship set out onward, stirring up the deep water, left behind the land of the Danes. By the mast there was then a

segl sale fæst; sund-wudu þunede;
no þær weg-flotan wind ofer yðum
siðes getwæfde; sæ-genga for,
fleat famig-heals forð ofer yðe,
bunden-stefna ofer brim-streamas,
þæt hie Geata clifu ongitan meahton,
cuþe næssas; ceol up geþrang,
lyft-geswenced on lande stod.
Hreþe wæs æt holme hyð-weard geara,
se þe ær lange tid leofra manna
fus æt faroðe feor wlatode;
sælde to sande sid-fæþme scip
oncer-bendum fæst, þy læs hym yþa ðrym
wudu wynsuman forwrecan meahte.
Het þa up beran æþelinga gestreon,
frætwe ond fæt-gold; næs him feor þanon
to gesecanne sinces bryttan,
Higelac Hreþling, þær æt ham wunað
selfa mid gesiðum sæ-wealle neah.
Bold wæs betlic, brego-rof cyning,
heah on healle, Hygd swiðe geong,
wis wel-þungen, þeah ðe wintra lyt
under burh-locan gebiden hæbbe,
Hæreþes dohtor; næs hio hnah swa þeah,
ne to gneað gifa Geata leodum,
maþm-gestreona. Mod-þryðo wæg
Fremu, folces cwen, firen' ondrysne;
nænig þæt dorste deor geneþan
swæsra gesiða, nefne sin-frea,
þæt hire an dæges eagum starede,
ac him wæl-bende weotode tealde

certain ocean-vestment, a sail fastened to a rope; the sailing-
wood groaned; there the wind did not hinder the wave-
floater from its voyage over the swells; the sea-walker pro-
ceeded, foamy-necked floated away over the waves,
bound-prowed over the ocean currents, so that they could
make out the Geats' cliffs, familiar headlands; the craft
pressed up, stood weather-beaten on land. At the sea the 1914
harbor-watch was ready at once, who for a long while had
been looking keenly far over the ocean for the esteemed
men; he moored the broad-breasted ship to the sand, firmly
with an anchor line, lest the force of the waves be able to
drive away the delightful wood. He directed then that the
nobles' treasures be brought up, equipment and plated gold;
he did not have far from there to go looking for the distribu-
tor of wealth, Hygelac son of Hrethel, where he himself with
his comrades stayed at home near the sea-scarp.

The building was splendid, the king nobly valiant, exalted 1925
in the hall, Hygd very young, wise, accomplished, though
she had lived few winters within the fortress, Hæreth's
daughter; she was not illiberal, though, nor too sparing of
gifts for the people of the Geats, of inherited treasures.
Fremu, the people's queen, practiced arrogance, terrible
outrages; none so bold of her own intimates, excepting her
great lord, dared venture to set eyes on her by day, but
he could count on hand-tied restraints appointed for him;

hand-gewriþene; hraþe seoþðan wæs
æfter mund-gripe mece geþinged,
þæt hit sceaden-mæl scyran moste,
cwealm-bealu cyðan. Ne bið swylc cwenlic þeaw
idese to efnanne, þeah ðe hio ænlicu sy,
þætte freoðu-webbe feores onsæce
æfter lige-torne leofne mannan.
Huru þæt onhohsnode Hemminges mæg:
ealo-drincende oðer sædan,
þæt hio leod-bealewa læs gefremede,
inwit-niða, syððan ærest wearð
gyfen gold-hroden geongum cempan,
æðelum diore, syððan hio Offan flet
ofer fealone flod be fæder lare
siðe gesohte; ðær hio syððan well
in gum-stole, gode mære,
lif-gesceafta lifigende breac,
hiold heah-lufan wið hæleþa brego,
ealles mon-cynnes mine gefræge
þone selestan bi sæm tweonum,
eormen-cynnes; forðam Offa wæs
geofum ond guðum, gar-cene man,
wide geweorðod, wisdome heold
eðel sinne; þonon Eomer woc
hæleðum to helpe, Hemminges mæg,
nefa Garmundes, niða cræftig.

XXVIII

Gewat him ða se hearda mid his hond-scole
sylf æfter sande sæ-wong tredan,
wide waroðas. Woruld-candel scan,
sigel suðan fus. Hi sið drugon,

shortly thereafter, following his arrest a sword was selected, so that a pattern-welded weapon was allowed to settle it,
make a public execution. Such is not a queenly virtue for a 1940
noblewoman to practice, even if she is peerless, that a peace-weaver should seek the life of a valued man after a feigned offense. To be sure, Hemming's kinsman put a check to that: ale-drinkers told another story, that she committed fewer wrongs against the people, malicious abuses, from the moment she was given, decked with gold, to the young champion, the brave prince, after she went by her father's direction on a trip over the glinting flood to Offa's hall; there afterward while she lived she made very good use of her condition in life on the throne, renowned for goodness, held deep affection for the lord of heroes, the best, I have heard, of all mankind, of the human race, between the oceans. Offa, that spear-bold man, was therefore honored far and wide in gifts and in war, ruled in wisdom his native land; from him arose Eomer as a help to heroes, Hemming's kinsman, Garmund's grandson, strong in strife.

XXVIII

Then the hardy man set out himself with his crew along 1963
the sand, treading the sea-plain, the broad strand. The world-candle gleamed, the sun ardent from the south. They

elne geeodon, to ðæs ðe eorla hleo,
bonan Ongenþeoes burgum in innan,
geongne guð-cyning godne gefrunon
hringas dælan. Higelace wæs
sið Beowulfes snude gecyðed,
þæt ðær on worðig wigendra hleo,
lind-gestealla lifigende cwom,
heaðo-laces hal to hofe gongan.
Hraðe wæs gerymed, swa se rica bebead,
feðe-gestum flet innanweard.
Gesæt þa wið sylfne se ða sæcce genæs,
mæg wið mæge, syððan man-dryhten
þurh hleoðor-cwyde holdne gegrette,
meaglum wordum. Meodu-scencum hwearf
geond þæt heal-reced Hæreðes dohtor,
lufode ða leode, lið-wæge bær
hæleðum to handa. Higelac ongan
sinne geseldan in sele þam hean
fægre fricgcean; hyne fyrwet bræc,
hwylce Sæ-Geata siðas wæron:
"Hu lomp eow on lade, leofa Biowulf,
þa ðu færinga feorr gehogodest
sæcce secean ofer sealt wæter,
hilde to Hiorote? Ac ðu Hroðgare
wid-cuðne wean wihte gebettest,
mærum ðeodne? Ic ðæs mod-ceare
sorh-wylmum seað, siðe ne truwode
leofes mannes; ic ðe lange bæd
þæt ðu þone wæl-gæst wihte ne grette,
lete Suð-Dene sylfe geweorðan
guðe wið Grendel. Gode ic þanc secge
þæs ðe ic ðe gesundne geseon moste."

undertook a trek, went heroically to where they had heard the shelter of men, the slayer of Ongentheo, good young war-king, parceled out rings inside the stronghold. Beowulf's arrival was promptly reported to Hygelac, that the protection of warriors, of shield-wielders had come living into the precinct, walking into court unscathed by war-play. Space was made inside the hall at once for the guests on foot, as the powerful man directed.

The one who had survived those trials sat opposite the 1977
man himself, kinsman with kinsman, after the chieftain had greeted his loyal man with ceremonious speech, hearty words. Hæreth's daughter wound her way through the house with mead-vessels, treated the people kindly, brought drinking-cups to heroes' hands. Hygelac began questioning his comrade pleasantly in the high hall; he was curious what the adventures of the Sea-Geats had been:

"How did things turn out for you on your trip, dear 1987
Beowulf, after you suddenly determined to go look for action far over the salt water, combat at Heorot? Did you at all ease the celebrated suffering of that renowned lord Hrothgar? I seethed with heavy waves of apprehension over that, did not feel assured about the valued man's undertaking; I repeatedly asked you not to approach the butchering spirit at all, let the South-Danes themselves settle their war with Grendel. I give thanks to God that I have been permitted to see you again safe and sound."

Biowulf maðelode, bearn Ecgðioes:
"Þæt is undyrne, dryhten Higelac,
mæru gemeting monegum fira,
hwylc orleg-hwil uncer Grendles
wearð on ðam wange, þær he worna fela
Sige-Scyldingum sorge gefremede,
yrmðe to aldre; ic ðæt eall gewræc,
swa begylpan ne þearf Grendeles maga
ænig ofer eorðan uht-hlem þone,
se ðe lengest leofað laðan cynnes,
fære bifongen. Ic ðær furðum cwom
to ðam hring-sele Hroðgar gretan;
sona me se mæra mago Healfdenes,
syððan he mod-sefan minne cuðe,
wið his sylfes sunu setl getæhte.
Weorod wæs on wynne; ne seah ic widan feorh
under heofones hwealf heal-sittendra
medu-dream maran. Hwilum mæru cwen,
friðu-sibb folca flet eall geondhwearf,
bædde byre geonge; oft hio beah-wriðan
secge sealde ær hie to setle geong.
Hwilum for duguðe dohtor Hroðgares
eorlum on ende ealu-wæge bær,
þa ic Freaware flet-sittende
nemnan hyrde, þær hio nægled sinc
hæleðum sealde. Sio gehaten is,
geong gold-hroden, gladum suna Frodan;
hafað þæs geworden wine Scyldinga,
rices hyrde, ond þæt ræd talað,
þæt he mid ðy wife wæl-fæhða dæl,
sæcca gesette. Oft seldan hwær

Beowulf made a speech, Ecgtheo's offspring: "It is no se- 1999
cret, lord Hygelac, an encounter well known to many peo-
ple, what a time of trial arose for Grendel and me in that
place, where he had always inflicted so very much pain and
misery on the Victory-Scyldings; I avenged all that, so that
no kinsman of Grendel on earth need boast of that uproar
in the dead of night, one who lives longest of that despica-
ble breed in the grasp of peril. There first I came to the ring-
hall to meet Hrothgar; the famous son of Healfdene, after
he understood my intentions, immediately assigned me a
seat by his own sons. The company was in contentment; 2014
never in all my life have I seen under heaven's vault greater
mead-revelry of hall-occupants. From time to time the fa-
mous queen, peace-pledge of peoples, roamed all through
the building, urged on the young men; she often gave a
wrought ring to a warrior before she went to her seat. At
times in the company's presence Hrothgar's daughter con-
veyed ale-cups to the men from end to end, whom I heard
the hall-occupants name Freawaru, where she brought a
studded vessel to heroes. She is promised, young and gold- 2024
bangled, to the gracious son of Froda; the friend of the
Scyldings, caretaker of the realm, has determined and counts
it advisable that by means of that woman he should settle a
sum of fatal feuds and conflicts. As a rule, the murderous

æfter leod-hryre   lytle hwile
bon-gar bugeð,   þeah seo bryd duge.
"Mæg þæs þonne ofþyncan   ðeoden Heaðo-Beardna
ond þegna gehwam   þara leoda
þonne he mid fæmnan   on flett gæð,
dryht-bearn Dena,   duguða biwenede.
On him gladiað   gomelra lafe,
heard ond hring-mæl   Heaða-Beardna gestreon,
þenden hie ðam wæpnum   wealdan moston—

XXVIIII–XXX

"oð ðæt hie forlæddan   to ðam lind-plegan
swæse gesiðas   ond hyra sylfra feorh.
"Þonne cwið æt beore   se ðe beah gesyhð,
eald æsc-wiga,   se ðe eall geman,
gar-cwealm gumena   —him bið grim sefa—
onginneð geomor-mod   geongum cempan
þurh hreðra gehygd   higes cunnian,
wig-bealu weccean,   ond þæt word acwyð:
'Meaht ðu, min wine,   mece gecnawan,
þone þin fæder   to gefeohte bær
under here-griman   hindeman siðe,
dyre iren,   þær hyne Dene slogon,
weoldon wæl-stowe,   syððan Wiðergyld læg,
æfter hæleþa hryre,   hwate Scyldungas?
Nu her þara banena   byre nathwylces
frætwum hremig   on flet gæð,
morðres gylpeð,   ond þone maðþum byreð,
þone þe ðu mid rihte   rædan sceoldest.'
Manað swa ond myndgað   mæla gehwylce
sarum wordum,   oð ðæt sæl cymeð
þæt se fæmnan þegn   fore fæder dædum

spear will rest idle only a little while after a national calamity, no matter how good the bride.

“The lord of the Heatho-Bards and every courtier of that 2032
nation will have the capacity to regret it when he, lordly son of Danes, walks onto the floor with the splendidly attended woman. On him there will gleam the heirlooms of the elders, the hard and ring-patterned treasures that belonged to the Heatho-Bards for as long as they had the power to wield those weapons—

XXVIIII–XXX

“until their close companions led them, and their own 2039
lives, to their ruin at the play of shields.

“Then one who sees the ring, an old ash-fighter who re- 2041
members all, men’s death by spear, will speak over drink—he will have a grim resolve—will begin with complaining intent to probe the thoughts of a young champion through the reflection of innermost feelings, to stir up violent trouble, and he will make this comment: ‘Can you, my friend, recognize the sword that your father carried to battle under masked helmet for the final time, precious iron, where the Danes cut him down, keen Scyldings, got control of the battlefield, when Withergyld fell, after the defeat of heroes? Now the son of one or another of the killers is walking here on this floor, priding himself on the gear, boasts of the murder and
bears the valuables that you by right should possess.’ He will 2057
press him so and remind him at all times with hurtful talk until the occasion will arise when the lady’s attendant for

æfter billes bite   blod-fag swefeð,
ealdres scyldig;   him se oðer þonan
losað lifigende,   con him land geare.
Þonne bioð abrocene   on ba healfe
að-sweord eorla;   syððan Ingelde
weallað wæl-niðas,   ond him wif-lufan
æfter cear-wælmum   colran weorðað.
Þy ic Heaðo-Beardna   hyldo ne telge,
dryht-sibbe dæl   Denum unfæcne,
freondscipe fæstne.
                        "Ic sceal forð sprecan
gen ymbe Grendel,   þæt ðu geare cunne,
sinces brytta,   to hwan syððan wearð
hond-ræs hæleða.   Syððan heofones gim
glad ofer grundas,   gæst yrre cwom,
eatol æfen-grom   user neosan,
ðær we gesunde   sæl weardodon.
Þær wæs Hondscio   hild onsæge,
feorh-bealu fægum;   he fyrmest læg,
gyrded cempa;   him Grendel wearð,
mærum magu-þegne   to muð-bonan,
leofes mannes   lic eall forswealg.
No ðy ær ut ða gen   idel-hende
bona blodig-toð,   bealewa gemyndig,
of ðam gold-sele   gongan wolde,
ac he mægnes rof   min costode,
grapode gearo-folm.   Glof hangode
sid ond syllic,   searo-bendum fæst;
sio wæs orðoncum   eall gegyrwed
deofles cræftum   ond dracan fellum.
He mec þær on innan   unsynnigne,

the father's deeds will sleep painted in blood after the bite of a sword, paying with his life; the other will get away from there alive, knows the region well. Then the sworn oaths of men on both sides will be broken, after violence engulfs Ingeld, and his love for the woman will grow colder after the upsurge of troubles. For that reason I do not regard the fidelity of the Heatho-Bards, their part in the truce with the Danes, as unfeigned, as unshakable friendship.

"I shall say more now about Grendel, so that you will 2069
know for certain, disperser of valuables, what the hand-to-hand combat of heroes afterward came to. After heaven's gem had slipped past the plain of earth, the angry demon, terrible and twilight-fierce, came looking for us where we inhabited the hall unmolested. There combat was fatal to Handsceoh, the attack deadly to the fated man; he fell first, that belted champion; Grendel came to be for him, for that brilliant young thane, his devourer, swallowed the entire body of that cherished man. None the sooner would the bloody-toothed killer, intent on destruction, depart yet empty-handed from the gold-hall, but, assertive of his strength, he made trial of me, the ready-handed one grasped
me. His glove hung wide and weird, fastened with cunning 2085
clasps; it was all ingeniously constructed with the devil's devices and dragon skins. The bold deed-doer wanted to put

dior dæd-fruma gedon wolde
manigra sumne; hyt ne mihte swa,
syððan ic on yrre upprihte astod.
To lang ys to reccenne hu ic ðam leod-sceaðan
yfla gehwylces ondlean forgeald;
þær ic, þeoden min, þine leode
weorðode weorcum. He on weg losade,
lytle hwile lif-wynna breac;
hwæþre him sio swiðre swaðe weardade
hand on Hiorte, ond he hean ðonan,
modes geomor mere-grund gefeoll.
Me þone wæl-ræs wine Scildunga
fættan golde fela leanode,
manegum maðmum, syððan mergen com,
ond we to symble geseten hæfdon.
Þær wæs gidd ond gleo; gomela Scilding,
fela-fricgende feorran rehte;
hwilum hilde-deor hearpan wynne,
gomen-wudu grette, hwilum gyd awræc
soð ond sarlic, hwilum syllic spell
rehte æfter rihte rum-heort cyning;
hwilum eft ongan eldo gebunden,
gomel guð-wiga gioguðe cwiðan,
hilde-strengo; hreðer inne weoll
þonne he wintrum frod worn gemunde.
Swa we þær inne andlangne dæg
niode naman, oð ðæt niht becwom
oðer to yldum. Þa wæs eft hraðe
gearo gyrn-wræce Grendeles modor,
siðode sorh-full; sunu deað fornam,
wig-hete Wedra. Wif unhyre

me all guiltless there within as one of many; it could not turn
out that way after I stood upright in anger. It is too long to
recount how I paid the marauder his due for every wrong;
there, my lord, I brought honor to your people by acting.
He broke away, savored the sweetness of life a little while; 2096
still, his right hand guarded his exit at Heorot, and from
there, abject, broken in spirit, he fell to the bottom of his
lagoon. The friend of the Scyldings rewarded me for that
deadly attack with heaps of plated gold, many valuables, af-
ter morning arrived and we had sat down to banquet. There 2105
was story-telling and entertainment; the ancient Scylding,
well informed, recounted from far back; at times the battle-
bold man touched the lyre with pleasure, the diverting
wood; at times he pursued a tale, true and tragic; at times
the big-hearted king duly offered an unusual account; at
times, in turn, hobbled by age, the old war-maker sang dirges
to his youth, his war powers; the breast welled up inside
him when, made wise by the years, he called many things to
mind. Thus we took our diversions indoors the entire day, 2115
until another night came to mortals. Then in turn Grendel's
mother was ready right off to avenge the injury, came trav-
eling full of grief; death and the enmity of the Weders had

hyre bearn gewræc,   beorn acwealde
ellenlice;   þær wæs Æschere,
frodan fyrn-witan   feorh uðgenge.
Noðer hy hine ne moston,   syððan mergen cwom,
deað-werigne   Denia leode
bronde forbærnan,   ne on bel hladan
leofne mannan;   hio þæt lic ætbær
feondes fæðmum   under firgen-stream.
Þæt wæs Hroðgare   hreowa tornost
þara þe leod-fruman   lange begeate.
Þa se ðeoden mec   ðine life
healsode hreoh-mod   þæt ic on holma geþring
eorlscipe efnde,   ealdre geneðde,
mærðo fremede;   he me mede gehet.
Ic ða ðæs wælmes,   þe is wide cuð,
grimne gryrelicne   grund-hyrde fond;
þær unc hwile wæs   hand gemæne;
holm heolfre weoll,   ond ic heafde becearf
in ðam guð-sele   Grendeles modor
eacnum ecgum;   unsofte þonan
feorh oðferede;   næs ic fæge þa gyt,
ac me eorla hleo   eft gesealde
maðma menigeo,   maga Healfdenes.

XXXI

"Swa se ðeod-kyning   þeawum lyfde;
nealles ic ðam leanum   forloren hæfde,
mægnes mede,   ac he me maðmas geaf,
sunu Healfdenes   on minne sylfes dom;
ða ic ðe, beorn-cyning,   bringan wylle,
estum geywan.   Gen is eall æt ðe
lissa gelong;   ic lyt hafo
heafod-maga   nefne, Hygelac, ðec."

carried off her son. The abominable female avenged her
child, bravely killed a man; there the life was expelled from
Æschere, the wise old counselor. Neither could they, the 2124
Danish people, after morning arrived, cremate the man
weary unto death in a fire, nor lay the beloved one on a pyre;
she carried off the corpse in her fiend's embrace under the
cascading river. For Hrothgar that was the most agonizing
disaster that had befallen the ruler for a long time. The lord,
inflamed in his heart, then implored me by your life that I
should accomplish a manly deed in the tumult of waves, risk
my life, achieve glory; he promised me reward. I found the 2135
grim, ghastly guard of the bottom of the deep, then, who is
widely known; for a time we went hand to hand; the water
surged with gore, and in that war-hall I cut off the head of
Grendel's mother with an immense blade; with no small ef-
fort I extricated my life from that; I was not yet fated to
die, but the protector of men again gave me many valuables,
Healfdene's son.

XXXI

"Thus, the king lived up to his usual ways; by no means 2144
had I forfeited the prize, the reward of my strength, but he
gave me treasures, Healfdene's son, of my own choosing;
I will bring them to you, your majesty, present them with
good will. All favors are still dependent on you; I have few
close relatives, except, Hygelac, for you."

Het ða in beran   eafor-heafod-segn,
heaðo-steapne helm,   hare byrnan,
guð-sweord geatolic,   gyd æfter wræc:
"Me ðis hilde-sceorp   Hroðgar sealde,
snotra fengel;   sume worde het
þæt ic his ærest ðe   est gesægde:
cwæð þæt hyt hæfde   Hiorogar cyning,
leod Scyldunga   lange hwile;
no ðy ær suna sinum   syllan wolde,
hwatum Heorowearde,   þeah he him hold wære,
breost-gewædu.   Bruc ealles well!"
Hyrde ic þæt þam frætwum   feower mearas
lungre, gelice   last weardode,
æppel-fealuwe;   he him est geteah
meara ond maðma.   Swa sceal mæg don,
nealles inwit-net   oðrum bregdon
dyrnum cræfte,   deað renian
hond-gesteallan.   Hygelace wæs
niða heardum   nefa swyðe hold,
ond gehwæðer oðrum   hroþra gemyndig.
Hyrde ic þæt he ðone heals-beah   Hygde gesealde,
wrætlicne wundur-maððum,   ðone þe him Wealhðeo geaf,
ðeodnes dohtor,   þrio wicg somod
swancor ond sadol-beorht;   hyre syððan wæs
æfter beah-ðege   breost geweorðod.
Swa bealdode   bearn Ecgðeowes,
guma guðum cuð,   godum dædum,
dreah æfter dome;   nealles druncne slog
heorð-geneatas;   næs him hreoh sefa,
ac he man-cynnes   mæste cræfte

He then commanded to be brought in the boar's head 2152
emblem, the battle-tall helmet, the hoary mail-shirt, the stately war-sword, and offered an account in the sequel: "Hrothgar gave me this war-gear, the wise monarch; he enjoined that I should first explain to you in a few words his good will: he said that King Heorogar owned it, that man of the Scyldings, for a long while; yet he did not care to give the breast-covering to his son, bold Heoroweard, though he was dear to him. Enjoy all of it well!"

I heard that four matching steeds, dapple-dun, forthwith 2163
brought up the rear of that equipment; he bestowed on him the gift of horses and treasures. That is what a kinsman ought to do, not to weave a web of malice round another with covert craftiness, plot the death of a comrade. To Hygelac, firm in adversity, his nephew was very loyal, and each watched out for the benefit of the other. I heard that he gave the ringed collar to Hygd, that amazing, stately ornament, which Wealhtheo, a lord's daughter, had given him, together with three horses, graceful and bright-saddled; in consequence of receiving the necklace, her breast was afterward ennobled.

Ecgtheo's offspring had thus shown himself brave, a man 2177
renowned in war, by his good deeds, had acted in accordance with honor; by no means did he strike down close associates as they drank; he did not have a fierce temperament, but, brave in battle, with the greatest of human skill he managed

ginfæstan gife þe him God sealde
heold hilde-deor. Hean wæs lange,
swa hyne Geata bearn godne ne tealdon,
ne hyne on medo-bence micles wyrðne
dryhten Wedera gedon wolde;
swyðe wendon þæt he sleac wære,
æðeling unfrom. Edwenden cwom
tir-eadigum menn torna gehwylces.
Het ða eorla hleo in gefetian,
heaðo-rof cyning Hreðles lafe
golde gegyrede; næs mid Geatum ða
sinc-maðþum selra on sweordes had;
þæt he on Biowulfes bearm alegde,
ond him gesealde seofan þusendo,
bold ond brego-stol. Him wæs bam samod
on ðam leodscipe lond gecynde,
eard eðel-riht, oðrum swiðor
side rice þam ðær selra wæs.

Eft þæt geiode ufaran dogrum
hilde-hlæmmum, syððan Hygelac læg,
ond Heardrede hilde-meceas
under bord-hreoðan to bonan wurdon,
ða hyne gesohtan on sige-þeode
hearde hilde-frecan, Heaðo-Scilfingas,
niða genægdan nefan Hererices:
syððan Beowulfe brade rice
on hand gehwearf; he geheold tela
fiftig wintra —wæs ða frod cyning,
eald eþel-weard— oð ðæt an ongan
deorcum nihtum draca ricsian,
se ðe on heaum hofe hord beweotode,

the abundant gifts that God had granted him. For a long time he had been lowly, as the sons of the Geats had not thought him good, nor had the lord of the Weders cared to put him in possession of much on the mead-bench; they had rather thought that he was shiftless, a slack lordling. A reversal of fortune for all his troubles came to the man blessed with glory.

Then the men's protector, the war-strong king, directed that Hrethel's legacy, trimmed with gold, be fetched in; there was not then among the Geats a better jeweled treasure in the form of a sword; he laid it in Beowulf's lap and gave him seven thousand hides of land, a hall and a lord's throne. The land in that nation was proper to both of them together, the country and ancestral domain, the broad rule more especially to one of them, who was superior in rank.

In turn it happened through the tumult of battle in later days, after Hygelac had fallen and war-swords had come to be the killers of Heardred under shield-cover, when hardy war-makers, Battle-Scylfings, came looking for him among the victory-people, violently assailed Hereric's nephew: afterward thc broad realm passed to the hand of Beowulf; he kept it well for fifty winters—the king was then old, an aged guardian of the homeland—until a certain one grew accustomed to holding sway on dark nights, a dragon, which kept watch over a hoard in a high hall, a mighty stone fortress;

stan-beorh stearcne; stig under læg
eldum uncuð. Þær on innan giong
niðða nathwylc, se ðe neh geþrong
hæðnum horde; hond eðe gefeng
searo since fah. Ne he þæt syððan bemað,
þeah ðe he slæpende besyred wurde
þeofes cræfte: þæt sie ðiod onfand,
bu-folc biorna, þæt he gebolgen wæs.

XXXII

Nealles męt gewealdum wyrm-horda cræft,
sylfes willum, se ðe him sare gesceod,
ac for þrea-nedlan þeo nathwylces
hæleða bearna hete-swengeas fleah,
ærnes þearfa, ond ðær inne fealh
secg syn-bysig sona in þa tide,
þæt þær ðam gyste gryre-broga stod;
hwæðre earm-sceapen ealdre neþde,
forht on ferhðe þa hyne se fær begeat,
sinc-fæt sohte. Þær wæs swylcra fela
in ðam eorð-sele ær-gestreona,
swa hy on gear-dagum gumena nathwylc,
eormen-lafe æþelan cynnes,
þanc-hycgende þær gehydde,
deore maðmas. Ealle hie deað fornam
ærran mælum, ond se an ða gen
leoda duguðe, se ðær lengest hwearf,
weard wine-geomor, wende þæs ylcan,
þæt he lytel fæc long-gestreona
brucan moste. Beorh eall gearo
wunode on wonge wæter-yðum neah,
niwe be næsse, nearo-cræftum fæst;

below lay a path unknown to humans. Therein went some- 2214
one or other, who pressed near to the heathen treasury; his
hand easily grasped a work of art trimmed with treasure.
Neither did the dragon conceal it afterward, though sleep-
ing it had been beguiled by the wiles of a thief: the people
discovered, human inhabitants, that it was enraged.

XXXII

The one who had offended it sorely had not willingly 2221
tested the security of serpent-hoards, by his own choice, but
out of dire compulsion the slave of who knows which of the
children of heroes had fled angry blows, a person in need of
shelter, and therein on that occasion the man hemmed in by
hostility penetrated without delay, so that grim terror rose
up in the visitor there; yet the wretch risked his life, fearful
at heart when the peril overtook him, and went after a pre-
cious vessel. There were many such heirlooms in that earth- 2231
hall, as I know not who in days long gone had hidden them
there with a purpose in mind, the immense legacy of a no-
ble race, costly goods. Death had carried off all of them in
former times, and of those people's number he alone who
roamed there longest, a custodian disconsolate over friends,
expected still the same, that he would be allowed to enjoy
that long-accumulated wealth a brief moment. A stronghold
waited all ready on land near the watery waves, a new one
by a headland, designed to be difficult of access; therein the

þær on innon bær eorl-gestreona
hringa hyrde hord-wyrðne dæl,
fættan goldes, fea worda cwæð:
"Heald þu nu, hruse, nu hæleð ne mostan,
eorla æhte. Hwæt, hyt ær on ðe
gode begeaton; guð-deað fornam,
feorh-bealo frecne fyra gehwylcne
leoda minra, þone ðe þis lif ofgeaf;
gesawon sele-dreamas. Nah hwa sweord wege
oððe forð bere fæted wæge,
drync-fæt deore; duguð ellor sceoc.
Sceal se hearda helm hyrsted-golde,
fætum befeallen; feormynd swefað,
þa ðe beado-griman bywan sceoldon;
ge swylce seo here-pad, sio æt hilde gebad
ofer borda gebræc bite irena,
brosnað æfter beorne. Ne mæg byrnan hring
æfter wig-fruman wide feran,
hæleðum be healfe. Næs hearpan wyn,
gomen gleo-beames, ne god hafoc
geond sæl swingeð, ne se swifta mearh
burh-stede beateð. Bealo-cwealm hafað
fela feorh-cynna forð onsended."
Swa giomor-mod giohðo mænde
an æfter eallum, unbliðe hwearf
dæges ond nihtes, oð ðæt deaðes wylm
hran æt heortan. Hord-wynne fond
eald uht-sceaða opene standan,
se ðe byrnende biorgas seceð,
nacod nið-draca, nihtes fleogeð
fyre befangen; hyne fold-buend

collector of the rings brought the portion of the men's treasures worth hoarding, of plated gold, and spoke a few words:

"Hold now, earth, now that heroes cannot, the posses- 2247
sions of men. To be sure, good people once got it from you;
war-death, fearful and deadly peril snatched away every soul
of my people who yielded up this life; they had seen their
pleasant times in the hall. I have none to bear a sword or
bring forth a plated goblet, a precious drinking-vessel; the
troop has rushed abroad. The hard helmet shall be stripped 2255
of gold ornaments and plates; the caretakers are sleeping
who should polish the battle-masks; likewise the army-shirt,
which in warfare endured the bite of iron implements over
crashing shields, decays after its man. The mail-shirt's ring
cannot travel far following a war-maker, by the side of he-
roes. There is no lyre's contentment, no harp's entertain-
ment, neither does a good hawk swoop through the hall, nor
does the swift steed trample the fortress area. Deadly pesti-
lence has dispatched many of the race of the living."

So with downcast spirit he rehearsed his wrongs, one af- 2267
ter all, roamed unhappy day and night, until the tide of death
touched him at the heart. An old vandal of the early hours
found the joy-giving hoard standing open, one that goes
looking for strongholds as it burns, a bare, violent dragon,
flies by night engulfed in flame; those settled on the land

swiðe ondrædað. He gesecean sceall
hearh on hrusan, þær he hæðen gold
warað wintrum frod; ne byð him wihte ðy sel.
Swa se ðeod-sceaða þreo hund wintra
heold on hrusan hord-ærna sum
eacen-cræftig, oð ðæt hyne an abealch
mon on mode; man-dryhtne bær
fæted wæge, frioðo-wære bæd
hlaford sinne. Ða wæs hord rasod,
onboren beaga hord, bene getiðad
fea-sceaftum men; frea sceawode
fira fyrn-geweorc forman siðe.
Þa se wyrm onwoc, wroht wæs geniwad;
stonc ða æfter stane, stearc-heort onfand
feondes fot-last; he to forð gestop
dyrnan cræfte dracan heafde neah.
Swa mæg unfæge eaðe gedigan
wean ond wræc-sið, se ðe waldendes
hyldo gehealdeþ. Hord-weard sohte
georne æfter grunde, wolde guman findan,
þone þe him on sweofote sare geteode;
hat ond hreoh-mod hlæw oft ymbehwearf
ealne utanweardne; ne ðær ænig mon
on þam westenne— hwæðre wiges gefeh,
beadwe weorces; hwilum on beorh æthwearf,
sinc-fæt sohte; he þæt sona onfand,
ðæt hæfde gumena sum goldes gefandod,
heah-gestreona. Hord-weard onbad
earfoðlice oð ðæt æfen cwom;
wæs ða gebolgen beorges hyrde,
wolde se laða lige forgyldan

live in heavy dread of it. Its way is to go looking for a temple
in the earth where, old in winters, it keeps watch over hea-
then gold; it is none the better for that.

So the nation's adversary for three hundred winters held 2278
a certain exceedingly secure hoard-hall underground, until
one human provoked it to anger; he took the plated cup to
his lord, asked his master for clemency. Then the treasure
was explored, the hoard of rings violated, the wretched
man's request granted; his lord beheld for the first time the
ancient handicrafts of men. Then the serpent awoke; con-
flict was brought to life again; it snuffled then across the
stone, strong-hearted, picked up the trace of an enemy; he
had stepped too close in his stealthy cunning near the drag-
on's head. So a man if undoomed can readily survive dis- 2291
tress and a miserable plight who enjoys the ruler's favor. The
hoard's keeper went looking intently over the ground,
wanted to find the human who had caused it offense in its
sleep; hot and with fierce intent, it often circled the bar-
row all around the outside; not a person there in the wilder-
ness—yet it savored conflict, the craft of warfare; at times
it would make its way into the stronghold, went looking for
the precious vessel; it discovered right away that some man
had tampered with the gold, the high treasures. The hoard- 2302
keeper waited impatiently till evening came; then the custo-
dian of the stronghold was furious; the enemy intended to
take satisfaction with flames for the costly vessel. Then day

drinc-fæt dyre.   Þa wæs dæg sceacen
wyrme on willan;   no on wealle læng
bidan wolde,   ac mid bæle for,
fyre gefysed.   Wæs se fruma egeslic
leodum on lande,   swa hyt lungre wearð
on hyra sinc-gifan   sare geendod.

XXXIII

Ða se gæst ongan   gledum spiwan,
beorht hofu bærnan—   bryne-leoma stod
eldum on andan;   no ðær aht cwices
lað lyft-floga   læfan wolde.
Wæs þæs wyrmes wig   wide gesyne,
nearo-fages nið   nean ond feorran,
hu se guð-sceaða   Geata leode
hatode ond hynde;   hord eft gesceat,
dryht-sele dyrnne,   ær dæges hwile.
Hæfde land-wara   lige befangen,
bæle ond bronde;   beorges getruwode,
wiges ond wealles;   him seo wen geleah.
Þa wæs Biowulfe   broga gecyðed
snude to soðe,   þæt his sylfes ham,
bolda selest,   bryne-wylmum mealt,
gif-stol Geata.   Þæt ðam godan wæs
hreow on hreðre,   hyge-sorga mæst;
wende se wisa   þæt he wealdende
ofer ealde riht,   ecean Dryhtne
bitre gebulge;   breost innan weoll
þeostrum geþoncum,   swa him geþywe ne wæs.
Hæfde lig-draca   leoda fæsten,
eal lond utan,   eorð-weard ðone
gledum forgrunden;   him ðæs guð-kyning,

was departed, to the serpent's satisfaction; it did not care to wait longer within the walls, but it set out in a blaze, equipped with fire. The onset was awful for the people in that region, just as it shortly was to be concluded grievously for their treasure-giver.

XXXIII

Then the stranger began to spew flames, to burn up the 2312
bright manors—firelight arose in enmity to humans; the cruel flier did not intend to leave anything there alive. The serpent's devastation was widely apparent, the hatred of the intensely hostile creature near and far, how the warlike destroyer detested and humiliated the Geatish people; it hurried back to the hoard again, the secret troop-hall, before daytime. It had engulfed the inhabitants of the region in flames, burning and conflagration; it trusted in the tumulus, warfare and walls; that expectation played it false.

Then Beowulf was soon informed for certain about the 2324
terror, that his own home, the best of halls, had melted in surging flames, the throne of the Geats. To the good man that was heartfelt distress, the severest mental affliction; the wise one imagined that he had bitterly enraged the ruler contrary to old law, the eternal Lord; dark thoughts welled up in his breast, as was not usual for him. The firedrake had ground down the people's stronghold and all the region surrounding, the earth-fortress, with wildfire; for that the war-

Wedera þioden   wræce leornode.
Heht him þa gewyrcean   wigendra hleo
eall irenne,   eorla dryhten,
wig-bord wrætlic;   wisse he gearwe
þæt him holt-wudu   helpan ne meahte,
lind wið lige.   Sceolde liþend daga,
æþeling ær-god   ende gebidan,
worulde lifes,   ond se wyrm somod,
þeah ðe hord-welan   heolde lange.
Oferhogode ða   hringa fengel
þæt he þone wid-flogan   weorode gesohte,
sidan herge;   no he him þa sæcce ondred,
ne him þæs wyrmes wig   for wiht dyde,
eafoð ond ellen,   forðon he ær fela
nearo neðende   niða gedigde,
hilde-hlemma,   syððan he Hroðgares,
sigor-eadig secg,   sele fælsode,
ond æt guðe forgrap   Grendeles mægum
laðan cynnes.
                    No þæt læsest wæs
hond-gemota   þær mon Hygelac sloh,
syððan Geata cyning   guðe ræsum,
frea-wine folca   Fres-londum on,
Hreðles eafora   hioro-dryncum swealt,
bille gebeaten.   Þonan Biowulf com
sylfes cræfte,   sund-nytte dreah;
hæfde him on earme   ealra þritig
hilde-geatwa   þa he to holme þrong.
Nealles Hetware   hremge þorfton
feðe-wiges,   þe him foran ongean
linde bæron;   lyt eft becwom

king, lord of Weders, taught him a lesson. The shelter of 2337
warriors, lord of men, then ordered that a splendid shield be
made for him all of iron; he knew well that wood of the for-
est could not help him, linden-wood against flames. That
mariner, a nobleman good in the old ways, was to encounter
the end of his days, of life in the world, and the serpent to-
gether with him, though it had held hoarded riches for long.
The procurer of rings then scorned to approach the wide- 2345
flier with a troop, a vast army; he did not dread the encoun-
ter, neither did he have any regard for the serpent's fight-
ing ability, its strength and courage, because, venturing into
tight spots, he had survived many hostilities, war-clashes,
since he, a man endowed with triumphs, had purged Hroth-
gar's hall and in combat had crushed the kin of the hated
family of Grendel.

It was not the least of those hand-to-hand encounters in 2354
which Hygelac was killed, after the king of the Geats, lord
and friend of peoples, in a war-raid in Frisia, Hrethel's heir,
died under blood-drinking swords, beaten by blades. Beowulf
got away from there under his own power, made use of his
swimming ability. On his arm he had, in all, thirty sets of
armor when he forced his way to the sea. The Hetware had
no need to exult in combat on foot, who carried before
them linden shields; few came back from that warrior to

fram þam hild-frecan   hames niosan.
Oferswam ða sioleða bigong   sunu Ecgðeowes,
earm an-haga   eft to leodum;
þær him Hygd gebead   hord ond rice,
beagas ond brego-stol;   bearne ne truwode,
þæt he wið æl-fylcum   eþel-stolas
healdan cuðe,   ða wæs Hygelac dead.
No ðy ær fea-sceafte   findan meahton
æt ðam æðelinge   ænige ðinga
þæt he Heardrede   hlaford wære,
oððe þone cynedom   ciosan wolde;
hwæðre he him on folce   freond-larum heold,
estum mid are,   oð ðæt he yldra wearð,
Weder-Geatum weold.
                                        Hyne wræc-mæcgas
ofer sæ sohtan,   suna Ohteres;
hæfdon hy forhealden   helm Scylfinga,
þone selestan   sæ-cyninga
þara ðe in Swio-rice   sinc brytnade,
mærne þeoden.   Him þæt to mearce wearð:
he þær for feorme   feorh-wunde hleat,
sweordes swengum,   sunu Hygelaces,
ond him eft gewat   Ongenðioes bearn
hames niosan   syððan Heardred læg,
let ðone brego-stol   Biowulf healdan,
Geatum wealdan;   þæt wæs god cyning.

XXXIIII

Se ðæs leod-hryres   lean gemunde
uferan dogrum,   Eadgilse wearð
fea-sceaftum freond;   folce gestepte
ofer sæ side   sunu Ohteres,

visit their home. Ecgtheo's son then swam over the expanse 2367
of ocean, a pitiable solitary back to his people; there Hygd offered him treasury and rule, rings and throne; she did not have confidence in her child that he would know how to hold his native seats against foreigners, now that Hygelac was dead. The dispossessed could not by any means persuade the noble to be Heardred's lord or to consent to accept the kingdom, but he supported him among the people with benign instruction, graciously with good will, until he grew older and ruled the Weder-Geats.

Exiles came looking for him over the sea, the sons of 2379
Ohthere. They had renounced the helm of the Scylfings, the best sea-king who distributed wealth in the kingdom of the Swedes, a renowned lord. That was the ultimate boundary for him: for his hospitality he earned by lot a mortal wound by sword-strokes, Hygelac's son, and the offspring of Ongentheo set out again to visit his home after Heardred lay dead, let Beowulf hold the throne, rule the Geats; that was a good king.

XXXIIII

He kept in mind repayment for that national calamity 2391
in later days, became a friend to destitute Eadgils; with an army he supported Ohthere's son over the broad sea with

wigum ond wæpnum; he gewræc syððan
cealdum cear-siðum, cyning ealdre bineat.
Swa he niða gehwane genesen hæfde,
sliðra geslyhta, sunu Ecgðiowes,
ellen-weorca, oð ðone anne dæg
þe he wið þam wyrme gewegan sceolde.
Gewat þa twelfa sum torne gebolgen
dryhten Geata dracan sceawian;
hæfde þa gefrunen hwanan sio fæhð aras,
bealo-nið biorna; him to bearme cwom
maðþum-fæt mære þurh ðæs meldan hond.
Se wæs on ðam ðreate þreotteoða secg,
se ðæs orleges or onstealde,
hæft hyge-giomor, sceolde hean ðonon
wong wisian. He ofer willan giong
to ðæs ðe he eorð-sele anne wisse,
hlæw under hrusan holm-wylme neh,
yð-gewinne; se wæs innan full
wrætta ond wira. Weard unhiore,
gearo guð-freca gold-maðmas heold
eald under eorðan; næs þæt yðe ceap
to gegangenne gumena ænigum.
Gesæt ða on næsse nið-heard cyning
þenden hælo abead heorð-geneatum,
gold-wine Geata. Him wæs geomor sefa,
wæfre ond wæl-fus, wyrd ungemete neah,
se ðone gomelan gretan sceolde,
secean sawle hord, sundur gedælan
lif wið lice; no þon lange wæs
feorh æþelinges flæsce bewunden.
Biowulf maþelade, bearn Ecgðeowes:

warriors and weapons; after that he avenged those cold, lamentable exploits, deprived the king of life.

So he had passed through every trouble, every dire con- 2397
flict, feat of courage, Ecgtheo's son, until that one day when
he was to contend with the serpent. As one of twelve men
the lord of the Geats, swollen with anger, set out then to see
the dragon; now he had learned from what the vendetta had
arisen, fatal violence against men; the notorious precious
vessel had come into his possession through the hand of the
informer. In that group he was the thirteenth man, the one
who had caused the origin of that conflict, a despondent
captive, abject, had to show the way from there to the place.
He went against his will to where he knew there was a cer- 2409
tain earth-hall, a cavern under the ground near the sea-
currents, the tumult of waves; inside, it was full of orna-
ments and metal bands. An unsavory warden, an alert
war-maker watched over the golden treasures, that old one
under the earth; that was not an easy bargain for any man to
realize. The king hardy in adversity then sat on the headland
while the gold-friend of Geats saluted his close comrades.
His mood was mournful, restless and ready for death, his 2419
destiny incalculably near, he who was to face the ancient
one, go after its soul's hoard, divide life from body; the
prince's soul was not to be clothed in flesh very long. Beowulf
spoke, Ecgtheo's offspring:

"Fela ic on giogoðe guð-ræsa genæs,
orleg-hwila; ic þæt eall gemon.
Ic wæs syfan-wintre þa mec sinca baldor,
frea-wine folca æt minum fæder genam;
heold mec ond hæfde Hreðel cyning,
geaf me sinc ond symbel, sibbe gemunde;
næs ic him to life laðra owihte,
beorn in burgum, þonne his bearna hwylc,
Herebeald ond Hæðcyn oððe Hygelac min.
Wæs þam yldestan ungedefelice
mæges dædum morþor-bed stred,
syððan hyne Hæðcyn of horn-bogan,
his frea-wine flane geswencte,
miste mercelses ond his mæg ofscet,
broðor oðerne blodigan gare.
Þæt wæs feohleas gefeoht, fyrenum gesyngad,
hreðre hyge-meðe; sceolde hwæðre swa þeah
æðeling unwrecen ealdres linnan.
"Swa bið geomorlic gomelum ceorle
to gebidanne, þæt his byre ride
giong on galgan. Þonne he gyd wrece,
sarigne sang, þonne his sunu hangað
hrefne to hroðre, ond he him helpe ne mæg
eald ond infrod ænige gefremman,
symble bið gemyndgad morna gehwylce
eaforan ellor-sið; oðres ne gymeð
to gebidanne burgum in innan
yrfe-weardas, þonne se an hafað
þurh deaðes nyd dæda gefondad.
Gesyhð sorh-cearig on his suna bure
win-sele westne, windge reste,

"I survived many military attacks in my youth, periods of 2426
combat; I remember all that. I was seven winters old when
my ruler of treasures, lord and friend of peoples, got me
from my father; King Hrethel kept me and watched over
me, gave me valuables and hospitality, kept our kinship in
mind; as a soldier in his strongholds I was never in any way
less dear to him than his children, Herebeald and Hæthcyn
or my Hygelac. For the eldest a bed of murder was spread 2435
unfittingly by the actions of his kinsman, when Hæthcyn
struck down his lord and friend with an arrow from a horn-
bow, missed the mark and shot his kinsman, one brother the
other, with a bloody dart. That was an inexpiable killing, a
wrong cruelly done, wearying to contemplate at heart; the
prince nonetheless had to lose his life unavenged.

"It is similarly grievous for an old man to live to see his 2444
young boy mount the gallows. Then he may tell a tale, a song
full of pain, when his son hangs to the raven's delight, and
he, old and decrepit, can offer him no help, is continually
reminded every morning of his offspring's departure; he has
no thought of living to see another heir among the manors,
when the one has had his fill of deeds through death's compulsion. He will look sadly at his son's chamber, the desolate
wine-hall, wind-swept place of rest, dreary, emptied; the rid-

reotge berofene; ridend swefað,
hæleð in hoðman; nis þær hearpan sweg,
gomen in geardum, swylce ðær iu wæron.

XXXV

"Gewiteð þonne on sealman, sorh-leoð gæleð
an æfter anum; þuhte him eall to rum,
wongas ond wic-stede.
"Swa Wedra helm
æfter Herebealde heortan sorge
weallinde wæg; wihte ne meahte
on ðam feorh-bonan fæghðe gebetan;
no ðy ær he þone heaðo-rinc hatian ne meahte
laðum dædum, þeah him leof ne wæs.
He ða mid þære sorhge, þe him sio sar belamp,
gum-dream ofgeaf, Godes leoht geceas;
eaferum læfde, swa deð eadig mon,
lond ond leod-byrig, þa he of life gewat.
"Þa wæs synn ond sacu Sweona ond Geata
ofer wid wæter wroht gemæne,
here-nið hearda, syððan Hreðel swealt,
oð ðe him Ongenðeowes eaferan wæran
frome fyrd-hwate, freode ne woldon
ofer heafo healdan, ac ymb Hreosna Beorh
eatolne inwit-scear oft gefremedon.
Þæt mæg-wine mine gewræcan,
fæhðe ond fyrene, swa hyt gefræge wæs,
þeah ðe oðer his ealdre gebohte,
heardan ceape: Hæðcynne wearð,
Geata dryhtne guð onsæge.
Þa ic on morgne gefrægn mæg oðerne
billes ecgum on bonan stælan,

ers sleep, heroes in concealment; there is no lyre's music there, entertainments in the household such as once had been.

XXXV

"He will go then to his bedstead, will chant dirges, one 2460
after another; it would seem to him all too spacious, grounds
and residence.

"Similarly, the helm of the Weders felt surging, heartfelt 2462
sorrow after Herebeald; he could by no means take satisfac-
tion for the offense on the killer, any more than he could
hate the warrior for the hated deed, though he was not dear
to him. Then with that grief he whom the pain had encom-
passed gave up human joys, chose God's light; to his sons he
left, as a prosperous man does, land and stronghold, when
he departed from life.

"Then there was incursion and strife of Swedes and Geats 2472
across the broad water, a quarrel between them, after Hre-
thel had died, until Ongentheo's heirs were full of vigor and
keen for campaigning, would keep no friendship over the
sea but often worked terrible, malicious slaughter around
the Hill of the Hreosas. My close kinsmen avenged that, the
feuding and the violence, as was well known, though one of
them paid with his life, a hard bargain: the war was fatal to
Hæthcyn, lord of Geats. Then, as I have heard, on the mor- 2484
row one kinsman exacted on the killer vengeance for the

þær Ongenþeow Eofores niosað;
guð-helm toglad, gomela Scylfing
hreas hilde-blac; hond gemunde
fæhðo genoge, feorh-sweng ne ofteah.
"Ic him þa maðmas þe he me sealde
geald æt guðe, swa me gifeðe wæs
leohtan sweorde; he me lond forgeaf,
eard eðel-wyn. Næs him ænig þearf
þæt he to Gifðum oððe to Gar-Denum
oððe in Swio-rice secean þurfe
wyrsan wig-frecan, weorðe gecypan;
symle ic him on feðan beforan wolde,
ana on orde, ond swa to aldre sceall
sæcce fremman, þenden þis sweord þolað
þæt mec ær ond sið oft gelæste,
syððan ic for dugeðum Dæghrefne wearð
to hand-bonan, Huga cempan—
nalles he ða frætwe Fres-cyninge,
breost-weorðunge bringan moste,
ac in campe gecrong cumbles hyrde,
æþeling on elne; ne wæs ecg bona,
ac him hilde-grap heortan wylmas,
ban-hus gebræc. Nu sceall billes ecg,
hond ond heard sweord ymb hord wigan."
Beowulf maðelode, beot-wordum spræc
niehstan siðe: "Ic geneðde fela
guða on geogoðe; gyt ic wylle,
frod folces weard fæhðe secan,
mærðu fremman, gif mec se man-sceaða
of eorð-sele ut geseceð."

other with the edge of a sword, where Ongentheo paid a visit to Eofor; his war-helmet was shattered, the ancient Scylfing collapsed battle-ashen; the hand remembered offenses enough, did not withhold the deathblow.

"I repaid in battle the treasures he had given me, such was my good fortune with a bright sword; he gave me land, estate and a desirable abode. He had no need to look to the Gifthas or to the Spear-Danes or in Sweden for an inferior war-maker, hire him for a price; I intended always to be to the fore of him in the ranks, alone in the vanguard, and thus I shall always pursue a conflict, as long as this sword holds out which has often supported me early and late, after I came to be, in the presence of the armies, hand-killer of Dæghrefn, champion of the Hugas—he was by no means permitted to bring those trappings, that breast-ornament, to the Frisian king, but the keeper of the ensign succumbed on the battlefield, a prince in a show of bravery; a blade was not the cause of his death, but a battle-grasp broke the beat of his heart, shattered his bone-house. Now shall weapon's edge, hand and hard sword, do battle for the hoard."

Beowulf made a speech, spoke a solemn vow for the last time: "I survived many conflicts in my youth; old guardian of the nation, I intend still to pursue a feud, accomplish a feat, if the vicious harm-doer will come to face me out of the earth-hall."

Gegrette ða gumena gehwylcne,
hwate helm-berend hindeman siðe,
swæse gesiðas: "Nolde ic sweord beran,
wæpen to wyrme, gif ic wiste hu
wið ðam aglæcean elles meahte
gylpe wiðgripan, swa ic gio wið Grendle dyde;
ac ic ðær heaðu-fyres hates wene,
oreðes ond attres; forðon ic me on hafu
bord ond byrnan. Nelle ic beorges weard
oferfleon fotes trem, ac unc feohte sceal
weorðan æt wealle, swa unc wyrd geteoð
metod manna gehwæs. Ic eom on mode from,
þæt ic wið þone guð-flogan gylp ofersitte.
Gebide ge on beorge byrnum werede,
secgas on searwum, hwæðer sel mæge
æfter wæl-ræse wunde gedygan
uncer twega. Nis þæt eower sið,
ne gemet mannes nefne min anes,
þæt he wið aglæcean eofoðo dæle,
eorlscype efne. Ic mid elne sceall
gold gegangan, oððe guð nimeð,
feorh-bealu frecne frean eowerne."
Aras ða bi ronde rof oretta,
heard under helme, hioro-sercean bær
under stan-cleofu, strengo getruwode
anes mannes; ne bið swylc earges sið!
Geseah ða be wealle se ðe worna fela
gum-cystum god guða gedigde,
hilde-hlemma, þonne hnitan feðan,
stondan stan-bogan, stream ut þonan
brecan of beorge; wæs þære burnan wælm

Then he addressed each of the men, keen helmet-wearers, 2516
for the final time, his personal comrades: "I would not bear
a sword, a weapon against the reptile, if I knew how I could
otherwise honorably grapple with the troublemaker, as I
once did with Grendel; but I expect hot war-flame there,
exhalations and poison; therefore I have on me shield and
mail-shirt. I do not intend to flee a foot's pace from the
guardian of the barrow, but it will turn out for us in a fight by
the wall as the ruler of humanity allots destiny to us. I am
determined in my mind, so that I will forgo a vow against
the war-flier. Wait on the barrow equipped with mail-shirts, 2529
men in armor, to see which of the two of us can better sur-
vive his wounds after the deadly onslaught. It is not your
undertaking, nor is it in the ability of anyone but me alone
that he pit his strength against the troublemaker, do a manly
deed. By valor I shall gain the gold, or warfare, violent, mor-
tal peril, will carry off your lord."

The bold warrior then rose with his shield by his side, 2538
hardy under helmet, bore battle-shirt under the stony preci-
pice, trusted in the strength of one person; such is not a
coward's venture! He who, good in many qualities, had sur-
vived a great many wars, battle-tumults, when infantry
clashed, then saw arches of stone standing in the wall, a
stream gushing out of them from the barrow; the brook's

heaðo-fyrum hat,   ne meahte horde neah
unbyrnende   ænige hwile
deop gedygan   for dracan lege.
Let ða of breostum,   ða he gebolgen wæs,
Weder-Geata leod   word ut faran,
stearc-heort styrmde;   stefn in becom
heaðo-torht hlynnan   under harne stan.
Hete wæs onhrered,   hord-weard oncniow
mannes reorde;   næs ðær mara fyrst
freode to friclan.   From ærest cwom
oruð aglæcean   ut of stane,
hat hilde-swat;   hruse dynede.
Biorn under beorge   bord-rand onswaf
wið ðam gryre-gieste,   Geata dryhten;
ða wæs hring-bogan   heorte gefysed
sæcce to seceanne.   Sweord ær gebræd
god guð-cyning,   gomele lafe,
ecgum unslaw;   æghwæðrum wæs
bealo-hycgendra   broga fram oðrum.
Stið-mod gestod   wið steapne rond
winia bealdor,   ða se wyrm gebeah
snude tosomne;   he on searwum bad.
Gewat ða byrnende   gebogen scriðan,
to gescipe scyndan.   Scyld wel gebearg
life ond lice   læssan hwile
mærum þeodne   þoṇne his myne sohte,
ðær he þy fyrste   forman dogore
wealdan moste   swa him wyrd ne gescraf
hreð æt hilde.   Hond up abræd
Geata dryhten,   gryre-fahne sloh
incge-lafe,   þæt sio ecg gewac

current was hot with war-flames; it could not endure for any amount of time without flaming, deep inside near the hoard, on account of the dragon's fire. Now that he was enraged, 2550
the man of the Weder-Geats let words escape from his breast, thundered with a strong heart; his voice came in roaring battle-loud under hoary stone. Hatred was stirred up; the hoard-keeper recognized the voice of a man; there was no more time for suing for peace. First the breath of the troublemaker came out of the stone, hot war-flame; the earth resounded. Below the barrow the man swung his shield 2559
to face the dreadful stranger, lord of Geats; then the coiled one was incited in its heart to look for a fight. The good war-king had already drawn his sword, an ancient legacy not blunt of edge; for each of them, intent on aggression, there was peril from the other. The firm-minded leader of friends stood against the tall shield when the serpent suddenly coiled; he stood fast in his armor. Then the coiled burner 2569
started out slithering, rushing to its fate. The shield protected life and body of the famous lord well a lesser while than his wish would have been if on that occasion he were for the first time to have been permitted to prevail without fate having decreed triumph for him in battle. The lord of Geats lifted his hand, struck the fearsomely marked one with the resplendent heirloom, with the result that the

brun on bane,   bat unswiðor
þonne his ðiod-cyning   þearfe hæfde
bysigum gebæded.   Þa wæs beorges weard
æfter heaðu-swenge   on hreoum mode,
wearp wæl-fyre;   wide sprungon
hilde-leoman.   Hreð-sigora ne gealp
gold-wine Geata;   guð-bill geswac
nacod æt niðe,   swa hyt no sceolde,
iren ær-god.   Ne wæs þæt eðe sið,
þæt se mæra   maga Ecgðeowes
grund-wong þone   ofgyfan wolde;
sceolde ofer willan   wic eardian
elles hwergen,   swa sceal æghwylc mon
alætan læn-dagas.
Næs ða long to ðon
þæt ða aglæcean   hy eft gemetton.
Hyrte hyne hord-weard,   hreðer æðme weoll,
niwan stefne;   nearo ðrowode
fyre befongen   se ðe ær folce weold.
Nealles him on heape   hand-gesteallan,
æðelinga bearn   ymbe gestodon
hilde-cystum,   ac hy on holt bugon,
ealdre burgan.   Hiora in anum weoll
sefa wið sorgum;   sibb' æfre ne mæg
wiht onwendan   þam ðe wel þenceð.

XXXVI

Wiglaf wæs haten,   Weoxstanes sunu,
leoflic lind-wiga,   leod Scylfinga,
mæg Ælfheres;   geseah his mon-dryhten
under here-griman   hat þrowian.
Gemunde ða ða are   þe he him ær forgeaf,

glinting blade failed against bone, bit less strongly than
the king of nations had need of it, oppressed by troubles.
The warden of the barrow was then in a fierce temper af- 2580
ter that war-thrust, spewed deadly flame; the battle-lights
sprang far and wide. The gold-friend of the Geats boasted of
no glorious victories; his war-weapon had failed, naked in
combat, as it should not have, that iron good through the
ages. That was no easy undertaking, that the renowned son
of Ecgtheo would give up the battlefield; against his will he
was to take lodging elsewhere, just as every person is to let
go of these fleeting days.

It was not long then till the troublemakers met again. 2591
The hoard-guard took heart, its breast swelling with breath
once again. Engulfed in flames, he who had ruled the na-
tion suffered dire straits. His close comrades, sons of nobles,
did not stand around him in a troop valorously, but they re-
treated to the wood to save their lives. The heart in one of
them seethed with regret; nothing can ever alter kinship ties
for one who is right-minded.

XXXVI

He was called Wiglaf, Wihstan's son, an admirable shield- 2602
warrior, a man of the Scylfings, kinsman of Ælfhere; he saw
his lord enduring the heat under masked helmet. He recalled 2606
then the favors that he had bestowed on him, the well-

wic-stede weligne Wægmundinga,
folc-rihta gehwylc, swa his fæder ahte;
ne mihte ða forhabban, hond rond gefeng,
geolwe linde, gomel swyrd geteah;
þæt wæs mid eldum Eanmundes laf,
suna Ohteres; þam æt sæcce wearð,
wræccan wineleasum Weohstan bana
meces ecgum, ond his magum ætbær
brun-fagne helm, hringde byrnan,
eald-sweord etonisc; þæt him Onela forgeaf,
his gædelinges guð-gewædu,
fyrd-searo fuslic— no ymbe ða fæhðe spræc,
þeah ðe he his broðor bearn abredwade.
He frætwe geheold fela missera,
bill ond byrnan, oð ðæt his byre mihte
eorlscipe efnan swa his ær-fæder;
geaf him ða mid Geatum guð-gewæda
æghwæs unrim þa he of ealdre gewat
frod on forð-weg. Þa wæs forma sið
geongan cempan þæt he guðe ræs
mid his freo-dryhtne fremman sceolde.
Ne gemealt him se mod-sefa, ne his mæges laf
gewac æt wige; þæt se wyrm onfand,
syððan hie togædre gegan hæfdon.
  Wiglaf maðelode, word-rihta fela
sægde gesiðum— him wæs sefa geomor:
"Ic ðæt mæl geman, þær we medu þegun,
þonne we geheton ussum hlaforde
in bior-sele, ðe us ðas beagas geaf,
þæt we him ða guð-getawa gyldan woldon
gif him þyslicu þearf gelumpe,

appointed residence of the Wægmundings, all their ances-
tral rights such as his father had had; he could not then for-
bear: his hand gripped the boss, the yellow linden-wood,
drew his ancient sword; among men it was the legacy of Ean-
mund, Ohthere's son; in combat Wihstan had come to be
the killer of that friendless exile with the blade of a sword,
and to his family he conveyed the glinting, patterned hel-
met, the ringed mail, the sword of ogreish origin; Onela
turned that over to him, his relation's battle-dress, ready
war-tackle—he said nothing about hostility, though he had
butchered his brother's son. He kept that equipment many 2620
seasons, sword and mail-shirt, until his boy could accom-
plish manly deeds just like his forefather; then among the
Geats he gave him a boundless bounty of every kind of
battle-garment when he departed from life, aged on his way
forth. That was the first time for the young champion that
he was to undertake a military attack with his noble lord.
His spirit did not melt, nor did his kinsman's legacy fail in
action; the serpent found that out after they had come to-
gether.

Wiglaf made a speech, addressed quite a bit of instruc- 2631
tion to his companions—his mood was rueful: "I recall the
occasion, in the place where we were having mead, when in
the drinking-hall we swore to our lord, who gave us these
rings, that we would repay him for the war-equipment if

helmas ond heard sweord. Ðe he usic on herge geceas
to ðyssum siðfate sylfes willum,
onmunde usic mærða, ond me þas maðmas geaf,
þe he usic gar-wigend gode tealde,
hwate helm-berend— þeah ðe hlaford us
þis ellen-weorc ana aðohte
to gefremmanne, folces hyrde,
forðam he manna mæst mærða gefremede,
dæda dollicra. Nu is se dæg cumen
þæt ure man-dryhten mægenes behofað
godra guð-rinca; wutun gongan to,
helpan hild-fruman þenden hyt sy,
gled-egesa grim. God wat on mec
þæt me is micle leofre þæt minne lic-haman
mid minne gold-gyfan gled fæðmie.
Ne þynceð me gerysne þæt we rondas beren
eft to earde, nemne we æror mægen
fane gefyllan, feorh ealgian
Wedra ðeodnes. Ic wat geare,
þæt næron eald-gewyrht þæt he ana scyle
Geata duguðe gnorn þrowian,
gesigan æt sæcce; urum sceal sweord ond helm,
byrne ond beadu-scrud bam gemæne."
Wod þa þurh þone wæl-rec, wig-heafolan bær
frean on fultum, fea worda cwæð:
"Leofa Biowulf, læst eall tela,
swa ðu on geoguð-feore geara gecwæde
þæt ðu ne alæte be ðe lifigendum
dom gedreosan; scealt nu dædum rof,
æðeling an-hydig, ealle mægene
feorh ealgian; ic ðe fullæstu."

such need arose for him, helmets and hard swords. It is for
this reason he chose us of his own will from among his army
for this undertaking, considered us worthy of the honor, and
gave me these valuables: that he considered us good spear-
warriors, bold men in helmets—though this lord intended
to perform for us this work of valor alone, custodian of the
nation, because of all men he had accomplished the great-
est feats of glory, audacious deeds. Now the day has arrived 2646
when our lord has need of a force of good soldiers; let's go to
him, help our general now that there is this heat, this grim,
frightful conflagration. God is my witness that it is much
my preference that the flames engulf my body along with
my gold-giver. I think it unseemly that we bear shields back
home unless we can first fell the foe, preserve the life of the
lord of Weders. I know for a certainty that it would not be
just deserts for past accomplishments that he should bear
up alone under the anguish of the Geatish host, sink in bat-
tle; we two shall have sword and helmet, mail-shirt and ar-
mor in common."

He advanced then through the deadly fumes, brought his 2661
battle-crest to the assistance of his lord, spoke a few words:
"Beowulf, friend, bear all of it out well, as you said long ago
in the day of your youth that you would not let your glory
dim while you were alive. Now brave in accomplishments,
unwavering prince, you ought to defend your life with all
your strength; I shall support you."

Æfter ðam wordum   wyrm yrre cwom,
atol inwit-gæst   oðre siðe
fyr-wylmum fah   fionda niosian,
laðra manna.   Lig yðum for;
born bord wið rond.   Byrne ne meahte
geongum garwigan   geoce gefremman,
ac se maga geonga   under his mæges scyld
elne geeode,   þa his agen wæs
gledum forgrunden.   Þa gen guð-cyning
mod gemunde,   mægen-strengo sloh
hilde-bille,   þæt hyt on heafolan stod
niþe genyded;   Nægling forbærst,
geswac æt sæcce   sweord Biowulfes
gomol ond græg-mæl.   Him þæt gifeðe ne wæs
þæt him irenna   ecge mihton
helpan æt hilde;   wæs sio hond to strong,
se ðe meca gehwane   mine gefræge
swenge ofersohte   þonne he to sæcce bær
wæpen wundum heard;   næs him wihte ðe sel.
Þa wæs þeod-sceaða   þriddan siðe,
frecne fyr-draca   fæhða gemyndig,
ræsde on ðone rofan,   þa him rum ageald,
hat ond heaðo-grim,   heals ealne ymbefeng
biteran banum.   He geblodegod wearð
sawul-driore;   swat yðum weoll.

XXXVII

Ða ic æt þearfe gefrægn   þeod-cyninges
andlongne eorl   ellen cyðan,
cræft ond cenðu,   swa him gecynde wæs.
Ne hedde he þæs heafolan,   ac sio hand gebarn
modiges mannes   þær he his mæges healp,

After these words, a second time the serpent came wrath- 2669
ful, the terrible, malicious stranger wrapped in surging
flames, attacking its enemies, the hated humans. Fire came
forth in waves; his shield burned down to the boss. His mail-
shirt could not afford the young spear-warrior protection,
but the young man went briskly under his kinsman's shield,
now that his own was reduced to cinders. The war-king still
kept up his courage, thrust the war-sword with mighty force,
so that it stood at the head, impelled violently; Nægling
shattered, Beowulf's sword failed in combat, old and gray-
marked. It was not allowed him that the blade of any weapon 2682
of iron could help him in battle; the hand was too strong
that, I have heard, overtaxed with its stroke every sword
whenever it bore to battle a weapon hardened in wounds; he
was none the better for it.

For the third time, then, the people's scourge was intent 2688
on feuding, rushed upon the hero when the opportunity
permitted, hot and intent on combat, enclosed his entire
neck in its bitter fangs. He was smeared with his life's blood;
the gore welled up in waves.

XXXVII

I have heard the king's man by his side then showed his 2694
valor, strength and keenness, as was bred in him. He paid no
heed to the head, but the hand of the courageous man was

þæt he þone nið-gæst   nioðor hwene sloh,
secg on searwum,   þæt ðæt sweord gedeaf
fah ond fæted,   þæt ðæt fyr ongon
sweðrian syððan.   Þa gen sylf cyning
geweold his gewitte,   wæll-seaxe gebræd
biter ond beadu-scearp,   þæt he on byrnan wæg;
forwrat Wedra helm   wyrm on middan.
Feond gefyldan   —ferh ellen wræc—
ond hi hyne þa begen   abroten hæfdon,
sib-æðelingas;   swylc sceolde secg wesan,
þegn æt ðearfe!   Þæt ðam þeodne wæs
siðast sige-hwila   sylfes dædum,
worlde geweorces.
                    Ða sio wund ongon,
þe him se eorð-draca   ær geworhte,
swelan ond swellan;   he þæt sona onfand,
þæt him on breostum   bealo-niðe weoll
attor on innan.   Ða se æðeling giong,
þæt he bi wealle   wis-hycgende
gesæt on sesse;   seah on enta geweorc,
hu ða stan-bogan   stapulum fæste
ece eorð-reced   innan healde.
Hyne þa mid handa   heoro-dreorigne,
þeoden mærne,   þegn ungemete till,
wine-dryhten his   wætere gelafede
hilde sædne   ond his helm onspeon.
   Biowulf maþelode—   he ofer benne spræc,
wunde wæl-bleate;   wisse he gearwe
þæt he dæg-hwila   gedrogen hæfde,
eorðan wynne;   ða wæs eall sceacen
dogor-gerimes,   deað ungemete neah:

burnt when he assisted his kinsman, in that he struck the
violent stranger rather lower, that man in armor, so that the
patterned and plated sword penetrated, so that the flames
began to diminish after that. The king himself was still con- 2702
scious then, drew his deadly long-knife, bitter and battle-
sharp, which he wore on his mail-shirt; the helm of the Wed-
ers carved the reptile through the middle. They had felled
the enemy—bravery drove out life—and then they had both
cut it down, those related nobles; such ought a man to do, a
thane in time of need! It was for that lord the final moment
of victory among his own deeds, of his worldly works.

Then the wound that the earth-dragon had dealt him be- 2711
gan to burn and swell; he discovered straight away that poi-
son was seething with insidious effect inside his breast. The
sagacious prince went then to sit on a seat by the wall, to
gaze at the work of giants, how stone arches affixed to pil-
lars supported the ageless earth-hall inside. Then with his
hands the unutterably good attendant refreshed him with
water, bloodied as he was, that famous chieftain, his friend
and lord, sated with warfare, and unclasped his helmet.

Beowulf addressed him—he spoke, wounded as he was 2724
with a pitiably mortal wound; he knew for certain he had
lived out his days, his earthly joys; then the entire sum of his
hours had vanished, and death was immeasurably near:

"Nu ic suna minum   syllan wolde
guð-gewædu,   þær me gifeðe swa
ænig yrfe-weard   æfter wurde
lice gelenge.   Ic ðas leode heold
fiftig wintra;   næs se folc-cyning,
ymbe-sittendra   ænig ðara
þe mec guð-winum   gretan dorste,
egesan ðeon.   Ic on earde bad
mæl-gesceafta,   heold min tela,
ne sohte searo-niðas,   ne me swor fela
aða on unriht.   Ic ðæs ealles mæg
feorh-bennum seoc   gefean habban;
forðam me witan ne ðearf   waldend fira
morðor-bealo maga,   þonne min sceaceð
lif of lice.   Nu ðu lungre geong
hord sceawian   under harne stan,
Wiglaf leofa,   nu se wyrm ligeð,
swefeð sare wund,   since bereafod.
Bio nu on ofoste,   þæt ic ær-welan,
gold-æht ongite,   gearo sceawige
swegle searo-gimmas,   þæt ic ðy seft mæge
æfter maððum-welan   min alætan
lif ond leodscipe,   þone ic longe heold."

XXXVIII

Ða ic snude gefrægn   sunu Wihstanes
æfter word-cwydum   wundum dryhtne
hyran heaðo-siocum,   hring-net beran,
brogdne beadu-sercean   under beorges hrof.
Geseah ða sige-hreðig,   þa he bi sesse geong,
mago-þegn modig   maððum-sigla fealo,
gold glitinian   grunde getenge,

"Now I would give my son these war-garments if I had been
so fortunate that there remained any heir belonging to my
flesh after me. I governed this nation fifty winters. There
was not any king of neighboring peoples who dared con-
front me with war-friends, threaten alarm. I lived out at
home my allotment of time, managed well what was mine,
did not go looking for unwarranted aggression, did not
swear multitudes of oaths in injustice. Sickened as I am by
mortal wounds, I can take satisfaction in all that; on that
account the ruler of men need not accuse me of the murder
of kinsmen when the life departs from my body. Now go 2743
quickly to examine the hoard under hoary stone, friend
Wiglaf, now that the serpent is lying down, sleeps sorely
wounded, robbed of riches. Make no delay now, so that I
may perceive the wealth of the ancients, golden objects, see
plainly the brilliant jewelry, so that in view of those costly
things I will be able to give up more gently my life and my
nation, which I have held for long."

XXXVIII

After these words, I have heard, Wihstan's son then 2752
promptly obeyed his wounded lord, sickened by warfare,
bore his net of rings, the intertwined battle-shirt, under the
roof of the barrow. Glorious in victory, he then saw, when he
passed by that seat, the courageous young courtier, many
objects of value, glittering gold lying on the ground, wonders

wundur on wealle, ond þæs wyrmes denn,
ealdes uht-flogan, orcas stondan,
fyrn-manna fatu, feormendlease,
hyrstum behrorene; þær wæs helm monig
eald ond omig, earm-beaga fela
searwum gesæled. Sinc eaðe mæg,
gold on grunde, gum-cynnes gehwone
oferhigian, hyde se ðe wylle.
Swylce he siomian geseah segn eall gylden
heah ofer horde, hond-wundra mæst,
gelocen leoðo-cræftum; of ðam leoma stod,
þæt he þone grund-wong ongitan meahte,
wrætte giondwlitan. Næs ðæs wyrmes þær
onsyn ænig, ac hyne ecg fornam.
Ða ic on hlæwe gefrægn hord reafian,
eald enta geweorc anne mannan,
him on bearm hladon bunan ond discas
sylfes dome; segn eac genom,
beacna beorhtost. Bill ær gescod
—ecg wæs iren— eald-hlafordes
þam ðara maðma mund-bora wæs
longe hwile, lig-egesan wæg
hatne for horde, hioro-weallende
middel-nihtum, oð þæt he morðre swealt.
Ar wæs on ofoste, eft-siðes georn,
frætwum gefyrðred; hyne fyrwet bræc,
hwæðer collen-ferð cwicne gemette
in ðam wong-stede Wedra þeoden
ellen-siocne, þær he hine ær forlet.
He ða mid þam maðmum mærne þioden,
dryhten sinne driorigne fand

on the walls, and the lair of the serpent, of the old flier in the
dead of night, pitchers, the vessels of the ancients, standing
unattended, shorn of ornament; there was many an old and
rusty helmet, a heap of armlets spiraled ingeniously. Trea- 2764
sure, gold in the ground, can easily escape from every hu-
man being, let him hide it who will. Likewise he saw an en-
sign all of gold hanging high over the hoard, the greatest
piece of workmanship, woven by skilful hands; light glinted
from it, so that he could make out the ground, look over the
treasures. There was not any glimpse of the serpent there,
but a blade had borne him off. Then, I have heard, one man
in the mound plundered the hoard, the ancient work of gi-
ants, filled his arms with cups and plate as much as he liked;
he also took the pennon, that brightest of standards. The 2777
aged lord's sword, its blade of iron, had harmed the one that
had been the protector of the treasury for a long while, had
broadcast hot flame-horror on account of the hoard, seeth-
ing fiercely in the middle of the night, until it died a vio-
lent death. The messenger was in haste, eager to return, im-
pelled with the trappings; he was anxious to know whether
he would find the noble-hearted lord of Weders alive, ailing
after his bravery, in the setting where he had left him. Then 2788
with the riches he found the renowned chieftain, his lord,

ealdres æt ende; he hine eft ongon
wæteres weorpan, oð þæt wordes ord
breost-hord þurhbræc.
Biorn-cyning spræc
gomel on giohðe, gold sceawode:
"Ic ðara frætwa Frean ealles ðanc,
wuldur-cyninge wordum secge,
ecum dryhtne, þe ic her on starie,
þæs ðe ic moste minum leodum
ær swylt-dæge swylc gestrynan.
Nu ic on maðma hord mine bebohte
frode feorh-lege, fremmað gena
leoda þearfe; ne mæg ic her leng wesan.
Hatað heaðo-mære hlæw gewyrcean
beorhtne æfter bæle æt brimes nosan;
se scel to gemyndum minum leodum
heah hlifian on Hrones Næsse,
þæt hit sæ-liðend syððan hatan
Biowulfes Biorh, ða ðe brentingas
ofer floda genipu feorran drifað."
Dyde him of healse hring gyldenne
þioden þrist-hydig, þegne gesealde,
geongum gar-wigan, gold-fahne helm,
beah ond byrnan, het hyne brucan well:
"Þu eart ende-laf usses cynnes,
Wægmundinga; ealle wyrd forsweop
mine magas to metod-sceafte,
eorlas on elne; ic him æfter sceal."
Þæt wæs þam gomelan gingæste word
breost-gehygdum, ær he bæl cure,

bloodied, at life's end. He began to sprinkle water on him
again, until the pointed end of a sentence pierced his breast's
hoard.

The king spoke, the old one in extremis, gazed at the 2792
gold: "I will express in words thanks to the Lord of all, the
king of glory, the eternal ruler, for this gear that I look on
here, for allowing me to acquire such for my people before
my day of death. Now that I have bargained for a hoard of
treasures with the loss of my old life, tend still to the needs
of the nation; I cannot be here longer. Tell men renowned
for warfare to build after the blaze a dazzling mound on a
promontory in the ocean; it is to tower high on Whale's
Ness as a reminder to my people, so that seafarers will after-
ward call it Beowulf's Barrow, those who steer tall ships from
afar over the mists of the deep."

The bold-minded lord took from his neck his golden col- 2809
lar, gave it to his thane, the young spear-warrior, his gold-
adorned helmet, ring and mail, told him to make good use of
them: "You are the final remnant of our family, the Wæg-
mundings; events have swept all my kin to their appointed
end, men of valor; I shall go after them."

Those were the final words from the thoughts of the heart 2817
of the old man before he resigned himself to the flames, the

hate heaðo-wylmas;   him of hræðre gewat
sawol secean   soðfæstra dom.

XXXVIIII

Ða wæs gegongen   guman unfrodum
earfoðlice,   þæt he on eorðan geseah
þone leofestan   lifes æt ende
bleate gebæran.   Bona swylce læg,
egeslic eorð-draca   ealdre bereafod,
bealwe gebæded.   Beah-hordum leng
wyrm woh-bogen   wealdan ne moste,
ac him irenna   ecga fornamon,
hearde heaðo-scearpe   homera lafe,
þæt se wid-floga   wundum stille
hreas on hrusan   hord-ærne neah.
Nalles æfter lyfte   lacende hwearf
middel-nihtum,   maðm-æhta wlonc
ansyn ywde,   ac he eorðan gefeoll
for ðæs hild-fruman   hond-geweorce.
Huru þæt on lande   lyt manna ðah
mægen-agendra   mine gefræge,
þeah ðe he dæda gehwæs   dyrstig wære,
þæt he wið attor-sceaðan   oreðe geræsde,
oððe hring-sele   hondum styrede,
gif he wæccende   weard onfunde
buon on beorge.   Biowulfe wearð
dryht-maðma dæl   deaðe forgolden;
hæfde æghwæðer   ende gefered
lænan lifes.

Næs ða lang to ðon
þæt ða hild-latan   holt ofgefan,
tydre treow-logan   tyne ætsomne,

hot battle-surges; his soul set out from his breast to seek the judgment of the righteous.

XXXVIIII

Then it was an event ill to be endured for a man of few 2821
years that he saw on the ground that most beloved man fare
pitiably at life's end. The killer, the terrible earth-dragon,
likewise lay robbed of life, under the duress of destruction.
The coiled reptile would no longer be allowed to have con-
trol of the ring-hoard, but iron edges had taken him off, the
hard, battle-sharp leaving of hammers, so that the wide-flier,
stilled by wounds, fell to earth near the treasure-hall. By no 2832
means did it roam sporting in air in the middle of the night,
exulting in its ownership of riches, made a show of its ap-
pearance, but it fell to earth by the handiwork of a leader in
war. Certainly, not many a man on land who has the strength,
as I have heard, even if he dared all deeds, has succeeded in
rushing into the breath of a venomous attacker, or in dis-
turbing with his hands a ring-hall, if he found a waking
warder living in a barrow. A measure of noble treasures was
paid for with Beowulf's death; each of the two had reached
the end of this fleeting existence.

Then it was not long before those reluctant to fight gave 2845
up the woods, ten craven renegers together, who had not

ða ne dorston ær dareðum lacan
on hyra man-dryhtnes miclan þearfe;
ac hy scamiende scyldas bæran,
guð-gewædu þær se gomela læg;
wlitan on Wilaf. He gewergad sæt,
feðe-cempa frean eaxlum neah,
wehte hyne wætre; him wiht ne speow.
Ne meahte he on eorðan, ðeah he uðe wel,
on ðam frum-gare feorh gehealdan,
ne ðæs wealdendes wiht oncirran;
wolde dom Godes dædum rædan
gumena gehwylcum, swa he nu gen deð.
Þa wæs æt ðam geongan grim andswaru
eð-begete þam ðe ær his elne forleas.
Wiglaf maðelode, Weohstanes sunu;
sec sarig-ferð seah on unleofe:
"Þæt, la, mæg secgan se ðe wyle soð specan
þæt se mon-dryhten, se eow ða maðmas geaf,
eored-geatwe þe ge þær on standað,
þonne he on ealu-bence oft gesealde
heal-sittendum helm ond byrnan,
þeoden his þegnum, swylce he þrydlicost
ower feor oððe neah findan meahte—
þæt he genunga guð-gewædu
wraðe forwurpe ða hyne wig beget.
Nealles folc-cyning fyrd-gesteallum
gylpan þorfte; hwæðre him God uðe,
sigora waldend, þæt he hyne sylfne gewræc
ana mid ecge, þa him wæs elnes þearf.
Ic him lif-wraðe lytle meahte
ætgifan æt guðe, ond ongan swa þeah

dared to sport with spears at their lord's great need, but
shame-faced they bore shields and mail-shirts to where the
ancient one lay; they looked at Wiglaf. He sat exhausted, a
foot-soldier near the shoulders of his lord, tried to rouse him
with water; it was entirely in vain. Though he would well 2855
have liked it, he could not keep the life of the war-leader on
the earth, nor alter anything of the ruler's; God's judgment
would govern the doings of all men, just as it now still does.
Then it was easy to obtain from the young man a grim re-
sponse to one who had abandoned his valor.

Wiglaf made a speech, Wihstan's son; the heavy-hearted 2862
warrior looked at the unloved: "Whoever cares to tell the
truth can certainly say that this chieftain, who gave you
riches, the cavalry-gear you stand in there, as often as he
gave on the ale-bench a helmet and a mail-shirt to those who
sat in his hall, a lord to his thanes, the most forceful of such
that he could find anywhere far or near—that he had utterly
and senselessly squandered those war-garments when com-
bat encompassed him. The nation's king had no need at all
to boast of his war-comrades; yet God was generous to him,
wielder of victories, so that alone he acquitted himself with
a blade when he was in need of bravery. I could give him 2877
scant vital protection in combat, and set out nonetheless to

ofer min gemet   mæges helpan;
symle wæs þy sæmra   þonne ic sweorde drep
ferhð-geniðlan,   fyr unswiðor
weoll of gewitte.   Wergendra to lyt
þrong ymbe þeoden   þa hyne sio þrag becwom.
Nu sceal sinc-þego   ond swyrd-gifu,
eall eðel-wyn   eowrum cynne,
lufen alicgean;   lond-rihtes mot
þære mæg-burge   monna æghwylc
idel hweorfan,   syððan æðelingas
feorran gefricgean   fleam eowerne,
domleasan dæd.   Deað bið sella
eorla gehwylcum   þonne edwit-lif!"

XL

Heht ða þæt heaðo-weorc   to hagan biodan
up ofer ecg-clif,   þær þæt eorl-weorod
morgen-longne dæg   mod-giomor sæt,
bord-hæbbende,   bega on wenum,
ende-dogores   ond eft-cymes
leofes monnes.   Lyt swigode
niwra spella   se ðe næs gerad,
ac he soðlice   sægde ofer ealle:
"Nu is wil-geofa   Wedra leoda,
dryhten Geata   deað-bedde fæst,
wunað wæl-reste   wyrmes dædum;
him on efn ligeð   ealdor-gewinna
sex-bennum seoc;   sweorde ne meahte
on ðam aglæcean   ænige þinga
wunde gewyrcean.   Wiglaf siteð

help my kinsman beyond my means; it was ever the weaker
as I struck our mortal enemy with my sword: the flames
welled less forcefully from its wits. Too few defenders
thronged about their lord when the time arrived. Now pre- 2884
cious gifts and sword-bequests, all the gladness and comfort
of a homeland, shall fail for your family; every one of your
kin will go deprived of property after the nobles receive
news from far off of your flight, your dishonorable doings.
Death is better for every man than a life of disgrace!"

XL

Then he directed that the results of battle be announced 2892
to the entrenchment up over the cliff's edge, where the host
of men had sat sorrowing the morning-long day, shield-
bearers, in expectation both of a day of finality and of the
beloved man's return. He who rode the headland hardly kept
quiet about the recent news, but he spoke frankly in the
hearing of all:

"Now the patron of the people of the Weders, lord of 2900
Geats, is confined fast to his deathbed, resides in mortal rest
by the doing of the serpent; beside him lies his life's enemy,
sickened by knife-wounds; he could not cause a wound to
the adversary with a sword by any means. Wiglaf sits over

ofer Biowulfe, byre Wihstanes,
eorl ofer oðrum unlifigendum,
healdeð hige-mæðum heafod-wearde
leofes ond laðes.
"Nu ys leodum wen
orleg-hwile, syððan underne
Froncum ond Frysum fyll cyninges
wide weorðeð. Wæs sio wroht scepen
heard wið Hugas, syððan Higelac cwom
faran flot-herge on Fresna land,
þær hyne Hetware hilde genægdon,
elne geeodon mid ofer-mægene,
þæt se byrn-wiga bugan sceolde,
feoll on feðan; nalles frætwe geaf
ealdor dugoðe. Us wæs a syððan
Merewioingas milts ungyfeðe.
"Ne ic te Sweo-ðeode sibbe oððe treowe
wihte ne wene, ac wæs wide cuð
þætte Ongenðio ealdre besnyðede
Hæðcen Hreþling wið Hrefna Wudu,
þa for onmedlan ærest gesohton
Geata leode Guð-Scilfingas.
Sona him se froda fæder Ohtheres,
eald ond egesfull ondslyht ageaf,
abreot brim-wisan, bryd ahredde,
gomelan io-meowlan golde berofene,
Onelan modor ond Ohtheres,
ond ða folgode feorh-geniðlan
oð ðæt hi oðeodon earfoðlice
in Hrefnes Holt hlafordlease.
Besæt ða sin-herge sweorda lafe

Beowulf, Wihstan's son, one man over another void of life, holds a weary-minded wake over friend and foe.

"Now a time of strife is to be expected for the nation, af- 2910
ter the king's fall is widely bruited to Franks and Frisians.
Hostility with the Hugas was made hard after Hygelac came
faring with a flotilla in the Frisians' domain, where the Het-
ware assailed him with attacks, accomplished it bravely with
superior force that the mailed warrior had to give way, fell
among the infantry; the leader did not by any means give
spoils to his troops. The good will of the Merovingian was
ever afterward unobtainable for us.

"Neither do I expect peace or amity at all with the nation 2922
of Swedes, but it was widely reported that Ongentheo de-
prived Hæthcyn, son of Hrethel, of his life at Ravenswood,
when for arrogance the Geatish people first confronted the
War-Scylfings. The seasoned father of Ohthere, old and ter-
rible, paid him an attack in return, cut down the seafarer,
rescued his bride, the aged woman of old bereft of gold, the
mother of Onela and Ohthere, and then pursued his mor-
tal enemies until they narrowly escaped, leaderless, into Ra-
venswood. His vast army then besieged the remnant left by 2936

wundum werge;   wean oft gehet
earmre teohhe   ondlonge niht,
cwæð, he on mergenne   meces ecgum
getan wolde,   sum' on galg-treowum
fuglum to gamene.   Frofor eft gelamp
sarig-modum   somod ær-dæge,
syððan hie Hygelaces   horn ond byman,
gealdor ongeaton,   þa se goda com
leoda dugoðe   on last faran.

XLI

"Wæs sio swat-swaðu   Sweona ond Geata,
wæl-ræs weora   wide gesyne,
hu ða folc mid him   fæhðe towehton.
Gewat him ða se goda   mid his gædelingum,
frod fela-geomor   fæsten secean,
eorl Ongenþio   ufor oncirde;
hæfde Higelaces   hilde gefrunen,
wlonces wig-cræft;   wiðres ne truwode,
þæt he sæ-mannum   onsacan mihte,
heaðo-liðendum   hord forstandan,
bearn ond bryde;   beah eft þonan
eald under eorð-weall.   Þa wæs æht boden
Sweona leodum,   segn Higelaces
freoðo-wong þone   forð ofereodon,
syððan Hreðlingas   to hagan þrungon.
Þær wearð Ongenðio   ecgum sweorda,
blonden-fexa   on bid wrecen,
þæt se þeod-cyning   ðafian sceolde
Eafores anne dom.   Hyne yrringa
Wulf Wonreding   wæpne geræhte,
þæt him for swenge   swat ædrum sprong

swords, wearied by wounds; through the entire night he repeatedly promised the wretched band grief, said in the morning he would spill blood with the sword's edge, some on gallows for birds' sport. Relief rose in turn for the dejected before dawn, when they recognized the call of Hygelac's horn and trumpet, when the good one came traveling on the trail of the troop of men.

XLI

"The bloody track of Swedes and Geats, the deadly on- 2946
slaught of men, was widely apparent, how the armies roused
up hostility between them. Then the good one set out with
his companions, old and deeply sorrowful, looking for a se-
cure place; the man Ongentheo turned farther away; he had
learned about Hygelac's war-making, the proud man's skill
at waging combat; he did not have confidence in resistance,
that he could oppose the mariners, defend the hoard, chil-
dren and bride, against the warring sailors; old, he retreated
from there behind earthen walls. Then chase was offered to 2957
the Swedish men; Hygelac's standards overran the place of
refuge after the sons of Hrethel thronged the defenses.
There gray-haired Ongentheo was brought to bay by the
blades of swords, so that the high king had to endure the
sole judgment of Eofor. Wulf, son of Wanred, angrily struck
him with his weapon, so that on account of the blow blood

forð under fexe. Næs he forht swa ðeh,
gomela Scilfing, ac forgeald hraðe
wyrsan wrixle wæl-hlem þone,
syððan ðeod-cyning þyder oncirde.
Ne meahte se snella sunu Wonredes
ealdum ceorle ondslyht giofan,
ac he him on heafde helm ær gescer,
þæt he blode fah bugan sceolde,
feoll on foldan; næs he fæge þa git,
ac he hyne gewyrpte, þeah ðe him wund hrine.
Let se hearda Higelaces þegn
bradne mece, þa his broðor læg,
eald-sweord eotonisc entiscne helm
brecan ofer bord-weal; ða gebeah cyning,
folces hyrde, wæs in feorh dropen.
Ða wæron monige þe his mæg wriðon,
ricone arærdon, ða him gerymed wearð,
þæt hie wæl-stowe wealdan moston.
Þenden reafode rinc oðerne,
nam on Ongenðio iren-byrnan,
heard swyrd hilted, ond his helm somod,
hares hyrste Higelace bær.
He ðam frætwum feng ond him fægre gehet
leana mid leodum, ond gelæste swa;
geald þone guð-ræs Geata dryhten,
Hreðles eafora, þa he to ham becom,
Iofore ond Wulfe mid ofer-maðmum,
sealde hiora gehwæðrum hund þusenda
landes ond locenra beaga —ne ðorfte him ða lean oðwitan
mon on middan-gearde, syððan hie ða mærða geslogon—
ond ða Iofore forgeaf angan dohtor,
ham-weorðunge, hyldo to wedde.

flowed forth in streams from under his locks. He was not 2967
cowed, however, the ancient Scylfing, but he quickly repaid
the onslaught with a worse exchange, after the high king
turned there. The deft son of Wanred could not give a coun-
terblow to the old man, but he had cleft the helmet on his
head, so that he had to retreat drenched in blood, fell on
the earth; he was not yet doomed to die, but he recovered,
though he felt the wound. Hygelac's hardy thane, now that 2977
his brother had fallen, let his broad blade, an old, ogreish
sword, break the giant-made helmet over the phalanx of
shields; then the king withdrew, warder of the nation, was
cut to the quick. They were many who bandaged his kins-
man, raised him up at once when the opportunity arose, that
they were able to take control of the battlefield. Then one
warrior plundered another, took from Ongentheo his iron
mail-shirt, his hard, hilted sword, and his helmet besides,
conveyed the hoary one's gear to Hygelac. He took posses- 2989
sion of those trappings and handsomely promised him rec-
ompense back among their people, and he kept his word
about that; when he came home, the lord of Geats, Hreth-
el's heir, repaid Eofor and Wulf for that martial deed with
treasure on treasure, gave each of them the value of a hun-
dred thousand in land and interlocked rings—no one on
middle-earth needed to criticize him for those rewards, af-
ter they had achieved those glorious feats—and then he
gave to Eofor his only daughter, honor to a home, as a pledge
of fealty.

"Þæt ys sio fæhðo ond se feondscipe,
wæl-nið wera, ðæs ðe ic wen hafo,
þe us seceað to Sweona leoda,
syððan hie gefricgeað frean userne
ealdorleasne, þone ðe ær geheold
wið hettendum hord ond rice
æfter hæleða hryre, hwate Scilfingas,
folc-red fremede, oððe furður gen
eorlscipe efnde. Nu is ofost betost
þæt we þeod-cyning þær sceawian
ond þone gebringan, þe us beagas geaf,
on ad-fære. Ne scel anes hwæt
meltan mid þam modigan, ac þær is maðma hord,
gold unrime grimme geceapod,
ond nu æt siðestan sylfes feore
beagas gebohte; þa sceall brond fretan,
æled þeccean— nalles eorl wegan
maððum to gemyndum, ne mægð scyne
habban on healse hring-weorðunge,
ac sceal geomor-mod, golde bereafod
oft nalles æne el-land tredan,
nu se here-wisa hleahtor alegde,
gamen ond gleo-dream. Forðon sceall gar wesan
monig morgen-ceald mundum bewunden,
hæfen on handa, nalles hearpan sweg
wigend weccean, ac se wonna hrefn
fus ofer fægum fela reordian,
earne secgan hu him æt æte speow,
þenden he wið wulf wæl reafode."

Swa se secg hwata secggende wæs,
laðra spella; he ne leag fela

"That is the feud and the enmity, deadly hostility of men, 2999
as I expect, for which the Swedish people will come in
search of us, the keen Scylfings, after they discover that our
lord is no longer living, who guarded the hoard and king-
dom against opponents after the fall of champions, fur-
thered the people's interests, or what is more, accomplished
heroic acts. Now it is best not to delay our viewing the high
king there and bringing him who gave us rings in a funeral
cortege. No little something will be melted with the coura- 3010
geous man, but there is a treasure hoard there, limitless gold
grimly purchased, and only just now he paid for those rings
with his own life; flames shall consume them, the fire enfold
them—no man by any means wear the valuables in remem-
brance, nor a lovely young woman have a neck-ornament
at her throat, but shall tread foreign ways not once but of-
ten, sick at heart, stripped of gold, now that the commander
has laid aside laughter, diversions and delights. Therefore 3021
many a morning-cold spear will be wrapped in palms, held
in hands, not the music of the harp waking the warriors,
but the wan and ready raven articulating much over the
doomed, telling the eagle how it fared for carrion when it
vied with the wolf at despoiling the dead."

The man was thus a teller of auguries, of repugnant news; 3028

wyrda ne worda. Weorod eall aras;
eodon unbliðe under Earna Næs,
wollen-teare wundur sceawian.
Fundon ða on sande sawulleasne
hlim-bed healdan þone þe him hringas geaf
ærran mælum; þa wæs ende-dæg
godum gegongen, þæt se guð-cyning,
Wedra þeoden wundor-deaðe swealt.
Ær hi þær gesegan syllicran wiht,
wyrm on wonge wiðerræhtes þær
laðne licgean; wæs se leg-draca
grimlic gryre-fah gledum beswæled;
se wæs fiftiges fot-gemearces
lang on legere; lyft-wynne heold
nihtes hwilum, nyðer eft gewat
dennes niosian; wæs ða deaðe fæst,
hæfde eorð-scrafa ende genyttod.
Him big stodan bunan ond orcas,
discas lagon ond dyre swyrd,
omige þurhetone, swa hie wið eorðan fæðm
þusend wintra þær eardodon,
þonne wæs þæt yrfe eacen-cræftig,
iu-monna gold galdre bewunden,
þæt ðam hring-sele hrinan ne moste
gumena ænig, nefne God sylfa,
sigora soð-cyning sealde þam ðe he wolde
—he is manna gehyld— hord openian,
efne swa hwylcum manna swa him gemet ðuhte.

XLII

Þa wæs gesyne þæt se sið ne ðah
þam ðe unrihte inne gehydde

he did not equivocate much in regard to words or deeds.
The troop all rose; they went unhappy under Eagles' Ness
with welling tears to regard that wonder. On the sand they
found then occupying a place of rest the one now soulless
who had given them rings in former times; the closing day
had come then to the good one, so that the war-king, lord of
Weders, died a strange death. They had already seen there 3038
the fantastic creature, the repellent reptile lying opposite
there on the ground; the firedrake, grim and with grisly
markings, was scorched by the sparks; it was fifty feet long
as laid out; for a time it had exulted in air by night, came
down in turn to find its den; it was in the firm grasp of death
then; its use of caverns had come to an end. By it stood cups 3047
and pitchers; dishes and precious swords lay eaten away by
rust, inasmuch as they had remained there in the earth's em-
brace a thousand winters, while that mighty inheritance, the
gold of the ancients, was wrapped in a spell, so that no man
was permitted to touch that ring-hall, unless God himself,
the true king of victories—he is the refuge of humankind—
allowed one whom he wished to open the hoard, whatsoever
person he thought fit.

XLII

It was then apparent that the attempt by the one who 3058
had wrongly hidden the valuables within walls had not suc-

wrætte under wealle. Weard ær ofsloh
feara sumne; þa sio fæhð gewearð
gewrecen wraðlice. Wundur hwar þonne
eorl ellen-rof ende gefere
lif-gesceafta, þonne leng ne mæg
mon mid his magum medu-seld buan.
Swa wæs Biowulfe, þa he biorges weard
sohte, searo-niðas —seolfa ne cuðe
þurh hwæt his worulde gedal weorðan sceolde—
swa hit oð domes dæg diope benemdon
þeodnas mære þa ðæt þær dydon,
þæt se secg wære synnum scildig,
hergum geheaðerod, hell-bendum fæst,
wommum gewitnad, se ðone wong strude.
Næs he gold-hwæte, gearwor hæfde
agendes est ær gesceawod.
Wiglaf maðelode, Wihstanes sunu:
"Oft sceall eorl monig anes willan
wræc adreogan, swa us geworden is.
Ne meahton we gelæran leofne þeoden,
rices hyrde ræd ænigne,
þæt he ne grette gold-weard þone,
lete hyne licgean þær he longe wæs,
wicum wunian oð woruld-ende;
heold on heah-gesceap. Hord ys gesceawod,
grimme gegongen; wæs þæt gifeðe to swið
þe ðone þeod-cyning þyder ontyhte.
Ic wæs þær inne ond þæt eall geondseh,
recedes geatwa, þa me gerymed wæs,
nealles swæslice sið alyfed
inn under eorð-weall. Ic on ofoste gefeng

ceeded. The guardian had killed one of a few; then the feud
was avenged fiercely. It is a mystery, after all, where a coura-
geous person will reach the end of his allotted life, when a
man can no longer occupy the mead-hall among his kin. So 3066
it was for Beowulf when he went looking for the barrow's
guardian, treacherous quarrels—he himself did not know
what should be the cause of his parting from the world—so
deeply did the famed chieftains who placed it there declare
it all the way to doomsday, that the man would be gravely
guilty, confined in heathen shrines, clasped in the bonds of
hell, tormented by trials, who plundered the place. He had
not by any means expected a curse on gold, rather the own-
er's favor.

Wiglaf made a speech, Wihstan's son: "Many a man shall 3076
often suffer wrack for the will of one alone, as has happened
to us. We could not prevail upon our beloved lord, safeguard
of the realm, with any persuasion that he not approach the
gold-guardian, let him lie where he had long been, keep to
those places to the world's end; he held to his high destiny.
The hoard is revealed, grimly attained; that fate was too
powerful that impelled the nation's king to this place. I was 3087
inside there and looked through it all, the hall's splendors,
when I was afforded the opportunity, permitted passage
under circumstances by no means agreeable, in under the

micle mid mundum   mægen-byrðenne
hord-gestreona,   hider ut ætbær
cyninge minum.   Cwico wæs þa gena,
wis ond gewittig;   worn eall gespræc
gomol on gehðo,   ond eowic gretan het,
bæd þæt ge geworhton   æfter wines dædum
in bæl-stede   beorh þone hean,
micelne ond mærne,   swa he manna wæs
wigend weorðfullost   wide geond eorðan,
þenden he burh-welan   brucan moste.
Uton nu efstan   oðre siðe,
seon ond secean   searo-gimma geþræc,
wundur under wealle;   ic eow wisige,
þæt ge genoge   neon sceawiað
beagas ond brad gold.   Sie sio bær gearo,
ædre geæfned,   þonne we ut cymen,
ond þonne geferian   frean userne,
leofne mannan   þær he longe sceal
on ðæs waldendes   wære geþolian."
   Het ða gebeodan   byre Wihstanes,
hæle hilde-dior   hæleða monegum,
bold-agendra,   þæt hie bæl-wudu
feorran feredon,   folc-agende,
godum togenes: "Nu sceal gled fretan
—weaxan wonna leg—   wigena strengel,
þone ðe oft gebad   isern-scure,
þonne stræla storm   strengum gebæded
scoc ofer scild-weall,   sceft nytte heold,
fæðer-gearwum fus   flane fulleode."
   Huru se snotra   sunu Wihstanes
acigde of corðre   cyniges þegnas

earthen walls. In haste I took with my hands a great, heavy load of hoarded riches, carried them out here to my king. He was still alive then, conscious and alert; the old one said a great deal in sorrow, and enjoined me to address you, requested that you build in accordance with your friend's accomplishments the high barrow in the pyre-place, spacious and grand, as he was the worthiest warrior of men far and wide over the earth while he was permitted the use of
fortress-riches. Let us now go at once another time, to view 3101
and visit the heap of intricate ornaments, marvels within walls. I shall show you the way, so that you will examine from near enough the rings and plated gold. Let the bier be ready, prepared at once, when we come out, and then convey our lord, the beloved man, to where he shall long endure in the ruler's covenant."

Wihstan's son, a hero courageous in war, then ordered 3110
that many champions, hall-possessors, be directed to bring firewood from afar, men with followers, to the good one: "Now the blaze shall consume—the pale flame rise up—the prince of warriors, who often lived through a tempest of iron, when a downpour of missiles launched by bowstrings shot over the wall of shields; the shaft did its duty, readily followed the barb with its feather-gear."

To be sure, the sage son of Wihstan summoned from the 3120

syfone tosomne,   þa selestan,
eode eahta sum   under inwit-hrof
hilde-rinca;   sum on handa bær
æled-leoman,   se ðe on orde geong.
Næs ða on hlytme   hwa þæt hord strude,
syððan orwearde   ænigne dæl
secgas gesegon   on sele wunian,
læne licgan;   lyt ænig mearn
þæt hi ofostlice   ut geferedon
dyre maðmas;   dracan ec scufun,
wyrm ofer weall-clif,   leton weg niman,
flod fæðmian   frætwa hyrde.
Þa wæs wunden gold   on wæn hladen,
æghwæs unrim,   æþeling boren,
har hilde-rinc   to Hrones Næsse.

XLIII

Him ða gegiredan   Geata leode
ad on eorðan   unwaclicne,
helmum behongen,   hilde-bordum,
beorhtum byrnum,   swa he bena wæs;
alegdon ða tomiddes   mærne þeoden
hæleð hiofende,   hlaford leofne.
Ongunnon þa on beorge   bæl-fyra mæst
wigend weccan;   wudu-rec astah
sweart ofer swioðole,   swogende leg
wope bewunden   —wind-blond gelæg—
oð þæt he ða ban-hus   gebrocen hæfde
hat on hreðre.   Higum unrote
mod-ceare mændon,   mon-dryhtnes cwealm;
swylce giomor-gyd   Geatisc meowle
æfter Biowulfe   bunden-heorde

host seven of the king's thanes altogether, the best, went as one of eight war-makers under the roof of malice; one bore in hand a burning light, who went in front. Then it was not decided by lot who would plunder the hoard, after the men saw any portion standing unguarded in that hall, lying vulnerable; little did anyone regret that they promptly brought out precious treasures; the dragon they also shoved, the serpent, over the steep embankment, let the waves take possession of, the flood embrace the keeper of those splendors. Then sinuous gold was piled on a wagon, a limitless count of everything, and the prince conveyed, the ancient war-maker, to Whale's Ness.

XLIII
The Geatish people then readied no mean pyre on the 3137
earth, with helmets hung about it, war-boards, bright mail-
shirts, as he had requested; in the midst, then, grieving
champions laid the renowned ruler, their beloved lord. War-
riors began to kindle on the mound then the greatest fune-
real fire; wood-smoke ascended swart over the blaze, roaring
flames interwoven with weeping—the wind currents sub-
sided—until it had broken down the bone-house hot in its
very heart. Desolate of mind they expressed their hearts' 3148
grief, the passing of their lord; likewise a Geatish woman
with hair bound up sorrowfully sang an elegy for Beowulf,

sang sorg-cearig, sæide geneahhe
þæt hio hyre here-geongas hearde ondrede,
wæl-fylla worn, werudes egesan,
hynðo ond hæft-nyd. Heofon rece swealg.
Geworhton ða Wedra leode
hlæw on hoe, se wæs heah ond brad,
weg-liðendum wide gesyne,
ond betimbredon on tyn dagum
beadu-rofes becn, bronda lafe
wealle beworhton, swa hyt weorðlicost
fore-snotre men findan mihton.
Hi on beorg dydon beg ond siglu,
eall swylce hyrsta swylce on horde ær
nið-hedige men genumen hæfdon;
forleton eorla gestreon eorðan healdan,
gold on greote, þær hit nu gen lifað,
eldum swa unnyt swa hyt æror wæs.
Þa ymbe hlæw riodan hilde-diore,
æþelinga bearn, ealra twelfe,
woldon care cwiðan ond cyning mænan,
word-gyd wrecan, ond ymb wer sprecan;
eahtodan eorlscipe ond his ellen-weorc
duguðum demdon— swa hit gedefe bið
þæt mon his wine-dryhten wordum herge,
ferhðum freoge, þonne he forð scile
of lic-haman læded weorðan.
Swa begnornodon Geata leode
hlafordes hryre, heorð-geneatas;
cwædon þæt he wære wyruld-cyninga
manna mildust ond mon-ðwærust,
leodum liðost ond lof-geornost.

said repeatedly that she dreaded hard invasions of armies, a profusion of mayhem, terror of troops, abasement and captivity. Heaven swallowed the smoke.

Then the people of the Weders made a mound on the 3156
promontory, which was tall and broad, widely visible to mariners, and in ten days constructed a champion's monument, surrounded with a wall what the conflagration had left, as worthily as very prudent people could devise it. In the barrow they placed rings and brooches, all such ornaments as grim-minded people had taken from the hoard; they left the earth holding warriors' treasure, gold in the dirt, where it
now still resides, as useless to men as it was before. Then 3169
battle-brave sons of nobles rode around the mound, twelve in all, wanted to voice their grief and lament their king, express it in words and speak of the man; they praised his manliness and honored his acts of heroism with glory—just as it is proper for a man to commend his friend and lord in speech, cherish him in his soul when he must be led forth from the flesh. Just so the Geatish people, his retinue, bemoaned the fall of their lord; they said that of worldly kings he was the most benevolent of men and the kindest, most generous to his people and most honor-bound.

JUDITH

. . . ne tweode
gifena in ðys ginnan grunde. Heo ðar ða gearwe funde
mund-byrd æt ðam mæran Þeodne, þa heo ahte mæste þearfe
hyldo þæs hehstan deman, þæt he hie wið þæs hehstan brogan
gefriðode, frymða waldend. Hyre ðæs fæder on roderum
torht-mod tiðe gefremede, þe heo ahte trumne geleafan
a to ðam Ælmihtigan.
7 Gefrægen ic ða Holofernus
win-hatan wyrcean georne ond eallum wundrum þrymlic
girwan up swæsendo. To ðam het se gumena baldor
ealle ða yldestan ðegnas; hie ðæt ofstum miclum
ræfndon, rond-wiggende, comon to ðam rican þeodne
feran, folces ræswan. Þæt wæs þy feorðan dogore
þæs ðe Iudith hyne, gleaw on geðonce,
ides ælf-scinu, ærest gesohte.

x

15 Hie ða to ðam symle sittan eodon,
wlance to win-gedrince, ealle his wea-gesiðas,
bealde byrn-wiggende. Þær wæron bollan steape
boren æfter bencum gelome, swylce eac bunan ond orcas
fulle flet-sittendum; hie þæt fæge þegon,
rofe rond-wiggende, þeah ðæs se rica ne wende,
egesful eorla dryhten.

. . . did not doubt favors in this wide world. Then she readily found there support from the acknowledged Lord when she had greatest need of the protection of the highest judge, that he would exempt her from the retribution of the highest, the crafter of origins. The noble-minded father in heaven granted her favor because she always had firm belief in the Almighty.

Then, I heard, Holofernes had a drinking-party arranged 7
and a magnificent banquet prepared with all extravagances. The leader of the men invited all the most eminent officers to it; they complied, those shield-fighters, with the greatest promptness, and came hurrying to their mighty lord, the people's leader. That was on the fourth day after Judith, brilliant in her plans, lady of supernatural beauty, first visited him.

X

They then went to sit down to the feast, proud ones at 15
the wine-service, all his criminal companions, bold fighters in mail. Tall flagons were set down endlessly there along the bench, likewise brimming cups and bowls for the visitors to the hall; they partook of that as doomed men, those fierce shield-warriors, though the powerful, dreadful lord of the men did not suspect so.

Ða wearð Holofernus,
gold-wine gumena, on gyte-salum,
hloh ond hlydde, hlynede ond dynede,
þæt mihten fira bearn feorran gehyran
hu se stið-moda styrmde ond gylede,
modig ond medu-gal, manode geneahhe
benc-sittende þæt hi gebærdon wel.
Swa se in-widda ofer ealne dæg
dryht-guman sine drencte mid wine,
swið-mod sinces brytta, oð þæt hie on swiman lagon,
oferdrencte his duguðe ealle, swylce hie wæron deaðe geslegene,
agotene goda gehwylces. Swa het se gumena aldor
fylgan flet-sittendum, oð þæt fira bearnum
nealæhte niht seo þystre.
Het ða niða geblonden
þa eadigan mægð ofstum fetigan
to his bed-reste beagum gehlæste,
hringum gehrodene. Hie hraðe fremedon,
anbyht-scealcas, swa him heora ealdor bebead,
byrn-wigena brego, bearhtme stopon
to ðam gyst-erne, þær hie Iudithðe
fundon ferhð-gleawe, ond ða fromlice
lind-wiggende lædan ongunnon
þa torhtan mægð to træfe þam hean,
þær se rica hyne reste on symbel
nihtes inne, Nergende lað,
Holofernus. Þær wæs eall gylden
fleoh-net fæger ond ymbe þæs folc-togan
bed ahongen, þæt se bealofulla
mihte wlitan þurh, wigena baldor,

Holofernes, the gold-friend of the men, was then in a 21
mood for pouring, laughed and roared, shouted and reveled,
so that the children of men could hear from far off how that
stout heart stormed and yelled, conceited and mead-mad,
repeatedly insisted that those on the bench should enjoy
themselves. So the villain through the whole day soaked his
commanders in wine, that firm-willed dispenser of riches,
until they lay unconscious, his entire staff drowned with
drink, as if they were struck dead, drained of all good. Thus 28
the leader of the men commanded that the occupants of the
hall be attended to, until the murky night overtook the sons
of mortals.

Steeped in viciousness, he then ordered that the blessed 34
young woman be fetched with all haste, laden with rings,
draped in bangles, to his bedchamber. They did immediately,
his underlings, as their leader had asked, prince of the mail-
coated warriors, marched in a trice to the guest-quarters,
where they found Judith, sage of spirit, and then those bear-
ers of linden shields set out to lead the radiant young woman
to the tall tent wherein the mighty Holofernes, despised by
the Savior, rested by night during the feasting. There was a 46
net all of gold to keep out flies, splendid and hung about the
general's bed so that the baleful captain of the fighters could

on æghwylcne þe ðær inne com
hæleða bearna, ond on hyne nænig
monna cynnes, nymðe se modiga hwæne
niðe rofra him þe near hete
rinca to rune gegangan.
54 Hie ða on reste gebrohton
snude ða snoteran idese; eodon ða sterced-ferhðe,
hæleð heora hearran cyðan þæt wæs seo halige meowle
gebroht on his bur-getelde. Þa wearð se brema on mode
bliðe, burga ealdor, þohte ða beorhtan idese
mid widle ond mid womme besmitan. Ne wolde þæt wuldres dema
geðafian, þrymmes hyrde, ac he him þæs ðinges gestyrde,
Dryhten, dugeða waldend.
61 Gewat ða se deoful-cunda,
gal-ferhð gumena ðreate
bealo-full his beddes neosan, þær he sceolde his blæd forleosan
ædre binnan anre nihte; hæfde ða his ende gebidenne
on eorðan unswæslicne, swylcne he ær æfter worhte,
þearl-mod ðeoden gumena, þenden he on ðysse worulde
wunode under wolcna hrofe.
Gefeol ða wine swa druncen
se rica on his reste middan, swa he nyste ræda nanne
on gewit-locan. Wiggend stopon
ut of ðam inne ofstum miclum,
weras win-sade, þe ðone wær-logan,
laðne leod-hatan, læddon to bedde
nehstan siðe.
Þa wæs Nergendes
þeowen þrymful, þearle gemyndig

look through it at every military man who came therein, and not a human being could look at him, unless that braggart commanded some one of those brave in iniquity to come nearer to him for a private communication.

They then brought the wise lady directly to his bed; the 54
hard-hearted heroes then went to inform their superior that the saintly woman had been brought to his sleeping tent. Then the famous governor of cities was pleased, thought he would sully the radiant lady with filth and defilement. The judge of glory, shepherd of the host, did not intend to permit that, but he directed the matter for them, the Lord, guider of armies.

That baleful devil's spawn set out then in extravagant 61
spirits with a band of men to visit his bed, where he was to lose his glory precipitously, in the space of a single night. That fierce-hearted lord of men had reached his ungentle end on earth, such as he had been striving toward the while he remained in this world under the vault of the sky.

The mighty one then fell into the middle of his bed, so 67
steeped in wine that he knew no reason in his wits. The soldiers marched out of the chamber in great haste, men glutted with wine, who had led the faith-breaker, that loathed tyrant, to bed for the last time.

Then the Savior's servant was empowered, pointedly 73

hu heo þone atolan eaðost mihte
ealdre benæman ær se unsyfra,
womfull, onwoce. Genam ða wunden-locc
Scyppendes mægð scearpne mece,
scurum heardne, ond of sceaðe abræd
swiðran folme; ongan ða swegles weard
be naman nemnan, Nergend ealra
woruld-buendra, ond þæt word acwæð:
"Ic ðe, frymða God ond frofre Gæst,
Bearn alwaldan, biddan wylle
miltse þinre me þearfendre,
ðrynesse ðrym. Þearle ys me nuða
heorte onhæted ond hige geomor,
swyðe mid sorgum gedrefed. Forgif me, swegles Ealdor,
sigor ond soðne geleafan, þæt ic mid þys sweorde mote
geheawan þysne morðres bryttan. Geunne me minra gesynta,
þearl-mod Þeoden gumena. Nahte ic þinre næfre
miltse þon maran þearfe. Gewrec nu, mihtig Dryhten,
torht-mod tires brytta, þæt me ys þus torne on mode,
hate on hreðre minum."
Hi ða se hehsta dema
ædre mid elne onbryrde, swa he deð anra gehwylcne
her-buendra þe hyne him to helpe seceð
mid ræde ond mid rihte geleafan. Þa wearð hyre rume on mode,
haligre hyht geniwod; genam ða þone hæðenan mannan
fæste be feaxe sinum, teah hyne folmum wið hyre weard
bysmerlice, ond þone bealofullan
listum alede, laðne mannan,
swa heo ðæs unlædan eaðost mihte

aware how she could very easily deprive the monster of life before the shameless criminal awoke. The Creator's handmaid, with hair tied up, took a sharp sword, hardened in showers [of battle], and drew it from the sheath with her right hand; she began then to name heaven's warden by name, the Savior of all mortals, and spoke these words:

"I want to request of you, God of origins and consoling 83
Spirit, Son of the almighty, triune force, your mercy upon me in my need. My heart is now violently inflamed and my mind is mournful, heavily oppressed with cares. Grant me, heaven's ruler, victory and true faith, so that with this sword I may be permitted to cut down this purveyor of murder. Grant me my deliverance, stern Lord of men. I never had greater need of your mercy. Avenge now, mighty Lord, noble-minded distributor of glory, what sits so bitterly in my breast, with such heat in my heart."

Then the highest judge inspired her straightway with 94
courage, as he does every earthly sojourner who seeks his help with good judgment and with true belief. Her spirits were then lifted, the confidence of the saintly one restored; grasped then the heathen man firmly by his scalp, pulled him toward her with her hands, insultingly, and cleverly placed the baleful, horrid man in such a way that she could

wel gewealdan. Sloh ða wunden-locc
þone feond-sceaðan fagum mece,
hete-þoncolne, þæt heo healfne forcearf
þone sweoran him, þæt he on swiman læg,
druncen ond dolh-wund. Næs ða dead þa gyt,
ealles orsawle; sloh ða eornoste
ides ellen-rof oðre siðe
þone hæðenan hund, þæt him þæt heafod wand
forð on ða flore. Læg se fula leap
gesne beæftan; gæst ellor hwearf
under neowelne næs ond ðær genyðerad wæs,
susle gesæled syððan æfre,
wyrmum bewunden, witum gebunden,
hearde gehæfted in helle-bryne
æfter hin-siðe. Ne ðearf he hopian no,
þystrum forðylmed, þæt he ðonan mote
of ðam wyrm-sele, ac ðær wunian sceal
awa to aldre butan ende forð
in ðam heolstran ham, hyht-wynna leas.

XI

Hæfde ða gefohten foremærne blæd
Iudith æt guðe, swa hyre God uðe,
swegles ealdor, þe hyre sigores onleah.
Þa seo snotere mægð snude gebrohte
þæs here-wæðan heafod swa blodig
on ðam fætelse þe hyre fore-genga,
blac-hleor ides, hyra begea nest,
ðeawum geðungen, þyder on lædde,
ond hit ða swa heolfrig hyre on hond ageaf,
hige-ðoncolre, ham to berenne,

most easily have her way with the wretch. The bound-haired 103
one then struck the rancorous, destructive adversary with
a decorated sword, so that she carved halfway through his
neck, so that he lay in a stupor, drunk and severely wounded.
He was not yet dead, completely soulless; the courageous
lady then struck the heathen dog smartly for the second
time, so that his head rolled away onto the floor. The foul, 111
lifeless trunk lay behind; the spirit moved off under a steep
cliff and was sunk there, moored to misery ever afterward,
trammeled by snakes, tied by torments, cruelly made cap-
tive in hellfire after his exodus. Hemmed in by shadows, he
need not hope that he will be allowed to escape that snake-
hall, but he shall remain there ever and a day, time without
end, in that dim realm, devoid of the comfort of hope.

XI

Judith had then carved out in conflict preeminent re- 122
nown, such as God granted her, heaven's ruler, who had al-
lotted her victory. Then the prudent young woman with-
out delay put the head of the war-wager, bloody as it was,
into the container in which her attendant, that lily-cheeked
lady, mindful of her duties, had brought their provisions,
and, gory as it was, Judith entrusted it to the hand of her
conscientious accomplice to bear home.

Iudith gingran sinre.
Eodon ða gegnum þanonne
þa idesa ba ellen-þriste,
oð þæt hie becomon, collen-ferhðe,
ead-hreðige mægð, ut of ðam herige,
þæt hie sweotollice geseon mihten
þære wlitegan byrig weallas blican,
Bethuliam. Hie ða beah-hrodene
feðe-laste forð onettan,
oð hie glæd-mode gegan hæfdon
to ðam weal-gate.
Wiggend sæton,
weras wæccende wearde heoldon
in ðam fæstenne, swa ðam folce ær
geomor-modum Iudith bebead,
searo-ðoncol mægð, þa heo on sið gewat,
ides ellen-rof. Wæs ða eft cumen
leof to leodum, ond ða lungre het
gleaw-hydig wif gumena sumne
of ðære ginnan byrig hyre togeanes gan
ond hi ofostlice in forlæton
þurh ðæs wealles geat, ond þæt word acwæð
to ðam sige-folce:
"Ic eow secgan mæg
þonc-wyrðe þing, þæt ge ne þyrfen leng
murnan on mode. Eow ys Metod bliðe,
cyninga wuldor; þæt gecyðed wearð
geond woruld wide þæt eow ys wuldor-blæd
torhtlic toweard ond tir gifeðe,
lysing þara læðða þe ge lange drugon."

The two daring women then both departed from there, 132
until they, those elated and triumphant young women, passed beyond the encampment, so that they could plainly see the walls of that lovely city glimmer, Bethulia. Bejeweled, they hurried on along the foot-path until, glad of heart, they had reached the gate in the wall.

The soldiers sat, waking men held watch in the strong- 141
hold, as Judith, a clever young woman, had enjoined the mournful people when she had departed, a courageous lady. Their beloved had returned to the people, and the prudent-minded woman straightway called for a certain man to come from the sprawling town to meet her and let her in without delay through the gate in the wall, and she made this announcement to the triumphant populace:

"I can tell you something worthy of gratitude, that you 152
no longer need have anxiety of mind. Providence is kind to you, the splendor of kings; it has been revealed throughout the wide world that resplendent, glorious honor has befallen you and glory is given you, redemption from the trials you have long endured."

Þa wurdon bliðe burh-sittende,
syððan hi gehyrdon hu seo halige spræc
ofer heanne weall. Here wæs on lustum.
Wið þæs fæsten-geates folc onette,
weras wif somod, wornum ond heapum,
ðreatum ond ðrymmum þrungon ond urnon
ongean ða Þeodnes mægð þusend-mælum,
ealde ge geonge. Æghwylcum wearð
men on ðære medo-byrig mod areted
syððan hie ongeaton þæt wæs Iudith cumen
eft to eðle, ond ða ofostlice
hie mid eað-medum in forleton.
Þa seo gleawe het, golde gefrætewod,
hyre ðinenne þancol-mode
þæs here-wæðan heafod onwriðan
ond hyt to behðe blodig ætywan
þam burh-leodum, hu hyre æt beaduwe gespeow.
Spræc ða seo æðele to eallum þam folce:
"Her ge magon sweotole, sige-rofe hæleð,
leoda ræswan, on ðæs laðestan
hæðenes heaðo-rinces heafod starian,
Holofernus unlyfigendes,
þe us monna mæst morðra gefremede,
sarra sorga, ond þæt swyðor gyt
ycan wolde, ac him ne uðe God
lengran lifes, þæt he mid læððum us
eglan moste. Ic him ealdor oðþrong
þurh Godes fultum. Nu ic gumena gehwæne
þyssa burg-leoda biddan wylle,
rand-wiggendra, þæt ge recene eow
fysan to gefeohte, syððan frymða God,

Then the citizens were overjoyed, after they heard how 159
the saint called over the high wall. The army was in high spirits. The people hurried toward the gate of the fortress, men and women both, in crowds and throngs, hosts and multitudes, old and young pressed forward and ran by the thousands to meet the Lord's handmaiden. The heart of every person in that mead-fortress was gladdened as soon as they understood that Judith had come back to her homeland, and then unhesitatingly they reverently let her in.

The sage, adorned with gold, then directed her conscien- 171
tious attendant to uncover the head of the war-wager and show it all bloody to the citizens as proof of how she had succeeded in the contest. The noblewoman then spoke to all the people:

"Here, you heroes renowned in victory, leaders of men, 177
you can gaze unobstructed at the head of the most despica-
ble heathen war-maker, lifeless Holofernes, who of all peo-
ple caused us the most loss of life, bitter pain, and would
have added yet more to that, had God granted him longer
existence, so that he could plague us with injuries. I drove
the life out of him through God's help. Now I want to re- 186
quest of every man of this citizenry, every shield-bearer, that
you prepare yourselves without delay for battle after the God

arfæst cyning,   eastan sende
leohtne leoman.   Berað linde forð,
bord for breostum   ond byrn-homas,
scire helmas   in sceaðena gemong;
fyllað folc-togan   fagum sweordum,
fæge frum-garas.   Fynd syndon eowere
gedemed to deaðe,   ond ge dom agon,
tir æt tohtan,   swa eow getacnod hafað
mihtig Dryhten   þurh mine hand."
  Þa wearð snelra werod   snude gegearewod,
cenra to campe.   Stopon cyne-rofe
secgas ond gesiðas,   bæron sige-þufas,
foron to gefeohte   forð on gerihte,
hæleð under helmum,   of ðære haligan byrig
on ðæt dæg-red sylf.   Dynedan scildas,
hlude hlummon.   Þæs se hlanca gefeah
wulf in walde,   ond se wanna hrefn,
wæl-gifre fugel.   Wistan begen
þæt him ða þeod-guman   þohton tilian
fylle on fægum;   ac him fleah on last
earn ætes georn,   urig-feðera;
salowig-pada   sang hilde-leoð,
hyrned-nebba.
                    Stopon heaðo-rincas,
beornas to beadowe,   bordum beðeahte,
hwealfum lindum,   þa ðe hwile ær
el-ðeodigra   edwit þoledon,
hæðenra hosp.   Him þæt hearde wearð
æt ðam æsc-plegan   eallum forgolden,
Assyrium,   syððan Ebreas
under guð-fanum   gegan hæfdon

of origins, that compassionate king, sends from the east his bright light. Bear forth your linden shields before your breast, garments of mail and bright helmets into the crowd of attackers; cut down their generals, their doomed captains, with decorated swords. Our enemies are sentenced to death, and you will have honor and glory from the encounter, as the mighty Lord has revealed to you through my hand."

Then that host of the keen and competent was instantly 199
ready for warfare. Peers and commoners, brave as kings, hefted triumph-banners, went forth to battle properly, heroes in helmets, from that holy city at the very break of day. Shields clattered, resounded aloud. The lean wolf in the wood exulted, and the dusky raven, that bloodthirsty bird. They both knew that the men intended to furnish them their fill of the fated; but behind them flew the ravenous eagle with rain-flecked plumage; dusky-feathered, horn-beaked, he sang a war-song.

The men, war-workers, marched to battle, covered over 212
with curved shields of linden, who for long had endured the insults of foreigners, the abuse of heathens. That was harshly paid back to all of them, the Assyrians, in the launch of ash-spears, after the Hebrews under battle-standards had ad-

to ðam fyrd-wicum.   Hie ða fromlice
leton forð fleogan   flana scuras,
hilde-nædran   of horn-bogan,
strælas stede-hearde.   Styrmdon hlude
grame guð-frecan,   garas sendon
in heardra gemang.   Hæleð wæron yrre,
land-buende,   laðum cynne,
stopon styrn-mode,   sterced-ferhðe,
wrehton unsofte   eald-geniðlan
medo-werige.   Mundum brugdon
scealcas of sceaðum   scir-mæled swyrd,
ecgum gecoste,   slogon eornoste
Assiria   oret-mæcgas,
nið-hycgende,   nanne ne sparedon
þæs here-folces,   heanne ne ricne,
cwicera manna   þe hie ofercuman mihton.

XII

Swa ða mago-þegnas   on ða morgen-tid
ehton el-ðeoda   ealle þrage,
oð þæt ongeaton   ða ðe grame wæron,
ðæs here-folces   heafod-weardas
þæt him swyrd-geswing   swiðlic eowdon
weras Ebrisce.   Hie wordum þæt
þam yldestan   ealdor-þegnum
cyðan eodon;   wrehton cumbol-wigan
ond him forhtlice   fær-spel bodedon,
medo-werigum   morgen-collan,
atolne ecg-plegan.   Þa ic ædre gefrægn
slege-fæge hæleð   slæpe tobredon
ond wið þæs bealo-fullan   bur-geteldes
werig-ferhðe   hwearfum þringan,

vanced as far as the defenders' encampment. Then they
smartly let fly forth a downpour of arrows, battle-adders
from bows like horns, missiles meant to stay in place. The 223
grim war-makers bellowed loud, cast javelins in a fierce
throng. The native heroes were enraged against that hated
race, marched stern of mind with fortified resolve, un-
gently roused their mead-wearied ancient adversaries. With
their hands the fighters drew from sheaths pattern-welded
swords, incomparable blades, and hewed without hesitation
the ill-intending champions of Assyria, spared none of that
army, high or low of living men whom they could over-
power.

XII

Thus the men-at-arms in the morning hours pursued the 236
foreigners the whole time, until those who were the cruel
chief-watchmen of that military people perceived that the
Hebrew men were confronting them with powerful sword-
strokes. They went to convey that in words to the most se-
nior aides to the prince; they roused the standard-bearers
and, without flinching, announced to those mead-muddled
men the sudden news, the morning-slaughter, the terrible
blade-games. Then, as I have heard, those heroes doomed 246
to be struck down started out of sleep, and, weary of heart,
they began to throng in groups around the sleeping-tent of

Holofernus. Hogedon aninga
hyra hlaforde hilde bodian,
ærðon ðe him se egesa on ufan sæte,
mægen Ebrea. Mynton ealle
þæt se beorna brego ond seo beorhte mægð
in ðam wlitegan træfe wæron ætsomne,
Iudith seo æðele ond se gal-moda,
egesfull ond afor. Næs ðeah eorla nan
þe ðone wiggend aweccan dorste
oððe gecunnian hu ðone cumbol-wigan
wið ða halgan mægð hæfde geworden,
Metodes meowlan.

Mægen nealæhte,
folc Ebrea, fuhton þearle
heardum heoru-wæpnum, hæste guldon
hyra fyrn-geflitu fagum swyrdum,
ealde æfðoncan; Assyria wearð
on ðam dæg-weorce dom geswiðrod,
bælc forbiged.

Beornas stodon
ymbe hyra þeodnes træf þearfe gebylde,
sweorcend-ferhðe. Hi ða somod ealle
ongunnon cohhetan, cirman hlude
ond gristbitian, Gode orfeorme,
mid toðon, torn þoligende. Þa wæs hyra tires æt ende,
eades ond ellen-dæda. Hogedon þa eorlas aweccan
hyra wine-dryhten; him wiht ne speow.
Þa wearð sið ond late sum to ðam arod
þara beado-rinca, þæt he in þæt bur-geteld
nið-heard neðde, swa hyne nyd fordraf.
Funde ða on bedde blacne licgan

Holofernes. They intended to announce the combat to their lord at once, before confusion should descend on them, the force of the Hebrews. They all supposed that the prince of men and the radiant young woman were in that handsome tent together, Judith the noble and the lecher, horrid and harsh. There was not, however, a single man who dared waken the warrior or find out what had come to pass between the standard-bearer and the blessed young woman, the handmaid of Providence.

The force advanced, the army of the Hebrews, fought 261
heatedly with hard battle-weapons, fiercely repaid their former oppression, their old enmity, with inlaid swords. In that day's work the stature of the Assyrians was diminished, their hubris humbled.

Men stood about their lord's tent emboldened by neces- 267
sity, with darkening expectations. All together then they began to cough, to make loud noises and to make gnashing sounds with their teeth, void of God, suffering anxiety. Their glory was then at an end, their prosperity and their prowess. The men thought to awaken their friend and lord; they hardly succeeded.

Then one of the war-wagers sooner or later grew confi- 275
dent enough that, with steeled will, he ventured into the tent, since necessity compelled him. He found then lying

his gold-gifan gæstes gesne,
lifes belidenne. He þa lungre gefeoll
freorig to foldan, ongan his feax teran,
hreoh on mode, ond his hrægl somod,
ond þæt word acwæð to ðam wiggendum
þe ðær unrote ute wæron:
"Her ys geswutelod ure sylfra forwyrd,
toweard getacnod, þæt þære tide ys
mid niðum neah geðrungen, þe we sculon nyde losian,
somod æt sæcce forweorðan. Her lið sweorde geheawen,
beheafdod healdend ure."
Hi ða hreowig-mode
wurpon hyra wæpen of dune, gewitan him werig-ferhðe
on fleam sceacan. Him onfeaht on last
mægen-eacen folc, oð se mæsta dæl
þæs heriges læg hilde gesæged
on ðam sige-wonge, sweordum geheawen,
wulfum to willan ond eac wæl-gifrum
fuglum to frofre. Flugon ða ðe lyfdon,
laðra lind-werod. Him on laste for
sweot Ebrea sigore geweorðod,
dome gedyrsod; him feng Dryhten God
fægre on fultum, frea ælmihtig.
Hi ða fromlice fagum swyrdum,
hæleð hige-rofe, her-pað worhton
þurh laðra gemong, linde heowon,
scild-burh scæron. Sceotend wæron
guðe gegremede, guman Ebrisce,
þegnas on ða tid þearle gelyste
gar-gewinnes. Þær on greot gefeoll
se hyhsta dæl heafod-gerimes

on the bed his ashen patron, void of spirit, deprived of life. Then he at once fell trembling to the ground, began to tear his hair, perplexed of mind, and also his garment, and delivered this message to the warriors who, disturbed, were there outside:

“Here is revealed our own imminent destruction, signi- 285
fied with violence that it is drawn near the time when we
shall of necessity be lost, perish together in conflict. Here
lies our protector slashed by a sword, beheaded.”

Full of grief, they then threw down their weapons, de- 289
parted sick at heart to fly in retreat. A mighty host attacked
them from behind, until the greatest part of that army lay
devastated by war on the field of victory, slashed by swords,
to the delight of wolves, and also for the enjoyment of blood-
thirsty birds. Those who survived fled, a shield-troop of the
despised. Behind them came a company of Hebrews blessed
by victory, magnified in glory; the Lord God, almighty ruler,
had come graciously to their aid. Those resolute heroes then 301
briskly laid a war-path through the host of enemies with in-
laid swords, hacked at the linden shields, carved up the pha-
lanx. The lancers were steeled for battle, Hebrew men, war-
riors of that age, deeply desirous of spear-conflict. There in
the dirt fell the greatest part of the head-count of the elders

Assiria ealdor-duguðe,
laðan cynnes. Lythwon becom
cwicera to cyððe. Cirdon cyne-rofe,
wiggend on wiðer-trod, wæl-scel on innan,
reocende hræw. Rum wæs to nimanne
lond-buendum on ðam laðestan,
hyra eald-feondum unlyfigendum
heolfrig here-reaf, hyrsta scyne,
bord ond brad swyrd, brune helmas,
dyre madmas. Hæfdon domlice
on ðam folc-stede fynd oferwunnen
eðel-weardas, eald-hettende
swyrdum aswefede. Hie on swaðe reston,
þa ðe him to life laðost wæron
cwicera cynna.
Þa seo cneoris eall,
mægða mærost, anes monðes fyrst,
wlanc, wunden-locc, wagon ond læddon
to ðære beorhtan byrig, Bethuliam,
helmas ond hup-seax, hare byrnan,
guð-sceorp gumena golde gefrætewod,
mare madma þonne mon ænig
ascegan mæge searo-þoncelra.
Eal þæt ða ðeod-guman þrymme geeodon,
cene under cumblum on comp-wige
þurh Iudithe gleawe lare,
mægð modigre. Hi to mede hyre
of ðam siðfate sylfre brohton,
eorlas æsc-rofe, Holofernes sweord
ond swatigne helm, swylce eac side byrnan
gerenode readum golde, ond eal þæt se rinca baldor,

of Assyria, that hated race. Few returned alive to their fami- 310
lies. Valiant, noble fighters turned in retreat among the car-
nage, the reeking corpses. There was opportunity for the
native inhabitants to take from their most hated enemies
of old, lifeless, the blood-soaked spoils of war, magnificent
equipment, shields and broadswords, bright helmets, exqui-
site treasures. Patriots had to their honor overmatched their
opponents on the field of battle, foes of old, put them to
sleep with swords. They rested on the grass, those who of
living races were, alive, the most despicable.

Then the whole population, that most glorious of na- 323
tions, for the duration of one month, the proud and the
braided-haired, wore and bore to the glorious city of Bethu-
lia helmets and hip-daggers, gray mail-coats, men's war gear
chased with gold, more heirlooms than any expert could de-
scribe. The men of the nation had acquired all that by force, 331
stoics under standards in pitched battle, through the wise
instruction of Judith, that brave young woman. As a re-
ward for that selfsame woman they brought from that foray,
men skilled with ash-spears, Holofernes's sword and blood-
stained helmet, likewise his broad coat of mail, trimmed

swið-mod sinces ahte   oððe sundor-yrfes,
beaga ond beorhtra maðma,   hi þæt þære beorhtan idese
ageafon gearo-þoncolre.
341   Ealles ðæs Iudith sægde
wuldor weroda Dryhtne,   þe hyre weorð-mynde geaf,
mærðe on moldan rice,   swylce eac mede on heofonum,
sigor-lean in swegles wuldre,   þæs þe heo ahte soðne geleafan
to ðam Ælmihtigan;   huru æt þam ende ne tweode
þæs leanes þe heo lange gyrnde.   Ðæs sy ðam leofan Drihtne
wuldor to widan aldre,   þe gesceop wind ond lyfte,
roderas ond rume grundas,   swylce eac reðe streamas
ond swegles dreamas,   ðurh his sylfes miltse.

with red gold, and everything that the soldiers' overbearing superior had owned of riches and of select heirlooms, ornaments and gleaming treasures, that they gave to the radiant, brilliant woman.

For all that Judith proclaimed glory to the Lord of hosts, 341
who had granted her renown, esteem in the realm of earth, likewise recompense in heaven, victory's prize in the glory on high, because she had true faith in the Almighty; indeed, in the end there was no doubt of the reward that she had long desired. Glory be to the dear Lord for ever and ever for that, who created the wind and the atmosphere, the firmament and the far-extending earth, likewise the raging sea-currents and the joys of heaven, by his own generosity.

Appendix

The Fight at Finnsburg

Introduction

This fragment of a poem treats of the same general conflict summarized in the so-called Finnsburg Episode of *Beowulf* (lines 1063–1159), but much remains mysterious about the two, as there is remarkably little overlap in the narratives. The Fragment (i.e., *The Fight at Finnsburg*) appears to relate the initial attack upon the Half-Danes during their visit to Frisia, whereas the Episode deals chiefly with the aftermath of that attack. For a reconstruction of the general outline of the story, see the commentary on lines 1068–1159 of *Beowulf* in the Notes to the Translations.

Agreement has not been reached on several matters of importance. In the Episode the Jutes and the Frisians appear to be identical, or very closely associated, and this presents an obstacle to the view that Hengest should be identical to that Hengest who with his brother Horsa is said by the Venerable Bede to have founded the royal dynasty of the Jutish kingdom of Kent. As leader of the Half-Danes at Finnsburg, to the contrary, Hengest would appear to be an enemy of the Jutes. Various explanations have been offered to remove this obstacle, including the idea that there is no reference to Jutes in the Episode (see the commentary on *Beowulf* 902). The name Guthlaf appears in both the Fragment and the Episode, but it is uncertain whether it refers to the same person in lines 16 and 33 of the Fragment. If so, it must be assumed that he and his son Garulf fight on opposite sides of the conflict. Why the visiting Danes were attacked in the first place is simply unknown, but since Danes and Jutes were age-old enemies—the Danes had conquered Jutland by the six century at the latest—some such incident as Beowulf predicts for the renewal of hostilities between the Danes and the Heatho-Bards (*Beowulf* 2020–69) may be imagined to have occurred at Finnsburg. Uncertainty as to whether the Jutes and the Frisians are identical leaves us in doubt about whether Finn was complicit in the initial Jutish attack upon the Danes, and thus whether his death amounts to vindication for the Danes or simply a shameful violation of their oath of loyalty. That they swore such an oath to him suggests that he had not been treacherous, but it is impossible to be certain.

The Fight at Finnsburg is commonly regarded as one of the few surviving examples, outside of Old Norse literature, of the early Germanic heroic lay, a short poetic form that many assume was the chief conduit for the transmission of history and legend in the early Germanic world. Although it is a fragment, it has the appearance of having belonged to a relatively brief poem regarding a particular tragic conflict, like the also-fragmentary Old High German *Hildebrandslied*. Certainly its style is different from that of the Episode in *Beowulf*, unlike which it focuses on the specifics of the action, with fine speeches, varied characters, and a particularized scene of battle. Nearly as remarkable are the features that the Fragment has in common with medieval Celtic literatures, especially the trope of the misperceived signs of an approaching battle (lines 1–12) and warriors' service in repayment for white mead (line 39).

The loose manuscript leaf on which the Fragment was recorded has been missing for more than three centuries. We are obliged to rely instead on the transcript of the leaf published in 1703 by George Hickes in his *Thesaurus* (see the introduction to *Beowulf*), a transcript that is plainly unreliable in some respects. There is thus no reason to accord excessive reverence to the particulars of Hickes's text.

"... hornas byrnað næfre."
Hleoþrode ða heaþo-geong cyning:
"Ne ðis ne dagað eastan, ne her draca ne fleogeð,
ne her ðisse healle hornas ne byrnað,
ac her forþ berað. Fugelas singað,
gylleð græg-hama, guð-wudu hlynneð,
scyld scefte oncwyð. Nu scyneð þes mona
waðol under wolcnum; nu arisað wea-dæda
ðe ðisne folces nið fremman willað.
Ac onwacnigeað nu, wigend mine,
habbað eowre linda, hicgeaþ on ellen,
winnað on orde, wesað on mode!"
Ða aras mænig gold-hladen ðegn, gyrde hine his swurde;
ða to dura eodon drihtlice cempan,
Sigeferð and Eaha, hyra sword getugon,
and æt oþrum durum Ordlaf and Guþlaf
and Hengest sylf, hwearf him on laste.
Ða gyt Garulfe Guðere styrde,
ðæt he swa freolic feorh forman siþe
to ðære healle durum hyrsta ne bære,
nu hyt niþa heard anyman wolde;
ac he frægn ofer eal undearninga,
deor-mod hæleþ, hwa ða duru heolde.

"... gables will never burn."

Then the battle-young king made a speech: "This is not 2
the dawn rising from the east, neither is this a dragon flying, nor is this the gables of this hall burning, but they are approaching. Birds are calling, the gray-coat howls, war-wood thunders, shield answers arrow-shaft. Now this errant moon gleams behind clouds; now there are arising grievous doings that aim to carry out this enmity of the people. But rouse yourselves, my fighters, take your linden-shields, devote your thoughts to bravery, fight in the front line, be in high spirits!"

Then many a gold-laden follower rose, girded himself 13
with his sword; then lordly champions went to the door, Sigeferth and Eahha, drew their swords, and at the other doors Ordlaf and Guthlaf, and Hengest himself, who moved in their wake.

Then further, Guthhere restrained Garulf, lest he convey 18
his lordly life and armor to the hall's doors at the first opportunity, now that hard, violent men intended to deprive him of them; but above the commotion he could plainly be heard, the hero of high courage, asking who held the door.

"Sigeferþ is min nama," cweþ he; "ic eom Secgena leod,
wreccea wide cuð; fæla ic weana gebad,
heordra hilda; ðe is gyt her witod
swæþer ðu sylf to me secean wylle."
Ða wæs on healle wæl-slihta gehlyn,
sceolde celæs bord cenum on handa,
ban-helm berstan, —buruh-ðelu dynede—
oð æt ðære guðe Garulf gecrang
ealra ærest eorð-buendra,
Guðlafes sunu, ymbe hyne godra fæla,
hwearf-latra hræw.
Hræfen wandrode
sweart and sealo-brun. Swurd-leoma stod,
swylce eal Finnes Buruh fyrenu wære.
Ne gefrægn ic næfre wurþlicor æt wera hilde
sixtig sige-beorna sel gebæran,
ne nefre swanas hwitne medo sel forgyldan,
ðonne Hnæfe guldan his hæg-stealdas.
Hig fuhton fif-dagas, swa hyra nan ne feol,
driht-gesiða, ac hig ða duru heoldon.
Ða gewat him wund hæleð on wæg gangan,
sæde þæt his byrne abrocen wære,
here-sceorp unhror, and eac wæs his helm ðyrel.
Ða hine sona frægn folces hyrde
hu ða wigend hyra wunda genæson,
oððe hwæþer ðæra hyssa . . .

"Sigeferth is my name," he said; "I am a man of the Sec- 24
gas, an adventurer widely known; I have survived straits,
fierce combats; thus it is yet to be seen which of the two you
yourself will obtain from me."

Then in the hall there was the crash of deadly blows; a 28
peerless board was to be in the hand of a bold man, a bone-
helmet was to burst—hall-planking resounded—until in the
battle Garulf succumbed first of all inhabitants of earth,
Guthlaf's son, surrounded by many a good man, the corpses
of those disinclined to retreat.

A raven circled, swart and darkly glossy. Sword-light 34
sprang up, as if all Finnsburg were ablaze. I have never heard
of sixty triumphant men who bore themselves better, more
worthily in manly conflict, nor ever of swains who rendered
better payment for white mead than Hnæf's lads repaid
him. They so fought for five days that none of them, noble
peers, fell, but they held the doors.

Then a wounded hero went walking away, said that his 43
ring-mail was broken, his army-gear useless, and also his hel-
met was pierced through. Then at once the people's guard-
ian asked him how the soldiers bore their wounds, or which
of the young men . . .

Note on the Texts

Because of the damaged state of the manuscript, as described in the introduction, the present edition has benefited from consultation of the paleographical and codicological studies listed in the bibliography. Except for the diacritics having been removed, the texts of *Beowulf* and *The Fight at Finnsburg* are practically identical to those found in *Klaeber's "Beowulf" and "The Fight at Finnsburg,"* ed. R. D. Fulk, Robert E. Bjork, and John D. Niles, corrected reprint (Toronto, 2009), which should be consulted for the sometimes complex logic of the establishment of these two texts, along with R. D. Fulk, "The Textual Criticism of Frederick Klaeber's *Beowulf*," in *Constructing Nations, Reconstructing Myth: Essays in Honour of T. A. Shippey,* ed. Andrew Wawn (Turnhout, Belg., 2007), pp. 131–53. As an aid to comprehension, hyphens have been added to compound nouns and adjectives and their derivatives, and even to some (excluding personal names) that are not technically compounds but in which the meaning of the separate constituents is particularly transparent.

Manuscript abbreviations are expanded silently; only emendations and restorations of lost characters are noted in the Notes to the Texts.

Notes to the Texts

The notes that follow are a listing of textual variants. An ellipsis (. . .) is used to indicate one or more illegible or lost letters, usually those burned away at the edges. The listed variants in many instances cannot express probabilities raised by fragments of letters and faded letters.

The Passion of Saint Christopher

1 þu eart: þ . . . 2 his handa: his han . . . mid: m . . . 3 gecwædon: . . . cwædon wære: wær wælhreowlice: wælhr . . . cempan: cempa . . . 5 tintrego: tintreg . . . beobread: beobrea . . . 6 Cristoforus: crist . . . forus fyres lig: fyre . . . lig ofere þæt: ofer . . . 7 stefne: stefn . . . gescyndnesse: gecyndnesse 9 þe he: þe . . . 11 micelre: miceles 12 Þa þæt: þæt þa 13 him: hin 14 þinne: þone 15 tide: t . . . 16 gegearwode: gegear . . . de 18 Se cyning: . . . cyning 22 halgan: halga . . . 23 For: f . . . 25 ðurh dryhten sylfne: drihten sylf 26 nym: ny . . . 28 tid: . . . t onfehð: . . . fehð 29 unne: . . . e 30 fram: fran 32 myndgien on: on 34 feowertig: feower 35 hyne: hyn . . . 37 dom: dem 38 wuldor-geworces: wuldorge . . . ces 42 sunu: sun . . . 43 tearum: tear . . .

The Wonders of the East

V = London, BL, Cotton Vitellius A. xv; *T* = London, BL, Cotton Tiberius B. v.

Minor differences of spelling between the two manuscripts are unrecorded; only substantive changes to the text of *V* are indicated.

1 land-bunis is: land buend *V*, lond buend *T* from: *so T*, . . . rom *V* lande: *so T*, . . . ande *V* 4 cepe-monnum: *so T*, cere monnum *V* 8 *leones:* leo . . . *V*, leuua *T* 9 is þonne: is *VT* ðam þe: *so T*, þonne þe *V* 15–16 Hascellentia . . . gefylled: *om. V* bugað to: bueð oð *T* 17 Þeos: Ðeos *T*, . . . os *V* 18 On: *so T*, . . . n *V* 19 ðam mæstan westene: *so T*, þære mæstan wæstme *V* 20 bugað: buað *VT* to: *so T*, . . . o *V* 23 geornfulnysse: *so T*, geneornesse *V* 24 þæt mon: *so T*, þæt mo . . . *V* þæt hi: *so T*, þæt *V* 31 beardas: *so T*, bear . . . as *V* 35 fet: so *T*, *om. V* 43 eallicra: fallicra *V*, fullicra *T* 44 stowum: *so T*, *om. V* ylpenda: *so T*, olfenda *V* 47 ðrys: drys *V*, þreosellices *T* 48 Gyf hi: gyf *V*, gif hi *T* 51 Hi beoð sweartes hiwes ond: *so T*, *om. V* 53 on Brixonte: *so T*, *om. V* 55 Brixonte: *so T*, bixon *V* men acende: menn akende *T*, *om. V* 57 dracan: *so T*, *om. V* hundteontige: hundteotige *V*, hundteontiges *T* fotmæla: *so T*, . . . t mæla *V* 59 From: fram *T*, . . . rom *V* læssan: *so T*, . . . ssan *V* 60 twi-men: *om. V*, twylice *T* 61 beoþ: *so T*, habbaþ *V* 63 him: *so T*, *om. V* 68 lawern-beame: lawernbeabe *V*, laurbeame *T* 70 hatte: *so T*, *om. V* 71 Ðonne is sum: *so T*, Ðon . . . um *V* frihteras: *so T*, fr . . . f teras *V* eall: *so T*, *om. V* 72 æfter: *so T*, æfte . . . *V* heafde: *so T*, heafd . . . *V* 78 micel: *so T*, . . . icel *V* onele on: onele *V*, onæle on *T* 79 Ðonne: *so T*, . . . ne *V* þæs læssan: ðæs læssan *T*, . . . s læssan *V* ond þæs: *so T*, ond þ . . . s *V* leones hatte: leuua hatte *T*, leones . . . e *V* 80 þæs cyninges ond: þæs cinges *T*, *om. V* ond Iobes templ: *so T*, . . . iobes temple *V* 81 ðanon . . . begymeþ: *so T*, *om. V* ond setl: setl *V*, *om. T* 86 Þær . . . him: *so T*, *om. V* Readan: *so T*, re . . . dan *V* 87 saro-gimmas: sarogi *V*, þa deorwurðan gimmas *T* 89 Þa syndan hunticgean: hundicgean *V*, þa syndan huntigystran fore hundum: *so T*, from *V* deor: *so T*, . . . eor *V* mid heora scinlace: mid heora scin . . . e, *om. T* 90 Ðonne: *so T*, . . . ne *V* wif: *so T*, . . . *V* 91 ond hy: ond hi *T*, . . . hy *V* fet: *so T*, . . . t *V* 92 unclennesse: micelnesse *V*, mycelnysse *T* 94 is: *so T*, *om. V* þa syndon: *so T*, þær syndon *V* 95 þæt rice is: *so T*, þæs rices *V* 95 him: *so T*, *om. V* 97 Ðis man-cyn: Ðis mannkynn *T*, . . . ancyn *V* geara: *so T*, . . . ara *V* fremfulle: fremfulfe *T*, . . . remfulle *V* 98 hwilc: hwylc *T*, . . . wilc *V* þonne: *so T*, . . . n *V* ær: *so T*, . . . *V* 99 Macedonisca Alexander: *so T*, . . . cedonisca . . . lexander *V* to com: *so T*, . . . o com *V* don: *so T*, on *V* 100 stanas: *so T*, . . . tanas *V* þonon: þanon *T*, . . . onon 101 Ðær: *so T*, . . . r *V* 102–8 Ðonne . . . byrnende: *so T*, *om. V*

The Letter of Alexander the Great to Aristotle

1 gesetenis: GE SE GE NIS 2 gemindig þin: gemindig frecennisse: freon nis se 3 niura: minra gleawnis to: glengista 4 to: . . . snyttro ond: snyttro abæded: abæded Indie: . . . die micle: . . . icle 5 write: . . . ite in: . . . 8 ful-cuþan wildru ond wæstmas: ful cuþan 10 mid: m . . . 11 gelyfe: . . . lyfe talige: tali . . . 14 oþor: . . . or nu ær: . . . ær 15 gewritum: gewri . . . um þære: . . . ære rynum: . . . num 16 Þa: . . . micelre: mi . . . re forestihtod: fore . . . ihtod 17 cartan: . . . artan 22 þæm: þæ . . . 23 mid: m . . . d cyning: cyni . . . ond on þæm: ond þæm wæron: w . . . ron 27 ond þa: . . . 28 Þar wæron: þar wæ . . . n trumlice: trum . . . ice be þæm: . . . æm 29 gyldne: . . . dne fingres: fin . . . es 30 þa þing: . . . þing gyldenne: . . . yldenne 32 wingearde: . . . ingearde wæstmas: wæst . . . as 34 hwite: . . . wite styþeo: styþeo hie uton wreðedon 38 eorðan: eorðan ond ic swiðe wundrade þa gesælignesse þære eorðan 39 missenlican: missen . . . ican læs: l . . . 43 woldon: wolde 44 þone þræd: þonne sumum: sunnan 46 freonda ond heded: freond . . . ond 48 eorcnan-stana: eorcnan stane 50 het: hie 62 Þa: . . . a 66 þusenda feþena: þusend . . . feþena 72 in: iu seo ærest: . . . o ærest mines: m . . . es 73 wære mid: wære . . . d 74 wundredon: . . . undredon hefignesse: hefig . . . esse 75 þa: þæta þæt usic: þus ic *altered from* þætus ic 78 writon: riton *altered from* writon 79 Indisce: mennisce 86 unhyrlicran: un . . . rlicran grund: gr . . . sliton: sli . . . n þæt: . . . 91 men þa: men . . . 92 wæs þæt: þæt 93 þus: þætus 96 ond þa eal: . . . a eal 97 ic: . . . c 106 wæron toweard: wæron 111 Eall: . . . ll hwistlunge: . . . istlunge 113 Sioðþan: . . . ioðþan 118 hricge: h . . . icge 120 deaðberende: dead berende 124 mihton: . . . ton swilc earfeþo: swi . . . eþo niht: . . . iht 125 eoforas: laforas þar: . . . ar 126 hreaþe-mys: . . . reaþe mys pulledon: wulledon 137 bitan: . . . itan 144 gebrohton: g . . . brohton 150 Patriacen: patria . . . cen 153 swiðor: swiðe 155 cunnenne: cun enne *altered from* cumenne 156 metes: mete 162 þegnes: . . . egnes feoh-bigenga: eoh bigenga 164 Swa sona: swa 168 þæt gesælde þat: þæt 169 þa wæs he swa gefeonde for: þa 173 ond het: . . . et 188 ond hie: . . . e 194 hæfde hie: hæfde 196 gesawe we: ge sawe 203 lond: . . . d 204 usse: . . . sse 211 snaw: sna . . . 217 siðþan:

sið þan . . . ððan 218 minra: m . . . nra snawas: . . . was wicum: . . . um 223 mid: m . . . Macedoniam: mac . . . niam Olimphiade: olimph . . . de 227 þonne ic: þonne 230 to him: . . . him Secgað: . . . ecgað mærlices: . . . lices gehatað: ge ha . . . 231 me: . . . e kyning: ky . . . ing geferest: geferest ond 233 forealdodan: for eal ðoðan 235 meþo: me . . . þo 236 gerefum: geref . . . 238 panthera: palthera gegyryde: g . . . gyryde 239 þæt hie: þæt . . . 240 wynsumo: wyn . . . umo lifdon ond: lifdon 241 bisceop: . . . isceop 243 halette: alette 245 him: hin 246 wif-gehrine: wig . . . ge hrine þone: þ . . . ne 248 se: s . . . ond het: on . . . het 249 Wæs: . . . 250 setl-gonges: setlgongen 254 on middum: . . . dum meahton hie: mea . . . e eac: . . . ac heanisse: . . . nisse 255 Þara: . . . a ond cwæð: . . . cwæð wætan: wæ . . . an 256 sægde: sæg . . . regnes: . . . gnes 257 weopen: wepen 258 ac þa: ac þ . . . nære: nær . . . nyten: . . . ten soþe: soþre 261 becuman . . . uman Olimphiade: olimphi . . . de 262 gesceaft: eþel 266 swa we: swa . . . 270 modes: . . . des 273 medmicelne: micelne 276 irenes: . . . nes 282 syrere: . . . e 286 ðeah þu: ðeah þu þu 289 þy: þæty wop: po . . . 290 ne moste: ne most . . . 294 swelce: . . . ce ond hleouige: . . . leonige min þrym: . . . n þrym maran wæron: maran . . . æron

Beowulf

V = London, BL, Cotton Vitellius A. xv; *L* = the later hand on fols. 179 and 198v of the same; *A* = Thorkelín A; *B* = Thorkelín B; *W* = Wanley 1705; *C* = Conybeare's collation of *V* (in Kiernan 2003); *M* = Madden's collation of *V* (in Kiernan 2003). When *A, B, W, C,* or *M* is cited, it is to be assumed that *V* is now defective. For an explanation of the identity of each of these witnesses to the text, and the quality of the testimony it brings to bear, see *Klaeber's Beowulf,* pp. xxv–xxix.

4 sceaþena: *so W* 6 eorlas: eorl *V* 15 aldor-lease: aldor . . . ease *V* 18 Beow: beowulf *V* 20 geong: ge . . . *V* 21 bearme: . . . rme *A* 47 gyldenne: gy . . . denne *V* 51 -rædende: rædenne *V* 53 Beow: beowulf *V* 60 ræswan: ræswa *V* 62 wæs Onelan: elan *V* 70 þonne: þone *V* 84 ecg-: secg *V* -sweoran: swerian *V* 92 worhte: worh . . . *AB* 101 fremman: fre . . . man *V* 107 Caines: *so V, altered from* cames

113 gigantas: gi . . . ntas *B* 139 ræste sohte: ræste *V* 148 Scyldinga: scyldenda *V* 149 gesyne wearð: wearð *V* 158 banan: banum *V* 159 ac se: . . . *V* 175 hærg-: hrærg *V* 204 -rofne: pofne *A*, forne *B* 240 Ic hwile: le *V* 250 næfne: næfre *V* 255 minne: mine *V* 280 edwenden: edwendan *AB* 302 sale: sole *V* 304 -bergan: beran *V* 306 grimmon: grummon *V* 307 sæl: æl *V* 312 hof: of *V* 332 æþelum: hæleþum *V* 357 anhar: un hár *V* 375 eafora: eaforan *V* 390 Wedera leodum word: word *V* 395 -getawum: geatawum *V* 403 hrof eode hilde-deor: hrof *V* 404 heard: *so B* heorðe: heoðe *V* 414 haðor: hador *V* 418 minne: mine *V* 447 dreore: deore *V* 457 Fore: fere *V* 461 Wedera: gara *V* 465 Deniga: deninga *V* 466 ginne: gim me *V* 499 Unferð: HVN ferð *V* 516 wylmum: wylm *V* 524 soðe: sode *A* 530 Unferð: hun ferð *V* 534 eafeþo: earfeþo *V* 567 sweordum: swe . . . *V*, speodum *A* 578 hwæþere: hwaþere *V* 581 wadu: wudu *V* 586 þæs fela: þæs *V* 591 Grendel: gre del *V* 652 Gegrette: grette *V* 684 he: het *V* 702 wide-: ride *AB* 707 scyn- syn *V* 714 wolc-: wole *A* 716 fætum: fættum *V* 722 æthran: . . . hran *V* 723 he gebolgen: . . . bolgen *V* 747 him: hi . . . *V* 752 sceata: sceatta *V* 780 betlic: hetlic *V* 811 he wæs: he *V* 836 hrof: hr . . . *B* 875 Sigemundes: sige munde *V* 902 eafoð: earfoð *V* 905 lemedon: lemede *V* 936 gehwylcum: ge hwylcne *V* 947 betesta: betsta *V* 949 nænigre: ænigre *V* 954 þin dom: þin *V* 963 hine: him *V* 965 mund-: hand *V* 976 nið-: mid *V* 986 hilde-: hilde hilde *B* 1004 gesecan: gc sacan *V* 1022 hilde-: hilte *V* 1026 sceotendum: scotenum *V* 1031 walu: walan *V* 1032 feola: fela *V* meahte: meahton *V* 1037 in under: munder *A* 1051 -lade: leade *V* 1068 eaferan: eaferum *V* 1073 lind-: hild *V* 1079 heo: he *V* 1106 scede: scolde *V* 1107 Ad: að *V* 1117 eame: earme *V* 1118 guðrec: guð rinc *V* 1128–29 Finne he: finnel *V* 1130 ne: he *V* 1151 roden: hroden *V* 1165 Unferþ: hun ferþ *V* 1174 þa þu: þu *V* 1176 hererinc: here ric *V* 1198 -maððum: mad mum *V* 1199 þære: here *V* 1200 fleah: fealh *V* 1218 þeod-: þeo *V* 1229 hold: hol (*altered from* heol) *V* 1234 grimme: grimne *V* 1261 Cain: camp *V* 1278 deoð: þeod *V* 1285 geþruen: geþuren *V* 1314 hwæþer: hwæþre *V* alwalda: alf walda *V* 1318 nægde: hnægde *AB* 1320 neod-laðum: neod laðu *V* 1328 Swylc: swy . . . *A* 1329 æþeling ær-god: ærgod *V* 1331 hwæder:

hwæþer *V* 1333 gefrecnod: ge frægnod *V* 1354 nemdon: nemdod *AB* 1362 standeð: stanðeð *V* 1372 hafelan beorgan: hafelan *V* 1375 ðrysmaþ: drysmaþ *V* 1379 sinnigne: fela sinnigne *V* 1382 wundnan: wundini *V* 1391 gang: gan *altered to* gang *in another hand V* 1404 þær gegnum: gegnum *V* 1407 ealgode: eahtode *V* 1424 fyrd-leoð: . . . leoð *V* 1488 Unferð: hunferð *V* 1506 -wylf: wyl *V* 1508 þæm: þæs *V* 1510 swencte: swecte *V* 1513 he in: he *V* 1520 hond sweng: hord swenge *V* 1523 Đa: da *AB* (*altered to* ða *with another ink B*) 1531 wunden-: wundel *V* 1537 feaxe: eaxle *V* 1541 and-: hand *V* 1545 seax: seaxe *V* 1546 brad ond: brad *V* 1559 þæt wæs: þæt *V* 1585 ðæs: to ðæs *V* 1599 abroten: abreoten *V* 1602 setan: secan *V* 1624 -laca: lace *V* 1663 ofost: oftost *V* 1707 freode: freoðe *V* 1735 wunað: wunad *A* 1737 sefan: sefað *A* 1741 weaxeð: weaxed *AB* 1750 fætte: fædde *V* 1759 betesta: betsta *V* 1774 edwenden: ed wendan *V* 1796 beweotede: be weotene *V* 1802–3 leoma ofer sceadwa scacan: scacan *V* 1805 farenne: farene ne *V* 1816 hæle: hella *V* 1830 Higelac: hige lace *V* 1833 wordum: weordum *V* nerige: herige *V* 1836 Hreþric: hreþrinc *V* 1837 geþingeð: geþinged *V* 1857 gemænu: ge mænum *V* 1861 gegretan: gegrettan *V* 1862 heafu: hea þu *V* 1868 hine: inne *V* 1871 betestan: betstan *V* 1875 hie: he *V* seoððan no: seoðða . . . *V* 1876 Wæs: þæs *A* 1880 born: beorn *V* 1883 agend-: aged *V* 1889 -stealdra heap: stealdra *V* 1893 gæstas: gæs . . . *A* 1902 maþme weorþra: maþma weorþre *V* 1903 naca: nacan *V* 1918 oncer-: oncear *V* 1926 heah on healle: hea healle *V* 1944 onhohsnode: on hoh nod *altered to* on hohsnod *V* Hemminges: hem ninges *V* 1947 syððan: fyððan *A* 1956 þone: þæs *V* 1960 Eomer: geomor *V* 1961 Hemminges: hem inges *V* 1981 heal-reced: reced *altered to* side ręced *V* 1983 hæleðum: hæðnum *but* ð *erased V* 1991 wid-: wið *V* 2000 Higelac: hige . . . *B* 2001 mæru: . . . *V* 2002 hwylc: hwyle *A*, hwylce *B* orleg-: or . . . *M* 2006 ne þearf: þearf *V* 2007 ænig: en . . . *B* 2008 se ðe: sede *A* 2009 fære: fæ . . . *A*, fer . . . *B* 2019 sealde: . . . *V* 2020 duguðe: . . . uguðe *with* ð *altered from* d *B* 2023 nægled: . . . gled *V* 2024 is: . . . se *B* 2026 hafað: iafað *A* 2037 -Beardna: bearna *V* 2039 XXVIIII–XXX: *om. V* 2042 geman: genam *but* na *added later B* 2043 sefa: . . . fa *A* 2044 geongum: geong . . . *AB* 2055 gylpeð: gylped *B* 2062 lifigende: . . . figende *A* 2063 abrocene: . . . orocene *AB* 2064 syððan: . . . ðan *AB* 2067 -Beardna: bearna *V* 2076 hild: hilde *V* 2079 magu-: magum *V* 2085 gearo-: geareo *A* 2093 hu ic ðam: hiedam *A* 2094 ond-: hond *V* 2097 breac: bræc *A*, brene *altered to* brec *B* 2108 gomen-: go mel *AB* 2113 inne: mne *A* 2128 fæðmum under: fæð . . . der *A* 2129 Hroðgare: hroð . . . *A*, Hrodgar . . . *B* 3136 grimne: grimme *V* 2139 guð-sele: sele *V* 2146 maðmas: . . . is *B* 2147 minne: . . . ne *V* 2168 renian: ren . . . *B* 2174 ðeodnes: ðeod . . . *A* 2176 breost: brost *V* 2177 bealdode: b . . . dode *A* 2178 guðum: guð . . . *A* 2186 dryhten: . . . nten *altered to* drihten *B* Wedera: wereda *V* 2187 wendon: . . . don *V* 2196 bam: . . . am *A* 2202 Heardrede: hearede *V* 2207 brade: bræde *or* brade *L* 2209 wintra: wintru *L* 2210 -weard: peard *L* an: ón *L* 2211 ricsian: rics an *altered from* ricran *(?) A* 2212 heaum hofe: hea . . . *L* 2213 stearcne: stearne *L* 2215 niðða: nið . . . *L*, mða *A* -hwylc se ðe neh geþrong: hwyl . . . h g . . . g *V* 2216 eðe gefeng: . . . *L* 2217 searo: . . . *L* fah: fac *with* h *above* c *L* bemað: . . . *L* 2218 þeah ðe he: þ . . . ð . . . *L* -syred: syre . . . *AB* wurde: . . . de *V* 2219 onfand: . . . *L* 2220 bu-: b . . . *V* biorna: beorn . . . *with* i *altered to* i *L* -bolgen: bolge . . . *L* 2221 męt gewealdum: . . . weoldum *L* 2223 þeo: þ . . . *L* 2224 fleah: fleoh *L* 2225 þearfa: þea . . . *L* fealh: weall *A* 2226 -bysig: . . . sig *L* in þa tide: mwatide *L* 2227 þær: . . . *L* gyste: gyst . . . *L* gryrebroga: . . . br . . . g . . . *L on fol. 179r* 2228 hwæðre earm-sceapen: hwæ . . . sc . . . pen *L on 179r*, . . . sceapen *L on 179v* ealdre neþde: . . . e *V* 2230 forht on ferhðe: forh . . . *V* 2230 fær: fæs *L* 2231 sohte: . . . *L* 2232 -sele: se . . . *B* 2237 se: si *L* 2239 wende: rihde *L* ylcan: yldan *L* 2244 innan: innon *L* 2245 hord-: hard *L* 2246 fea: fec *L* 2247 mostan: mæstan *(?) L* 2250 feorh-bealo: reorh bealc *L* fyra gehwylcne: fyrena gel ylcne *L* 2251 þone: þana *L* þis lif: þis *L* 2252 -dreamas: dream . . . *L* 2253 forð bere: f . . . *A* 2254 duguð: dug . . . *A* sceoc: seoc *V* 2255 hyrsted: . . . sted *V* 2268 hwearf: hwear . . . *M* 2275 swiðe ondrædað: . . . *V* 2276 hearh on: bearn . . . *B* 2279 hrusan: hrusam *V* 2296 hlæw: hlæwum *V* 2298 on þam: on þ . . . *A* 2298 wiges: hilde *V* 2299 beadwe: bea . . . *V* 2305 se laða: fela ða *V* 2307 læng: læg *V* 2325 ham: him *V* 2334 eal lond: ealond 2340 helpan: he . . . *V* 2341 liþend: þend *V* 2347 þa: þam *V* 2355 gemota: gemot *AB* 2361 ealra: . . . *V* 2362 þrong: . . . g *V* 2363 þorfton: þorf . . . on *B* 2383 ðe: ðe ðe *V* 2385 for feorme:

orfeorme *V* 2405 maðþum-: madþum *AB* 2448 helpe: helpan *V* 2457 reotge: reote *V* 2473 wid: rid *A* 2478 ge-: ge ge *V* 2488 hilde-blac: blac *V* 2503 -cyninge: cyning *V* 2505 cempan: campe *V* 2514 mærðu: mærðum *V* 2523 oreðes: reðes *V* attres: hattres *V* 2525 feohte: . . . *V* 2533 nefne: nefu *A* 2534 þæt: wat *V* 2545 stondan: stodan *V* 2564 unslaw: unglaw (*letter erased after* l) *V* 2566 wið: wid *A* 2589 ofer willan: willan *V* 2596 hand-: heand *V* 2612 Ohteres: ohtere *V* 2613 wræccan: wræcca *A* Weohstan: weohstanes *V* 2628 mæges: mægenes *V* 2629 þæt: þa *V* 2660 beadu-: byrdu *V* 2671 niosian: niosnan *B*, mosum *A* 2676 wæs: . . . *V* 2678 mod: m . . . *V* 2694 þearfe gefrægn: þearfe *V* 2698 mæges: mægenes *V* 2710 siðast: siðas *V* -hwila: hwile *V* 2714 -niðe: niði *B* 2723 helm: helo *A* 2727 wynne: wyn . . . *V* 2755 under: urder *V* 2765 grunde: grund *AB* 2769 leoma: leoman *V* 2771 wrætte: wræce *V* 2775 hladon: hlodon *V* 2792 -bræc. Biorncyning spræc: bræc *V* 2793 giohðe: giogoðe *V* 2799 mine: minne *V* 2814 -sweop: speof *V* 2819 hræðre: hwæðre *V* 2821 XXXVIIII: *om.* *V* guman: gumum *V* 2829 -scearpe: scear de *V* 2844 æghwæðer: æghwæðre *V* 2854 speow: speop *V* 2860 geongan: geongum *V* 2882 Wergendra: fergendra *V* 2884 Nu: hu *V* 2904 sex-: siex *V* 2911 underne: under *V* 2916 genægdon: ge hnægdon *V* 2921 Merewioingas milts: mere wio ingasmilts (*altered from* mere wio ingannilts) *V* 2929 ond-: hond *V* 2930 bryd ahredde: bryda heorde *V* 2931 gomelan: gomela *V* 2940 -treowum: treowu *V* 2941 fuglum to: to *V* 2946 Sweona: swona *V* 2958 Higelaces: higelace *V* 2959 forð: ford *V* 2961 sweorda: sweordum *V* 2965 -reding: reðing *V* 2972 ond-: hond- *V* 2978 bradne: brade *V* 2989 ðam: d . . . *B* 2990 mid: . . . *V* gelæste: gelæsta *V* 2996 syððan: syðða *V* 3000 ic wen: ic *V* 3005 Scilfingas: scildingas *V* 3007 Nu: me *V* 3012 geceapod: gecea . . . d *C* 3014 gebohte: . . . te *V* 3041 gryre-fah: gry . . . *B* 3060 wrætte: wræce *V* 3065 magum: . . . gum *V* 3073 strude: strade *V* 3078 adreogan: a dreogeð *V* 3086 ðone þeod-cyning: ðone *V* 3101 oðre siðe: oðre *V* 3102 searo-gimma: searo *V* 3119 fæðer-: fæder *V* 3122 tosomne: . . . ne *B* 3124 -rinca: rinc *V* 3130 -lice: -lic *AB* 3134 Þa: þæt *V* 3135 æþeling: æþelinge *V* 3136 hilde-rinc: hilde *V* 3139 helmum: helm *V* 3144 wudu-: wud *AB* 3145 swoðole: swicðole *V* leg: let *V* 3147 hæfde: hæfd . . .

V 3149 cwealm: . . . m *V*, cw aln *A* 3150 Geatisc: . . . iat . . . *L* 3151 æfter Biowulfe bunden-: . . . unden *L* 3152 sang: . . . *L* sæide geneahhe: sælðe . . . neahl . . . *L* 3153 hereg-: . . . g *V* -eongas: . . . gas *L* ondre-: ond . . . e *V* 3154 worn: wonn *L* werudes: . . . erudes *V* 3155 hynðo: hyðo *L* hæft-: . . . æft *V*, h . . . *L* 3157 hlæw: hlæ . . . *V* hoe: hde *A*, liðe *B* 3158 weg-: . . . g *V*, . . . et *B* 3159 betim-: beti . . . *L* 3160 -rofes: rofis *L* (rofes *V?*) 3168 æror: . . . r *V* 3170 twelfe: twelfa *L* 3171 care: . . . *V* ond cyning: kyning *L* 3172 wer: w . . . *L* 3174 gedefe: ged . . . *L* 3177 lic-haman: lachaman *L* læded: . . . ded *V* 3179 hryre: . . . re *L* 3180 -cyninga: cyning *L* 3181 mon-ðwærust: mondrærust *A*

Judith

1 ne tweode: . . . tweode 32 baldor: b *erased* 85 þearfende: þearf / fende 88 heorte: heorte ys 90 me: *inserted by same hand* 134 hie: hie hie 141 weal-gate: weal *added in a different ink, prob. same hand* 142 heoldon: heordon *altered later* (*by another hand?*) 144 Iudith: iudithe 150 forlæton: *altered* (*by the same hand?*) *from* forleten 158 lysing þara: þara 165 þeodnes: þeoðnes 179 starian: stariað 194 fyllað: fyllan 201 sige-þufas: þufas 207 Wistan: westan 234 ricne: rice 249 werig-ferhðe: weras ferhðe 251 hilde: hyldo 263 hæste: hæfte 266 dæg-weorce: dæge weorce 268 þearfe: þearle 287 sculon nyde: sculon 291 him on: him mon 292 mægen-eacen: mægen ecen *with* a *inserted in same hand* 297 lind-werod: lind w . . . 298 sigore: *inserted by same hand* 329 mare: mærra 332 on: ond 344–49 in . . . miltse: *added in an early modern hand*

The Fight at Finnsburg

1 hornas: nas 2 heaþo-: hearo 3 eastan: Eastun 11 linda: landa hicgeaþ: Hie geaþ 12 winnað: Windað 18 Garulfe: Garulf styrde: styrode 20 bære: bæran 25 wreccea: Wrecten weana: weuna 29 bord: borð cenum on: Genumon 34 hwearf-latra hræw: Hwearflacra hrær 36 Finnes Buruh: Finnsburuh 38 gebæran: gebærann 39 swanas: swa noc 45 here-sceorp unhror: Here sceorpum hror ðyrel: ðyrl

Notes to the Translations

For prose texts the numeral at the head of the comment refers to the relevant sentence number, the start of every fifth sentence being indicated in the margin; for poetic texts it corresponds to the line number.

The Passion of Saint Christopher

1 The text begins imperfect, due to the loss of several leaves from the manuscript. The approximate Latin source relates that Christopher comes to an unnamed city ruled by King Dagnus. (The city is identified as Samos in some Latin versions and in the *incipit* to the lost Old English text mentioned below. In some Latin versions, and in the *Old English Martyrology,* Christopher's adversary is the Emperor Decius.) There the inhabitants are astonished to see that the man has the head of a dog. Upon viewing a miracle (his planted walking-stick sprouts and blossoms), many are converted. Brought before Dagnus, Christopher refuses to worship idols, and the soldiers who arrested him, claiming to have been converted by him, are put to death. Dagnus imprisons him and sends two women to seduce him in his cell, but he converts them. As a consequence, they suffer horrible martyrdom, though not without heavenly signs of their sanctity. Many, seeing this, are converted, and the king summons Christopher to ask how he can convince him to sacrifice to heathen gods. The Old English fragment begins in the course of Christopher's refusal to submit. Christopher's enormous size has not heretofore been mentioned in the Latin. It should be noted that another Old English life of Saint Christopher was once preserved in London, British Library, Cotton Otho B. x, a manuscript badly damaged by the Cottonian fire of 1731. The explicit of this text recorded by Wanley in George Hickes's *Thesaurus* of 1703–5 (see

the bibliography) agrees with that of the present text, and so Wanley's incipit perhaps closely resembles the lost incipit of the present text: *Menn þa leofestan, on þære tide wæs geworden þe Dagnus se cync rixode on Samon þære ceastre, þæt sum man com on þa ceastre se wæs healf-hundisces mancynnes, ac he ne cuðe nan þinge to þam lyfiendan gode ne his naman ne cigde. Þa wæs him ætywed fram urum drihtne þæt he scolde fulluhte onfon* (Dearest people, at the time that Dagnus the king ruled in Samos it occurred that a certain man who was of the half-canine race of humans came into that city, but he did not know anything about the living God, nor did he invoke his name. Then it was revealed to him by our Lord that he should receive baptism).

2 A point after *weras* (men) (along with capitalization of the following word) shows that this was understood to be the object of *settan* (set). In the approximate Latin source, rather, a burning helmet is placed on Christopher's head, and the three men are the subject of the following sentence. Presumably, at some point in the course of transmission, the words *fyrenne helm* (burning helmet) were inadvertently omitted after *heafde* (head).

5 *Beo-bread,* literally "bee bread," is the term used in Old English to refer to honeycomb with the honey.

6 The Latin merely says that the bench was equal in measure to the man's stature, and thus probably what was meant was that it was as long as Christopher was tall. If this is so, he was presumably imagined to have been made to lie on the bench (or perhaps sit on it), with a fire ignited underneath.

7 MS *gecyndnesse* (nation, increase) is here assumed to be a corruption of *gescyndnesse* (disgrace), corresponding to *erubescentia* (embarrassment) in the approximate Latin source.

18 The Latin does not refer to three soldiers, saying instead that the king commanded the soldiers to shoot arrows three at a time.

20 The *Passio* says rather that the arrows were suspended by the wind to the saint's right and left. Perhaps *Godes mægen wæs . . . hangigende* (the might of God was hanging) is a corruption of *þurh Godes mægen wæron . . . hangigende* (through the power of God were hanging). (The word *þurh,* "through," has also been omitted from sentence 25.)

30 *Gehæl þu þone* is literally "heal him."

32 The verb *myndgien* (let them make mention) is supplied on the basis of the Latin *commemorantur* (which the context and alternate readings

suggest was intended to mean the same) and the genitive *þines naman* (your name) (since *myndgian* may take a genitive object).

34 Instead of manuscript *feower* (four), *feowertig* (forty) accords both with the Latin source and with the normal Old English method of expressing large numbers.

37 Manuscript *dem* is probably not a corruption of *deme* (I decree) (corresponding to *credo,* "I believe," in the Latin) but of dialectal *dom* (I do).

The Wonders of the East

1 For *T*'s *leuuae* (more commonly spelled *leucae* or *leugae*), "leagues," *V* has *leones* (lions), most likely due to confusion of two similar letters, *u* and *n,* and the habit of scribes of converting the Old English diphthong *eu* found in archaic texts to the more modern *eo.* It should be plain from the figures here that the author regarded the league as half again as long as the stade (not so later in the text), though usually the stade was reckoned at 600 feet and the league at either 3,000 feet or an hour's walk (about 3.5 miles). In the Latin text, the latter seems to have been understood to be the correct distance, since there a distance is sometimes reckoned in leagues plus a mile or half mile. (The Roman mile was shorter by 142 yards than the English mile.) Antimolima, it should be said, has not been identified. It seems likely that the name is a corruption, probably a conflation of *Antiocha* with the island *Oliva* or *Olinum* mentioned in some recensions of the Latin material.

10 Although the Latin is ambiguous, it probably means that the hens self-immolate, while the Old English translator plainly takes it to mean that the person who touches the birds is burned. Thus, the repetition in 14, though odd, is not as odd as it first appears, since there it is the animals themselves that burn.

13 The Latin says rather that the captors wear armor.

15 *Hascellentia* is apparently a transformation of *Seleucia,* referring to the ancient city near modern Baghdad. Although the reading *bueð oð* of *T* (missing from *V*) could be taken to mean "extends as far as" (an unusual sense), the Latin shows that *bugeð to* (is subject to) is intended.

47 The word *on* goes with *þær,* i.e., "wherein," though the syntax is unusual. The word *ðrys* may well be a dialectal genitive of the word for "three"

(as the Latin equivalent would seem to indicate), but if so, its unfamiliarity prompted the scribe of *V* to write *drys heowes* (in the form of a druid).

55 The Latin refers to one island in the Brixontes to the south.

63 As regards *el-reordige men* (speakers of barbaric tongues), see the commentary below on *The Letter of Alexander the Great to Aristotle* 146.

80–81 *T*, in agreement with the Latin, says rather that the temple was made with ironwork and brass. Given the disparities between *T* and *V* in regard to these two sentences, it appears that some copy of the text in the line of descent of *V* was damaged, and the scribe consulted the Latin to supply the missing words, translating very imperfectly. See the discussion in the facsimile of the Tiberius manuscript, ed. P. McGurk et al. (1983), pp. 94–95. Although the text of *T* is closer to the Latin, that of *V* (from *setl* to the end of the sentence) has been retained alongside the former for its intrinsic interest.

89 "With their illusion" renders restored *mid heora scinlace*. The Latin reads *cum illis* (with them), but there is reason to believe that the translator worked from a damaged or corrupt text and instead translated *cum illusione* (as argued by P. McGurk and Ann Knock in McGurk et al.: see the bibliography). Alternatively, *scin . . . e* might be restored as some nominal derivative of the verb *scyndan* (drive, impel) (*scindinge?*), which would make sense in context, but *lac* best fits the space for the missing letters.

92 The word *unclennesse* (filthiness) is substituted for *micelnesse* (great size) on the basis of the Latin. Presumably the four minims forming *un-* were mistaken by a prior copyist for *mi-*.

95 That is to say, the kings have subjugated the despots.

The Letter of Alexander the Great to Aristotle

4 Rather than "and of those things that are unseen where you are," the sense of the Latin is "and so that you might not consider it something strange."

8 That something is missing is implied by the *ond* (and) before *wecga* (of metals), and thus the words *wildru ond wæstmas* (wild animals and plants) are supplied on the basis of the Latin, which the translator has

misconstrued in minor ways, unless the Old English text is otherwise corrupt.

19 The Latin refers not to *Gande* but to *Ganges.*

22 "Fasiacen" refers to the region of the Phasis (modern Rioni) River in western Georgia. The Greek Alexander Romance more plausibly points to a form *Prasiake,* probably from Sanskrit *prāchyaka* (eastern).

23 Old English *hreðnisse* looks like a late spelling of *reðnisse* (ferocity), but what the translator no doubt intended was *hrædnisse* (swiftness), corresponding to Latin *celeritate.*

33 The word *hon* is otherwise unattested. It is sometimes rendered "tendrils" on the basis of the Latin *ligis* or *lignitis* (bindings), but the syntax of the Old English differs from that of the Latin, suggesting *hon* is instead a synonym for *wæstmas* (fruits). It is assumed here to be a noun related to the verb *hon* (hang), with the meaning "(hanging grape) clusters," the meaning of *racemi* in the Latin.

43 Old English *Patriacen* here corresponds to Latin *Bactriacen* (Bactria).

46 The Old English of the first clause does not quite make good sense and is rendered here loosely. The translator seems to have misconstrued the Latin, which says that Alexander felt that the difficulties that they faced were of his own doing.

48 The syntax of this sentence is rendered difficult by *þæt* (that) after *eorcnan-stana* (of precious stones), since it cannot be a relative pronoun.

98 The encampment was about two and a half miles on a side.

108 *Cerastes* is a horned and very flexible snake of Greek mythology after which the horned viper (Cerastes cerastes) is named.

111 The word *wyrm,* here rendered as "vermin" or "pest," could refer to any insect or crawling creature, including Beowulf's dragon. Here it encompasses both the scorpions and the snakes.

118 The Latin refers to the serpents' *pectora erecta,* which the translator has understood to mean not that the serpents held their heads and breasts erect in the air but that they traveled with their breasts turned up, i.e., crawling on their backs.

130 The *dentityrannus* (a semi-Latinization of *odontotyrannos*) of the source is a rhinoceros.

144 The Latin corresponding to the final clauses means "so that they might enjoy deserved punishment for what they had done."

146 Here, as commonly elsewhere, Old English *þæra el-reordigra* (literally, of those foreign speakers) renders Greco-Latin *barbarorum* (of barbarians), which literally denotes those whose language sounds like *bar bar.* The Old English word has been translated "gibberish-speaking" (or, elsewhere, "speakers of barbaric tongues") to convey a degree of implied contempt.

149 In the Latin it is Bactria that is described as endowed with gold and other riches.

156 The Latin says rather that Alexander posed as a merchant of wine and meat.

170 *Liber* is a name for Bacchus.

179 That is, the area through which they passed was a dried-up fen, according to the Latin.

181 The meaning of *acæglod* is uncertain, but "saw-like" is the sense of the corresponding Latin.

182 As the Latin makes plain, the allusion is to a crocodile head.

185 In the Latin, the river is called *Buemar.* Old English *Biswicmon* means essentially "deceive people."

192 It is uncertain whether the word in the manuscript is *rying* or *rynig.* The word is otherwise unattested, although its meaning is assured by the corresponding Latin *grunnitus* (grunting). About the use of swine, Gunderson (1980, 56) remarks, "The Megarians employed this stratagem against Antigonus Gonatas, causing him to order that elephants henceforth be trained to ignore swine."

198 The Latin manuscripts disagree about the form of the word corresponding to Old English *ictifafonas,* and although they seem to suggest an original *ichthyfaunos,* this may be a corruption of *ichthyophagos* (fish-eaters).

200 A cynocephalus has a human body with a dog's head.

219–20 In antiquity Ethiopia was thought to lie next to India. A people in India called Nysaeans (by Aristobulus, who accompanied Alexander in his Asian campaign) appear to have been associated here, incongruously, with Nysa, the mountain in Thrace sacred to Dionysus.

232 The words for "sun" and "moon" are masculine and feminine, respectively, in both Greek and Latin, the opposite of their genders in Old English.

243 The Latin says rather that the bishop had teeth like a dog's. Apparently there has been confusion of Latin *caninos* and *candidos.*

246 The Latin has the bishop refer to sexual intercourse (with boys, some manuscripts make explicit) or touching women.

250 The Latin explains rather that the tree of the sun speaks at sunrise and that of the moon at sunset.

258 The reader, though not the translator, may have forgotten by this point that the text has a narrator, as the letter consists of a long quotation beginning in sentence 2. Hence the intrusion of the narrator's *sægde Alexander* (said Alexander), which is unparalleled in the Latin.

262 The use of Latin *fata* indicates that Old English *gesceaft* (fate) is the concept intended; that *eþel* (homeland) came to be substituted for it is probably due to the fact that *eþel* used earlier in the sentence stands directly above it in the manuscript. The translator has rendered Latin *de tuo capite* literally as *be þinum heafde* (concerning your head), which apparently he took to mean "ahead of you," since he adds *ond fore* (and beforehand) as a second rendering. (He very often renders Latin words and phrases with two constructions, as has often been remarked, perhaps indicating he was working from a glossed text, since interlinear glosses are often supplied in pairs.) Rather, *capite* is a metonym for "life."

269 Alexander died of an unidentified malady, or perhaps he was poisoned, as indicated in the text below. At this point, however, the text is ambiguous as to whether a person is to be the cause of his death.

273 Manuscript *micelne* (large) is here emended to *medmicelne* (slight) on the basis of the Latin and the sense of the passage.

282 An Old English word corresponding to Latin *insidiatorem* (ambusher) appears to have been erased, though it is the first word on the page and has suffered extensive loss by fire damage. Old English *syrere* (plotter) is not otherwise attested, but among the many possibilities available, it concurs with normal derivational patterns, it fits the space available, and its unusual nature may explain why the word was expunged. Some noun close in meaning to this must have been intended, and it was probably agentive, given the reference to *his hond* (his hand) in the next clause, and given that *his* is unlikely to refer to *wyrde* (event), a feminine noun.

284 After the death of Alexander in 323BCE, the ruthless Olympias engaged in a prolonged struggle with Cassander, the even more ruthless

regent of Macedon. When she fell into his hands in 316 BCE, she was executed contrary to a prior agreement, and it is said that her remains were denied burial.

293 Here the translator has omitted the account in the Latin of the army's return to Porus, in the course of which they encounter more fantastic and dangerous beasts.

Beowulf

6–7 Scyld was a foundling, discovered adrift on the ocean in a small boat, and he was adopted by Danes and grew up to be their king. His dynasty is referred to as the Scyldings, though the term is also used in the poem to refer to Danes of all sorts.

18 The genealogy of the West Saxon King Æthelwulf, supported by the poetic meter in line 52, indicates that the son of Scyld was not named Beowulf (as the manuscript has it) but Beow or Beaw. The scribal alteration is a natural mistake in a poem about Beowulf.

19 Scania (Swedish *Skåne*) is the southernmost part of what is now Sweden, though it was under Danish rule until 1658. But perhaps, by synecdoche, all of Scandinavia is meant.

53 Since the first fitt (i.e., section) number appears on a separate line of the manuscript before the beginning of this verse, either the first 52 lines are intended as a prologue or the first scribe numbered his fitts retrospectively.

56–57 That is, Beow's son Healfdene was born.

62 The name of Healfdene's daughter, along with part of the name of Onela, king of the Swedes, was unfortunately omitted by the scribe.

78 *Heorot* means "Hart," an appropriate name for a building that probably was imagined as having projections atop the gables resembling horns, formed by crossing the elongated ends of the beams at the top of the endmost rafters.

82–85 It would appear that Heorot was burned in the course of a confrontation between Danes and Heatho-Bards after the marriage of Hrothgar's daughter Freawaru to the Bardish leader Ingeld failed to secure peace. See lines 2020–69. By "it was sooner yet," the poet seems to mean that the burning of the hall would ensue upon the outbreak of the conflict.

93 The Anglo-Saxons conceived of the world as a body of dry land surrounded by the ocean.

107–10 As the passage illustrates, the reference of pronouns in poetry can shift abruptly, and more than once, in a short space.

154–58 By the payment of a certain amount of property or money, a crime such as murder might be expiated under early Germanic custom. That an outcast creature such as Grendel might actually have been expected to make a settlement of money seems improbable; it may be that this passage is metaphorical, intended to highlight the way Grendel represents a kind of anti-thane and thus a foil to the young Beowulf.

168–69 The point of this obscure passage is here assumed to be that Grendel, being an outcast, is unlike a thane, who approaches the throne to receive rewards from his lord.

198, 200 "Wave-wanderer" is a kenning for a ship, and "swan-road" for the sea.

287–89 The sentinel's point is that although the Geats' arrival seemed a hostile action, Beowulf's words have revealed the case to be otherwise.

298 *Weder,* in the sense "Storm," is another term for a Geat.

330 The shafts of spears were made of ash-wood.

389 The scribe's eye appears to have skipped from one *leodum* (people) to another in his exemplar, causing the loss of a passage relating Wulfgar's return.

446 Presumably "hide my head" refers to funeral rites.

455 Wayland is the northern Hephaistos.

512 "Rowed" appears to be a metaphor for "swam" (cf. line 539), though some have interpreted it literally.

519 The Heatho-Reams are usually identified with a group living not far from present-day Oslo (in Romerike).

747–49 Not atypically, the pronoun reference changes in the middle of the sentence: Grendel reached toward him, and Beowulf seized his hand.

769 Despite much critical discussion, it is still not agreed precisely what this reference to *ealu-scerwen,* probably meaning "dispensing of ale," signifies. In context, a similar word in the Old English *Andreas* suggests that it should be a metaphor for "terror."

881 If English and Scandinavian legends about him were similar, Sigemund was not only uncle to Fitela but also father.

902 Here and below, *eotenum* literally means "ogres," which some take to be its meaning here, though most regard it as a reference to Jutes (properly *Eotum*).

915 The word *hine* (the final "him" in the translation) refers to Heremod, contrasted implicitly with Beowulf.

980 The son of Ecglaf is Unferth.

986 "Hand-vestiges" alludes to the leaving of the hand, arm, and shoulder behind as vestiges of the escaped monster, part of a poetic idiom, as in lines 970–72.

1018–19 Although the interpretation is contested, most scholars assume that this passage alludes to treachery on Hrothulf's part after the death of Hrothgar, as Scandinavian parallels seem to suggest. See further the commentary on lines 1163 and 1180–87.

1030–34 The Sutton Hoo helmet likewise bears a metal ridge on its crest. The "leaving of files" is a sword, i.e., what is left when the files have done their work. To say that it is *scur-heard* (shower-hard) probably is intended to mean that it is hard in the storm of battle, though the compound is apparently formed by analogy to poetic *regn-heard* (wonderfully hard) (as in line 326), mistakenly taken to mean "rain-hard."

1044 The friends of Ing (a god) are the Danes; their shelter is Hrothgar.

1064–65 Healfdene's battle-leader is Hrothgar. To touch the entertainment-wood is to play the lyre.

1068–1159 Much remains obscure and disputed about the story that the court poet narrates, the so-called Finnsburg Episode; the following is probably the most widely credited reconstruction. Hildeburh, a princess of the Half-Danes, is married to Finn Folcwalding, king of the Frisians. During a visit to the Frisian court, the Half-Danes appear to have been attacked treacherously by certain Jutes either allied with or identical to the Frisian party (but see the note on line 902). In the attack, the leader of the Half-Danes, Hildeburh's brother Hnæf, is killed, as is her unnamed Frisian son. At a stalemate, the two sides agree to a precarious truce. In the spring, with the return of sailing weather, Hengest, who appears to have assumed command of the Half-Danes, goaded by some of his own men, breaks the truce, and in the ensuing combat Finn is killed, the stronghold is plundered, and the visitors return home, bearing off the queen.

1074 Although the text refers to "sons and brothers," it seems that Hildeburh lost just one of each.

1107 "Resplendent" is a mere guess as to the meaning of *icge,* which, like the similar *incge* in line 2577, has not been explained conclusively.

1116 The bone-vessels are the son's body.

1163 The two good men are Hrothgar and Hrothulf, and with the addition of Unferth the poet seems to be constructing a sinister tableau, foreshadowing future treachery on Hrothulf's part: cf. the commentary on lines 1018–19 and 1180–87.

1180–87 If Hrothulf will later usurp the throne, as most scholars suppose (see the commentary on lines 1018–19 and 1163), this speech of Wealhtheo's is laden with irony and pathos.

1208 The "cup of waves" is the sea.

1214 *Heal swege onfeng* (the hall took up the sound) does not make unimpeachable sense, and it may well be that it is an error for *heals bege onfeng* (his neck received the collar).

1231 A peculiarity of Modern English is that all simple expressions for intoxication carry negative connotations, whereas Old English *druncne* apparently is ambiguous in this regard, signifying alternately stupid inebriation (cf. lines 480, 1467) and a pleasant state of satisfaction.

1391–94 Grendel's mother is actually referred to as "he" rather than "she" in these verses, and in a few other places.

1445 The bone-chamber is the body.

1459–60 The poison-twigs are most likely the interwoven design resulting from the pattern-welding commonly used in the period to forge sword-blades, which are poisonous only in a metaphorical sense ("deadly"). Battle-sweat is blood.

1555–56 That is, God settled the matter after Beowulf stood again.

1931–62 Much remains uncertain about this digression concerning a wicked princess tamed by marriage to Offa, king of the Angles, including the woman's name. In the critical literature on the poem, she is usually referred to as Modthryth(o) or Thryth, but the manuscript reading *mod þryðo* more likely means "arrogance," and the woman's name is here assumed to be Fremu (benefit). The description "Hemming's kinsman" is applied alternately to Offa (1943) and Eomer (1961).

2205–6 The Scylfings are Swedes; Hereric's nephew is Heardred, son of Hygelac.

2229 On the omission of a line here due to a dittograph in the manuscript, see the introduction to the poem.

2297–98 The syntax of the Old English is broken here, as the translation indicates, and the poetic form is irregular. Probably a line or two have been omitted by the scribe.

2387 The offspring of Ongentheo is Onela, who took the throne upon the death of his brother Ohthere, as a consequence of which Ohthere's sons Eanmund and Eadgils went into exile among the Geats.

2481 "One of them" refers not to Hæthcyn but to Hygelac.

2508 By "bone-house" is meant the body, i.e., what houses the bones; see also line 3147.

2559 We should expect *hilde-swat* (war-sweat) to be a kenning for blood (cf. lines 1286, 1460, 1606, 1668, 2693, and 2966) rather than fiery breath. Perhaps familiar *-swat* has been substituted by the scribe for rare *-swaþul* (flame), which occurs elsewhere only at line 782.

2888 "Wits," by metonymy, means "head."

2982 "His kinsman" is Eofor's brother Wulf.

3024–27 This is the only occurrence in *Beowulf* of the so-called beasts of battle topos, so common in Old English poetry, and it is an unusual instance, inasmuch as the beasts converse with each other, and they do not serve to mark the imminence of battle by their anticipation of feeding upon the slain.

3028 *Swa se secg hwata secggende wæs laðra spella* (The man was thus a teller of auguries, of repugnant news) could instead mean "The valiant man was saying repugnant news," though the syntax of this would be unusual.

Judith

1 On the loss of text at the beginning, see the introduction to the poem.

14 The phrase *ides ælf-scinu* (lady of supernatural beauty) is more literally "lady elf-radiant." It may be that *ælf-* implies an element of danger, as argued by Orchard (see the bibliography for *Judith*).

62 The off-verse was probably omitted inadvertently by the scribe, without affecting the sense of the passage.

152 The word *lysing* (release, redemption) is here supplied to govern the otherwise unaccompanied genitive *þara læðða* (the trials) and to mend the faulty meter.

210–11 The words *salowig-pada* (dusky-feathered) and *hyrned-nebba* (horn-beaked) probably describe the raven rather than the eagle in this more typical instance of the beasts of battle topos: see the commentary on *Beowulf* 3024–27.

271 Manuscript *gode* could mean "of good" rather than "of God," but the poetic meter would then be unusual.

275 "Confident" is an unusual, probably late, meaning for *arod,* which is more literally "trusted," to the verb *arian.*

321 "Rested" is litotes for "lay dead": see the discussion of understatement in the introduction to *Beowulf.*

The Fight at Finnsburg

1–12 Most likely someone keeping watch has reported seeing glimmering light outside the hall and has interpreted it as an early dawn, the flight of a fire-breathing dragon, or flames in the gables. Hnæf (the "battle-young king") responds that the light is none of these things, but the sign of an approaching troop, and he calls his men to arms.

5 "They are approaching" is a very uncertain rendering of an obscure construction, *forþ berað* (carry forth) without a direct object.

6 "Gray-coat howls" is the meaning that accords with the assumption that the poet is employing an allusion to the beasts of battle trope, as in *Beowulf* 3024–27 and *Judith* 205–12: see the commentary on these passages. Possibly the meaning is instead "gray-coat resounds," i.e., the mail-shirt makes a sound as it is brought out and readied for battle.

27 "Which of the two," i.e., victory or death.

29 "Peerless" is a mere guess as to the meaning of *celæs,* of which no fully satisfactory interpretation has been found.

30 In regard to *ban-helm* (bone-helmet), it is not plain whether "bone" refers to plating of bone decorating a helmet or to a skull.

Bibliography

For more detailed bibliographical guidance, consult Stanley B. Greenfield and Fred C. Robinson, *A Bibliography of Publications on Old English Literature to the End of 1972* (Toronto, 1980), and, subsequently, the annual bibliographies in the journals *Anglo-Saxon England* and *Old English Newletter.*

General

Förster, Max. *Die 'Beowulf'-Handschrift.* Berichte über die Verhandlungen der Sächsischen Akademie der Wissenschaften zu Leipzig, phil.-hist. Klasse 71. Leipzig, 1919.

Hickes, George. *Septentrionalium Thesaurus Grammatico-Criticus et Archaeologicus,* 2 vols. in 3 pts. Oxford, 1703–5.

Kiernan, Kevin S. *"Beowulf" and the "Beowulf" Manuscript.* Rev. ed. Ann Arbor, 1996.

——, ed. *Electronic Beowulf.* Version 2.0. 2 disks. London, 2003.

Malone, Kemp, ed. *The Nowell Codex.* Early English Manuscripts in Facsimile 12. Copenhagen, 1963.

——. "Readings from Folios 94 to 131, Cotton Vitellius A xv." In *Studies in Medieval Literature in Honor of Professor Albert Croll Baugh,* ed. MacEdward Leach, pp. 255–71. Philadelphia, 1961.

Orchard, Andy. *Pride and Prodigies: Studies in the Monsters of the Beowulf-Manuscript.* Rev. paperback ed. Toronto, 2003.

Rypins, Stanley I., ed. *Three Old English Prose Texts in MS. Cotton Vitellius A xv.* Early English Text Society o.s. 161. London, 1924.

Sisam, Kenneth. "The Beowulf Manuscript" and "The Compilation of the Beowulf Manuscript." In his *Studies in the History of Old English Literature,* pp. 61–64 and 65–96, resp. Oxford, 1953.

The Passion of Saint Christopher

Frederick, Jill. "'His ansyn wæs swylce rosan blostma': A Reading of the Old English *Life of St. Christopher.*" *Proceedings of the PMR Conference* 12–13 (1989): 137–48.

Lapidge, Michael. "Acca of Hexham and the Origin of the *Old English Martyrology.*" *Analecta Bollandiana* 123 (2005): 29–78.

Lionarons, Joyce Tally. "From Monster to Martyr: The Old English Legend of Saint Christopher." In *Marvels, Monsters, and Miracles: Studies in the Medieval and Early Modern Imaginations,* ed. Timothy S. Jones and David A. Sprunger, pp. 167–82. Studies in Medieval Culture 42. Kalamazoo, 2002.

McGowan, Joseph. "Readings from the *Beowulf* Manuscript, ff. 94r–98r (the *St. Christopher* Folios)." *Manuscripta* 39 (1995): 26–29.

Pulsiano, Phillip. "The Passion of Saint Christopher." In *Early Medieval English Texts and Interpretations: Studies Presented to Donald G. Scragg,* ed. Elaine Treharne and Susan Rosser, pp. 167–99. Medieval and Renaissance Texts and Studies 252. Tempe, 2002.

Rosenfeld, Hans-Friedrich. *Der hl. Christophorus: seine Verehrung und seine Legende.* Acta Academiae Aboensis, Humaniora X, 3. Åbo, 1937.

Rypins, Stanley I. "The Old English Life of St. Christopher." *Modern Language Notes* 35 (1920): 186–87.

Sisam, Kenneth. *Studies in the History of Old English Literature.* Oxford, 1953. (See esp. pp. 68–72.)

The Wonders of the East

Austin, Greta. "Marvelous Peoples or Marvelous Races? Race and the Anglo-Saxon *Wonders of the East.*" In *Marvels, Monsters, and Miracles: Studies in the Medieval and Early Modern Imaginations,* ed. Timothy S. Jones and David A. Sprunger, pp. 25–51. Studies in Medieval Culture 42. Kalamazoo, 2002.

Brynteson, William E. "*Beowulf,* Monsters, and Manuscripts: Classical Associations." *Res Publica Litterarum* 5.2 (1982): 41–57.

Cockayne, Thomas O., ed. *Narratiuncula Anglice conscriptæ.* London, 1861.

Donner, Morton. "Prudery in Old English Fiction." *Comitatus* 3 (1972): 91–96.

Förster, Max. "Zur ae. Mirabilien-Version." *Archiv für das Studium der neueren Sprachen und Literaturen* 117 (1906): 367–70.

Friedman, John Block. "The Marvels-of-the-East Tradition in Anglo-Saxon Art." In *Sources of Anglo-Saxon Culture,* ed. Paul E. Szarmach, pp. 319–41. Kalamazoo, 1986.

Holder, Alfred. "Collationen zu ags. Werken I. *De rebus in oriente mirabilis.*" *Anglia* 1 (1878): 331–37.

James, Montague R., ed. *Marvels of the East: A Full Reproduction of the Three Known Copies.* Oxford, 1929.

Kim, Susan M. "The Donestre and the Person of Both Sexes." In *Naked before God: Uncovering the Body in Anglo-Saxon England,* ed. Benjamin C. Withers and Jonathan Wilcox. Medieval European Studies 3. Morgantown, 2003.

———. "Man-Eating Monsters and Ants as Big as Dogs: The Alienated Language of the Cotton Vitellius A.XV 'Wonders of the East.'" In *Animals and the Symbolic in Mediaeval Art and Literature,* ed. L. A. J. R. Houwen, pp. 38–51. Mediaevalia Groningana 20. Groningen, 1997.

Knappe, Fritz, ed. "Der angelsächsische Prosastück Die Wunder des Ostens: Überlieferung, Quellen, Sprache und Text nach beiden Handschriften." PhD diss., University of Greifswald, Berlin, 1906.

Knock, Ann. "Analysis of a Translator: The Old English *Wonders of the East.*" In *Alfred the Wise: Studies in Honour of Janet Bately on the Occasion of Her Sixty-Fifth Birthday,* ed. Jane Roberts, Janet L. Nelson, and Malcolm Godden, pp. 121–26. Cambridge, 1997.

Lecouteux, Claude, ed. *De rebus in Oriente mirabilibus (Lettre de Farasmenes): Edition synoptique accompagnée d'une introduction et notes.* Beiträge zur klassischen Philologie 103. Meisenheim am Glan, 1979.

Malone, Kemp. "An Anglo-Latin Version of the Hjaðningavíg." *Speculum* 39 (1964): 35–44.

McGurk, P., et al., eds. *An Eleventh-Century Anglo-Saxon Illustrated Miscellany: British Library Cotton Tiberius B. V Part I, Together with Leaves from British Library Cotton Nero D. II.* Early English Manuscripts in Facsimile 21. Copenhagen, 1983.

Mittman, Asa Simon. *Maps and Monsters in Medieval England.* New York, 2006.

Olson, Mary C. *Fair and Varied Forms: Visual Textuality in Medieval Illuminated Manuscripts.* New York, 2003.

Pfister, Friedrich. "Auf den Spuren Alexanders des Grossen in der älteren englischen Literatur." *Germanisch-romanische Monatsschrift* 16 (1928): 81–86.

Rizzo, Carmela, ed. *Fabelwesen, mostri e portenti nell'immaginario occidentale: Medioevo germanico e altro.* Bibliotheca Germanica, Studi e Testi 15. Alessandria, 2004.

Rooney, Catherine. "Gerald of Wales and the Tradition of the Wonders of the East." *Quaestio* 4 (2003): 82–97.

Rossi-Reder, Andrea. "Wonders of the Beast: India in Classical and Medieval Literature." In *Marvels, Monsters, and Miracles: Studies in the Medieval and Early Modern Imaginations,* ed. Timothy S. Jones and David A. Sprunger, pp. 53–66. Studies in Medieval Culture 42. Kalamazoo, 2002.

Scheil, Andrew P. "Babylon and Anglo-Saxon England." *Studies in the Literary Imagination* 36.1 (2003): 37–58.

Sisam, Kenneth. *Studies in the History of Old English Literature.* Oxford, 1953. (See esp. pp. 80–82.)

Treharne, Elaine, ed. *Old and Middle English c. 890–c. 1450: An Anthology.* 3rd ed. Chichester, 2010.

The Letter of Alexander the Great to Aristotle

Baskervill, W. M. "The Anglo-Saxon Version of the *Epistola Alexandri ad Aristotelem.*" *Anglia* 4 (1881): 139–67.

Boer, W. W., ed. *Epistola Alexandri ad Aristotelem.* Beiträge zur klassischen Philologie 50. Meisenheim am Glan, 1973.

Bradley, Henry, and Kenneth Sisam. "Textual Notes on the Old English *Epistola Alexandri.*" *Modern Language Review* 14 (1919): 202–5.

Braun, A. *Lautlehre der angelsächsischen Version der 'Epistola Alexandri ad Aristotelem.'* PhD diss., University of Würzburg, Borna, 1911.

Busbee, Mark Bradshaw. "A Paradise Full of Monsters: India in the Old

English Imagination." *LATCH: A Journal for the Study of Literary Artifact in Theory, Culture, or History* 1 (2008): 51–72.

Butturff, Douglas R. "Style as a Clue to Meaning: A Note on the Old English Translation of the *Epistola Alexandri ad Aristotelem*." *ELN* 8.2 (1970): 81–86.

Davidson, Donald, and A. P. Campbell. "The Letter of Alexander the Great to Aristotle: The Old English Version Turned into Modern English." *Humanities Association Bulletin* 23.3 (1972): 3–16.

Davis, Norman. "'Hippopotamus' in Old English." *Review of English Studies* n.s. 4 (1953): 141–42.

Gunderson, Lloyd L. *Alexander's Letter to Aristotle about India.* Beiträge zur klassischen Philologie 110. Meisenheim am Glan, 1980.

Kim, Susan M. "'If One Who Is Loved Is Not Present, a Letter May Be Embraced Instead': Death and the *Letter of Alexander to Aristotle*." *Journal of English and Germanic Philology* 109 (2010): 33–51.

Klaeber, Frederick. "Notes on Old English Prose Texts." *Modern Language Notes* 18 (1903): 241–47.

McFadden, Brian. "The Social Context of Narrative Disruption in *The Letter of Alexander to Aristotle*." *Anglo-Saxon England* 30 (2001): 91–114.

Pfister, Friedrich. "Auf den Spuren Alexanders des Grossen in der älteren englischen Literatur." *Germanisch-romanische Monatsschrift* 16 (1928): 81–86.

Rypins, Stanley I. "Notes on *Epistola Alexandri ad Aristotelem*." *Modern Language Notes* 32 (1917): 94–95.

———. "The Old English *Epistola Alexandri ad Aristotelem*." *Modern Language Notes* 38 (1923): 216–20.

Stevick, Robert D. "Graphotactics of the Old English 'Alexander's Letter to Aristotle.'" *Studia Anglica Posnaniensia* 40 (2004): 3–13.

Swaen, A. E. H. "Is *seo hiow* = 'Fortune' a Ghost-Word?" *Englische Studien* 71 (1936): 153–54.

Beowulf

The treatment is necessarily very selective. For more detailed references, consult especially Bjork and Niles 1997, and Fulk, Bjork, and Niles 2009, cited below.

BIBLIOGRAPHY

Baker, Peter S., ed. *"Beowulf": Basic Readings.* New York, 1995.

Bjork, Robert E., and John D. Niles, eds. *A "Beowulf" Handbook.* Lincoln, 1997.

Bonjour, Adrien. *The Digressions in "Beowulf."* Oxford, 1950.

Brodeur, Arthur G. *The Art of "Beowulf."* Berkeley, 1959.

Chambers, R. W. *"Beowulf": An Introduction to the Study of the Poem.* 3rd ed., rev. C. W. Wrenn. Cambridge, 1959.

Chase, Colin, ed. *The Dating of "Beowulf."* Toronto, 1981.

Clark, George. *Beowulf.* Boston, 1990.

Dobbie, Elliott Van Kirk, ed. *"Beowulf" and "Judith."* The Anglo-Saxon Poetic Records 4. New York, 1953.

Fry, Donald K. *"Beowulf" and "The Fight at Finnsburh": A Bibliography.* Charlottesville, 1969.

——, ed. *The "Beowulf" Poet: A Collection of Critical Essays.* Englewood Cliffs, 1968.

Fulk, R. D., ed. *Interpretations of "Beowulf": A Critical Anthology.* Bloomington, 1992.

Fulk, R. D., Robert E. Bjork, and John D. Niles, eds. *Klaeber's "Beowulf" and "The Fight at Finnsburg."* Corrected reprint of the 4th ed. (2008). Toronto, 2009.

Gerritsen, Johan. "What Use Are the Thorkelin Transcripts of *Beowulf?*" *Anglo-Saxon England* 28 (1999): 23–42.

Grim. Johnson Thorkelin [Grímur Jónsson Thorkelín], ed. *De Danorum rebus gestis secul.* III *&* IV. *poëma danicum dialecto anglosaxonica.* Copenhagen, 1815.

Hasenfratz, Robert. *"Beowulf" Scholarship: An Annotated Bibliography, 1979–1990.* New York, 1993.

Hill, John M. *The Cultural World in "Beowulf."* Toronto, 1995.

——. *The Narrative Pulse of "Beowulf."* Toronto, 2008.

Irving, Edward B., Jr. *A Reading of "Beowulf."* New Haven, 1968.

——. *Rereading "Beowulf."* Philadelphia, 1989.

Joy, Eileen, and Mary K. Ramsey, eds. *The Postmodern "Beowulf."* Morgantown, W. Va., 2006.

Kemble, John Mitchell, ed. *The Anglo-Saxon Poems of "Beowulf."* London, 1833. (2nd ed. in 2 vols., 1835–1837.)

Kiernan, Kevin S. *"Beowulf" and the "Beowulf" Manuscript.* New Brunswick, 1981. (Rev. ed., Ann Arbor, 1996.)

——, ed. *Electronic "Beowulf."* 2 disks. London, 1999. (Version 2.0, London, 2003.)

——. *The Thorkelin Transcripts of "Beowulf."* Copenhagen, 1986.

Malone, Kemp, ed. *The Thorkelin Transcripts of "Beowulf" in Facsimile.* Early English Manuscripts in Facsimile 1. Copenhagen, 1951.

Nicholson, Lewis E., ed. *An Anthology of "Beowulf" Criticism.* Notre Dame, 1963.

Niles, John D. *"Beowulf": The Poem and Its Tradition.* Cambridge, Mass., 1983.

Orchard, Andy. *A Critical Companion to "Beowulf."* Cambridge, 2003.

Owen-Crocker, Gale. *The Four Funerals in "Beowulf."* Manchester, 2000.

Robinson, Fred C. *"Beowulf" and the Appositive Style.* Knoxville, 1985.

Schaubert, Else von, ed. *Heyne-Schückings Beowulf.* 18th ed. Paderborn, 1963.

Shippey, Thomas A. *Beowulf.* London, 1978.

Short, Douglas D. *"Beowulf" Scholarship: An Annotated Bibliography.* New York, 1980.

Sisam, Kenneth. *The Structure of "Beowulf."* Oxford, 1965.

Tolkien, J. R. R. "*Beowulf:* The Monsters and the Critics." *Proceedings of the British Academy* 22 (1936): 245–95.

Whitelock, Dorothy. *The Audience of "Beowulf."* Oxford, 1951.

Zupitza, Julius, ed. *"Beowulf" Reproduced in Facsimile from the Unique Manuscript British Museum MS. Cotton Vitellius A. xv.* Rev. Norman Davis. Early English Text Society o.s. 245. London, 1959.

Judith

Astell, Ann W. "Holofernes's Head: *tacen* and Teaching in the Old English *Judith.*" *Anglo-Saxon England* 18 (1989): 117–33.

Belanoff, Patricia A. "Judith: Sacred and Secular Heroine." In *Heroic Poetry in the Anglo-Saxon Period: Studies in Honor of Jess B. Bessinger,* ed. Helen Damico and John Leyerle, pp. 247–64. Studies in Medieval Culture 32. Kalamazoo, 1993.

Berkhout, Carl T., and James F. Doubleday. "The Net in *Judith* 46b–54a." *Neuphilologische Mitteilungen* 74 (1973): 630–34.

Brodeur, Arthur G. "A Study of Diction and Style in Three Anglo-Saxon Narrative Poems." In *Nordica et Anglica: Studies in Honour of Stefán Einarsson,* ed. Allan H. Orrick, pp. 98–114. The Hague, 1968.

Campbell, Jackson J. "Schematic Technique in *Judith.*" *ELH* 38 (1971): 155–72.

Chamberlain, David. "*Judith:* A Fragmentary and Political Poem." In *Anglo-Saxon Poetry: Essays in Appreciation for John C. McGalliard,* ed. Lewis E. Nicholson and Dolores Warwick Frese, pp. 135–59. Notre Dame, 1975.

Chickering, Howell. "Poetic Exuberance in the Old English *Judith.*" *Studies in Philology* 106.2 (2009): 119–36.

Cook, Albert S., ed. *"Judith," an Old English Epic Fragment.* 2nd ed. Boston, 1889.

de Lacy, Paul. "Aspects of Christianisation and Cultural Adaptation in the Old English *Judith.*" *Neuphilologische Mitteilungen* 97 (1996): 393–410.

Dobbie, Elliott Van Kirk, ed. *"Beowulf" and "Judith."* The Anglo-Saxon Poetic Records 4. New York, 1953.

Dockray-Miller, Mary. "Female Community in the Old English *Judith.*" *Studia Neophilologica* 70 (1998): 165–72.

Doubleday, J. F. "The Principle of Contrast in *Judith.*" *Neuphilologische Mitteilungen* 72 (1971): 436–41.

Estes, Heide. "Feasting With Holofernes: Digesting *Judith* in Anglo-Saxon England." *Exemplaria* 15 (2003): 325–50.

Fee, Christopher. "*Judith* and the Rhetoric of Heroism in Anglo-Saxon England." *English Studies* 78 (1997): 401–6.

Foster, Thomas G. *"Judith": Studies in Metre, Language and Style, with a View to Determining the Date of the Old English Fragment and the Home of Its Author.* Quellen und Forschungen 71, no. 4. Strassburg, 1892.

Fry, Donald K. "Imagery and Point of View in *Judith* 200b–231." *English Language Notes* 5.3 (1968): 157–59.

———. "Type-Scene Composition in *Judith.*" *Annuale Mediaevale* 12 (1972): 100–19.

Garner, Lori Ann. "The Art of Translation in the Old English *Judith*." *Studia Neophilologica* 73 (2001): 171–83.

Godfrey, Mary Flavia. "*Beowulf and Judith:* Thematizing Decapitation in Old English Poetry." *Texas Studies in Literature and Language* 35 (1993): 1–43.

Griffith, Mark, ed. *Judith*. Exeter, 1997.

Häcker, Martina. "The Original Length of the Old English *Judith*. More Doubt(s) on the 'Missing Text.'" *Leeds Studies in English* n.s. 27 (1996): 1–18.

Heinemann, Frederik J. "*Judith* 236–291a: A Mock Heroic Approach-to-Battle Type Scene." *Neuphilologische Mitteilungen* 71 (1970): 83–96.

Hermann, John P. "The Theme of Spiritual Warfare in the Old English *Judith*." *Philological Quarterly* 55 (1976): 1–9.

Hieatt, Constance B. "*Judith* and the Literary Function of Old English Hypermetric Lines." *Studia Neophilologica* 52 (1980): 251–57.

Huppé, Bernard F. *The Web of Words: Structural Analyses of the Old English Poems "Vainglory," "The Wonder of Creation," "The Dream of the Rood," and "Judith," with Texts and Translations*. Albany, 1970.

Kaske, R. E. "*Sapientia et fortitudo* in the Old English *Judith*." In *The Wisdom of Poetry: Essays in Early English Literature in Honor of Morton W. Bloomfield,* ed. Larry D. Benson and Siegfried Wenzel, pp. 13–29, 264–68. Kalamazoo, 1982.

Kim, Susan. "Bloody Signs: Circumcision and Pregnancy in the Old English *Judith*." *Exemplaria* 11 (1999): 285–307.

Klegraf, Josef, ed. and trans. *Die altenglische 'Judith': eine Ausgabe für den akademischen Unterricht*. Ausgewählte Texte aus der Geschichte der christlichen Kirche 3. Stuttgart, 1987.

Koppelman, Kate. "Fearing My Neighbor: The Intimate Other in *Beowulf* and the Old English *Judith*." *Comitatus* 35 (2004): 1–21.

Litton, Alfred G. "The Heroine as Hero: Gender Reversal in the Anglo-Saxon *Judith*." *CEA Critic* 56.1 (1993): 35–44.

Locherbie-Cameron, Margaret. "Wisdom as a Key to Heroism in *Judith*." *Poetica* (Tokyo) 27 (1988): 70–75.

Lochrie, Karma. "Gender, Sexual Violence, and the Politics of War in the Old English *Judith*." In *Class and Gender in Early English Literature,* ed. Britton J. Harwood and Gillian R. Overing, pp. 1–20. Bloomington, 1994.

Lucas, Peter J. "Franciscus Junius and the Versification of *Judith. Francisci Junii in Memoriam:* 1591–1991." In *The Preservation and Transmission of Anglo-Saxon Culture: Selected Papers from the 1991 Meeting of the International Society of Anglo-Saxonists,* ed. Paul E. Szarmach and Joel T. Rosenthal, pp. 369–404. Studies in Medieval Culture 40. Kalamazoo, 1997.

——. "*Judith* and the Woman Hero." *Yearbook of English Studies* 22 (1992): 17–27.

——. "The Place of *Judith* in the *Beowulf*-Manuscript." *Review of English Studies* n.s. 41 (1990): 463–78.

Magennis, Hugh. "Adaptation of Biblical Detail in the Old English *Judith:* The Feast Scene." *Neuphilologische Mitteilungen* 84 (1983): 331–37.

——. "Contrasting Narrative Emphases in the Old English Poem *Judith* and Ælfric's Paraphrase of the Book of Judith." *Neuphilologische Mitteilumgen* 96 (1995): 61–66.

——. "Gender and Heroism in the Old English *Judith.*" In *Writing Gender and Genre in Medieval Literature: Approaches to Old and Middle English Texts,* ed. Elaine Treharne, pp. 5–18. Cambridge, 2002.

Momma, Haruko. "Epanalepsis: A Retelling of the Judith Story in the Anglo-Saxon Poetic Language." *Studies in the Literary Imagination* 36.1 (Spring 2003): 59–73.

Mullally, Erin. "The Cross-Gendered Gift: Weaponry in the Old English *Judith.*" *Exemplaria* 17 (2005): 255–84.

Mushabac, Jane. "*Judith* and the Theme of *Sapientia et Fortitudo.*" *Massachusetts Studies in English* 4 (1973): 3–12.

Nelson, Marie. "*Judith:* A Story of a Secular Saint." *Germanic Notes* 21 (1990): 12–13.

——, ed. and trans. *Judith, Juliana, and Elene: Three Fighting Saints.* American University Studies, ser. 4: English Language and Literature 135. Bern, 1991.

——. "Judith, Juliana, and Elene: Three Fighting Saints, or How I Learned That Translators Need Courage Too." *Medieval Perspectives* 9 (1994): 85–98.

Nicholson, Lewis E. "Oral Techniques in the Composition of Expanded Anglo-Saxon Verses." *PMLA* 78 (1963): 287–92.

Olsen, Alexandra Hennessey. "Inversion and Political Purpose in the Old English *Judith.*" *English Studies* 63 (1982): 289–93.

Orchard, Andy. "Intoxication, Fornication, and Multiplication: The Burgeoning Text of *Genesis A*." In *Text, Image, Interpretation: Studies in Anglo-Saxon Literature and Its Insular Context in Honour of Éamonn Ó Carragáin,* ed. Alastair Minnis and Jane Roberts, pp. 333–54. Turnhout, Belg., 2007.

Orlandi, Paola. "La dimensione eroica nella *Giuditta* anglosassone." In *La funzione dell'eroe germanico: storicità, metafora, paradigma. Atti del Convegno internazionale di studio, Roma, 6–8 maggio 1993,* ed. Teresa Pàroli, pp. 75–91. Philologia 2. Rome, 1995.

Parker, Kathleen. "Is the Old English Judith Beautiful?" *Annali Istituto Universitario Orientale di Napoli, Sezione Germanica: Filologia germanica* n.s. 2.1–3 (1992): 61–77.

Pringle, Ian. "*Judith:* The Homily and the Poem." *Traditio* 31 (1975): 83–97.

Raffel, Burton. "*Judith:* Hypermetricity and Rhetoric." In *Anglo-Saxon Poetry: Essays in Appreciation for John C. McGalliard,* ed. Lewis E. Nicholson and Dolores Warwick Frese, pp. 124–34. Notre Dame, 1975.

Rapetti, Alessandra. "Three Images of Judith." *Études de Lettres (Univ. de Lausanne)* 2–3 (1987): 155–65.

Robinson, Fred C. "Five Textual Notes on the Old English *Judith.*" *ANQ* 15.2 (2002): 47–51.

Swanton, Michael. "Die altenglische Judith: Weiblicher Held oder frauliche Heldin." In *Heldensage und Heldendichtung im Germanischen,* ed. Heinrich Beck, pp. 289–304. Ergänzungsbände zum Reallexikon der germanischen Altertumskunde 2. Berlin, 1988.

Thijs, Christine. "Feminine Heroism in the Old English *Judith.*" *Leeds Studies in English* n.s. 37 (2006): 41–62.

Thormann, Janet. "The Jewish Other in Old English Narrative Poetry." *Partial Answers: Journal of Literature and the History of Ideas* 2 (2004): 1–19.

Timmer, B. J., ed. *Judith.* Exeter Medieval English Texts. Rev. reprint of 1952 ed. Exeter, 1978.

Tyler, Elizabeth M. "Style and Meaning in *Judith.*" *Notes & Queries* n.s. 39 (1992): 16–19.

Wenisch, Franz. "*Judith*—eine westsächsische Dichtung?" *Anglia* 100 (1982): 273–300.

Index

Roman numerals (vii, ix) refer to the page numbers of the Introduction. Two-part arabic numbers (3.199, 4.1252) refer to the Old English work and sentence number (for prose) or line number (for verse). The Old English works are numbered as follows: 1. *The Passion of Saint Christopher,* 2. *The Wonders of the East,* 3. *The Letter of Alexander the Great to Aristotle,* 4. *Beowulf,* 5. *Judith,* 6. *The Fight at Finnsburg.* Arabic numbers followed by *n* (4.1252n) refer to the Notes to the Translations.